Bridges On Buffalo '87

LANDSCAPE AND IDEOLOGY

LANDSCAPE

Ann Bermingham

AND IDEOLOGY

The English Rustic Tradition,

1740–1860

UNIVERSITY OF CALIFORNIA PRESS

BERKELEY · LOS ANGELES · LONDON

University of California Press
Berkeley and Los Angeles, California

University of California Press, Ltd.
London, England

Library of Congress Cataloging-in-Publication Data

Bermingham, Ann.
  Landscape and ideology.

  Bibliography: p.
  Includes index.
   1. Landscape painting, English. 2. Landscape
painting—18th century—England. 3. Landscape
painting—19th century—England. 4. Picturesque, The, in art.
I. Title
ND1354.4.B47 1986   758'.1'0942   85–24509
ISBN 0–520–05287–0 (alk. paper)

Printed in the United States of America

1   2   3   4   5   6   7   8   9

TO J·C·B· AND M·H·B·

CONTENTS

ILLUSTRATIONS

ix

FIGURES

ACKNOWLEDGMENTS

As much as anything else, this book was written to explain to myself why at a certain historical moment landscape painting should have expressed the deepest needs of a whole culture. That such a private quest should meet with such a public end is both exhilarating and daunting. I take heart in knowing that my ideas have been shaped by time, fortunate circumstances, and the assistance of others. I am pleased therefore to acknowledge those who have contributed to this work.

My advisor at the Fogg Museum, Henri Zerner, offered judicious criticism, and his enthusiasm for this study when he first read it as a dissertation was a sustaining source of encouragement. Similarly, T. J. Clark kindly provided me with important criticisms and suggestions. The merits of their recommendations at times exceeded the use I made of them, and the fact that I have not always taken their good advice should weigh on me and not on them. I am grateful to Mark Roskill, who, as my teacher at the University of Massachusetts, Amherst, first introduced me to questions of meaning in the visual image that have since guided my studies. I have benefited from lively consultations with D. A. Miller, whose advice, encouragement, and friendship have been major contributions to this work. Charles Rhyne, Leslie Parris, and Ian Fleming-Williams patiently listened and responded to my inquiries about Constable. I am indebted to Shelley Bennett, Ian Fleming-Williams, Robert Folkenflik, Karl Kroeber, and Ronald Paulson, all of whom read the manuscript and made helpful suggestions for revision. Two study groups have given me welcome support and criticism. The members of a Berkeley women's writing group, Ramsey Bell, Leah Freiwald,

Susan Harris, Katherine Hughes, and Nancy Ungar, provided the emotional and critical impetus to complete the manuscript. More recently Jerrine Mitchel, Paula Rea Radisich, Suzanne Rubenstein, and Joanna Stein, members of a Los Angeles group, Art Around 1800, advised me on revising certain parts of the manuscript. Those who assisted me in locating and gathering the necessary illustrations for this book include Selina Fox, Christopher Gattis, Joan Harvey, John Hayes, Evelyn Joll, Jeremy Maas, Caroline Odgers, and the staffs of Thomas Agnew and Sons, Ltd., the Witt Library, and the Tate Gallery department of publications. I wish to thank William McClung, John McGowan, Jeanne Sugiyama, Marilyn Schwartz, and Stephanie Fay of The University of California Press for their skill and care on behalf of this book and my colleagues in the Art History department at the University of California, Irvine, for their encouragement and understanding during the lengthy period this book has been in press.

Harvard University awarded a Traveling Fellowship that allowed me to do the initial research in England. The University of California, Santa Cruz, gave additional support in the form of a Faculty Research Grant. The University of California, Riverside, provided me with an efficient research assistant, Elizabeth Lopez, who helped me with the bibliography. My own campus, the University of California, Irvine, has been extraordinarily generous. Grants from the School of Fine Arts, the Faculty Career Development Program, and the Committee on Faculty Research have given me the necessary funds and, more important, the time to see this project through.

Finally, I must thank my parents, who have nurtured in me a love of art and confidence in my own creative process. I dedicate this work to them.

Long Beach, California
November 1984

INTRODUCTION

THE EMERGENCE of rustic landscape painting as a major genre in England at the end of the eighteenth century coincided with the accelerated enclosure of the English countryside. Beginning with the assumption that the parallelism of these events is not an accident but rather a manifestation of profound social change, this study attempts to illuminate the relationship between the aesthetics of the painted landscape and the economics of the enclosed one. Rustic landscape painting became a major genre in the 1780s and received its official endorsement in Joshua Reynolds's Discourse on Thomas Gainsborough. At the same time the improvement of the real landscape, increasing its agricultural yield, raised its commercial and monetary worth. Estates were valued not just because they conferred and embodied the prestige of lineage but also because they promised financial gains unknown to the grandfathers and great-grandfathers of the enclosing landowners. As a result of its new economic value, land at the end of the eighteenth century acquired new social and political value as well. Simultaneously, Nature, with its various representations in painting, poetry, letters, manners, dress, philosophy, and science, became a supreme social value and was called upon to clarify and justify social change. One now did something in a certain way because it was more "natural"; one said something in a certain way because it sounded more "natural"; something worked as it did because it was its "nature" to do so. In the eighteenth and nineteenth centuries almost all change was accommodated under the rubric of "nature" and "naturalness." Hence Nature becomes a key concept linking the cultural representations of social institutions and apparatuses with the economics of the enclosed landscape.

This study examines how rustic landscape painting intersected with the agrarian revolution, how the genre echoed prevailing cultural values that linked it directly to enclosure. Accordingly, I have looked at the formal means through which the genre indirectly inscribed these values, noting as well those instances where it registered contradictions in dominant ideologies, challenged them, or even transcended their values. I have also considered whether the very idea of art's adversarial relationship to the values of bourgeois culture does not itself allow these values to stay in place. With these considerations in mind, I examine the period from 1740 to 1860, analyzing the landscapes of Gainsborough, John Constable, the picturesque painters, and the Pre-Raphaelites and their associates. The period was the golden age of English landscape painting, and the number of major artists then working in the genre has never been equaled. This study deals with only a few of them, using their works as focal points for more general theoretical concerns. The most notable omission is J. M. W. Turner, whose work, falling outside the category of the "rustic," is not central to my topic.

If one were to imagine a physical shape for this study, it would consist of two funnels joined at their narrowest points. That is to say, the argument moves from a consideration of large cultural tendencies to a specific case, the art of John Constable, and then back by way of conclusion to a more general perspective. Although broad in scope, this book is not meant to be a comprehensive study of the development of English landscape painting but rather a critical investigation of the ideological significance of certain formal and aesthetic movements within it.[1] Unlike a survey, it does not rehearse the history of a particular stylistic development but uses historical information to speculate about the cultural meaning of the development. As a result, certain items that would figure in a survey, like the landscapes of the Norwich school painters, are overlooked while others that probably would not, like the outdoor conversation piece, receive attention here because they reveal important social changes relevant to the rustic landscape. In short, this study attempts to provide the reader with an approach to landscape painting that makes sense of its unique historical moment.

The weakness of most art-historical overviews of English landscape painting is that they assume a position of historical neutrality and objectivity that limits them to researching and retelling familiar events without ever interpreting them. Such "objectivity" is a myth that enforces the very cultural values it presumes to stand outside of.[2] It is a myth that enslaves art historians to "data" and allows the supposed objective presentation of them to go unquestioned; it falsely sets the art-historical method outside history and outside ideology. Because art history is an ideological process of interpretation, I outline here both my method and its theoretical assumptions and concerns.

The obvious danger of a sociohistorical approach is that it risks addressing too many levels, the formal and aesthetic as well as the political, social, and economic. The shifting and grinding of gears that accompany the move from one level to another are often abrupt and painfully audible. The sociohistorical approach assumes a relationship between the levels, yet it often fails to show the subtle and varying aspects of this relationship. In many cases economic determination crudely "explains" stylistic developments or limits the discussion to patrons, markets, and sales.[3] Such studies often assume an unproblematic relationship between economic, artistic, and intellectual developments. In contrast, I wish to show that the relationship is highly ambiguous, fraught with a number of contradictory movements. Moreover, since art history must treat individuals who relate to the larger socioeconomic sphere, both symbolically through the style and content of their art and existentially through the prejudices of their own class and their role as producers in the marketplace, this discussion is multidimensional, dealing with the art and, where pertinent, the life of the artist.

The word *ideology* in the title of this work describes the relationships between the various institutions and apparatuses (economic, political, social, and artistic) as well as their expressive contents.[4] Moreover, as Louis Althusser has pointed out, in its imaginary reproduction of the individual's imaginary relationship to the means of production, ideology describes the relationship of the political-legal and intellectual fields of the superstructure to the economic base.[5] Thus the study of a particular ideology (the point of view of a specific class) can clarify not only the connections between the various social institutions and apparatuses within the superstructure but also their relation to the base. I propose that there is an ideology of landscape and that in the eighteenth and nineteenth centuries a class view of landscape embodied a set of socially and, finally, economically determined values to which the painted image gave cultural expression. Rustic landscape painting is ideological in that it presents an illusionary account of the real landscape while alluding to the actual conditions existing in it. Hence although it neither reflects nor directly mirrors reality, the rustic landscape does not altogether dispense with it. Discovering the meaning of its illusionary representation requires interpreting the painted image: not only its content (the particular class view it inscribes) but also the way this content expresses itself and makes itself intelligible—the way it performs in the larger semiotic field. For the relationship of a particular class to the means of production is embedded not only in what is represented but also in the social code or system of representation itself.[6]

Because an artist's connection to dominant class ideologies is never simple, art is capable of showing contradictions within the various ideological functionings of the superstructure. Through the process of "internal distanciation," whereby the·work of art sets itself in a dialogical relation to specific ideologies, it betrays its own ideological underpinnings.[7] The discrepancies, blindnesses, and silences that the work of art maintains in the face of ideology are themselves ideological positions. Because art registers these positions, it is, instead of a one-dimensional "example" of ideology, as much a dynamic framer of ideology as politics itself. For this reason it is important not to overlook the work of art's contradictory character en route to larger social categories, for though art produces ideology and exists within it, it also registers the inconsistencies within ideologies and pinpoints the places where their totalizing worldview threatens to unravel.

In describing the ideological functions of rustic landscape during the enclosure period, I have relied on the method of semiological analysis put forth by Roland Barthes in his various studies of the sign systems of bourgeois culture.[8] His most significant contribution, from my point of view, is his analysis of the "naturalization" of the cultural codes fundamental to bourgeois realism.[9] His analysis stands behind my interpretation of the significance of the social value placed on nature and the natural during the enclosure period. Barthes's discussion of the way this naturalization works, of its semiological effectiveness, is as important as his analysis of the semiotic codes themselves. The ideological relevance of naturalization to the social and economic realities of the enclosure period and its embodiment in the arts of this period are discussed in chapter 1 and set a basis for the interpretation of other historical and artistic developments that unfold in the subsequent chapters. Studying the naturalization of the cultural codes as well as the codes themselves can illuminate the form and function of the ideology of the rustic landscape.

A number of works by historians and critics have been useful in my consideration of the activities of the enclosure period and their relation to the arts. E. P. Thompson's *Making of the English Working Class* provides the best introduction to the politics and effects of enclosure, most notably the transformation of the rural cottager into the industrial proletarian.[10] His analysis of not only the events themselves but also their ideological motivations and effects has influenced my own approach to the imagery of the rustic landscape. A complementary discussion by Raymond Williams of changing critical attitudes toward nature and the countryside as reflected in poetry and prose is *The Country and the City*.[11] Williams's analysis of literary representations of rural life in the eighteenth and nineteenth centuries has been especially suggestive for this study. Similarly, John Barrell's *Idea of Landscape and a Sense of Place, 1730–1840: An Approach to the Poetry of John Clare* and James Turner's *Politics of Landscape* illuminate the connection between rural economic change and its ideological inscription in nature poetry.[12]

Recent art-historical treatments of English landscape complement these literary studies. David Solkin's catalogue of the work of Richard Wilson and Michael Rosenthal's more directly relevant study of John Constable's Stour Valley landscapes are important socioeconomic studies of two major artists and their works.[13] Rosenthal's insightful analysis of Constable's formal development and its relationship to the social realities of the agrarian landscape of the Stour Valley provides an excellent basis for understanding Constable's art. A second fine book by John Barrell, *The Dark Side of the Landscape: The Rural Poor in English Painting, 1730–1840*,[14] published while this work was well in progress, addresses many of the themes of rustic landscape painting that are discussed here. Focusing on the representation of the rural poor in the genre and landscape paintings of Gainsborough, George Morland, and Constable, Barrell juxtaposes their representations with those of contemporary poets like Thomas Gray, Oliver Goldsmith, and John Clare. He shows that both painting and poetry shifted from the pastoral to the georgic mode of representation, exploring in the process the political, social, and economic stakes and strategies of such a shift and relating them to changes brought about by industrialism.

In addition to its reliance on these sociocultural discussions of landscape painting, my work is indebted to the Gainsborough catalogues of John Hayes and the Constable catalogues of Graham Reynolds and of Leslie Parris, Conal Shields, and Ian Fleming-Williams that are major contributions to the study of these artists' works as well as models of thoroughness and dependability.[15] In a more general way, the work of Kenneth Clark and Ernst Gombrich, illuminating the formal and perceptual dimensions of landscape representation, has provided me with important ideas to consider if not always to accept.[16] Finally, Ronald Paulson's writings detailing the important transition in English art from emblematic modes of representation to expressive ones have deepened my own appreciation of my subject.[17]

I see the eclecticism of my research as its strength; for a topic as all-embracing as ideology and art requires the consideration not only of the historical period and its forms of representation but also of the cultural mechanisms whereby social and economic realities become inscribed in a medium intrinsically different from that of "lived experience." Constructing an art-historical account of the meaning and significance of landscape means addressing all the ways it has been seen, recorded, represented, explained, understood, appreciated, and valued. This process has importance for the present historical moment. As the works of Gainsborough, Constable, and the Victorians show, art, like other ideological apparatuses, insulates society from desires that cannot otherwise be met or validated. The different responses of these artists represent differences of personality and situation and reveal both the ideological and the artistic range of aesthetic imagination. By inscribing the social values of industrialism, their landscapes become sites for the expression of society's positive as well as often ambivalent feelings about the changing social order. Thus the ideology of landscape as seen in the English rustic tradition suggests a history for our own century's troubled dealings with nature. Moreover, it implies that our feelings about nature are less censored versions of our feelings about ourselves and suggests that since the industrial revolution the figure in the landscape has been as much endangered as the landscape itself.

I shall no longer resist the Passion in me for things
of a natural kind; where neither *Art*, nor the *conceit*
or *caprice* of men has spoil'd their genuine order, by
breaking in upon the primitive *State*.

Anthony Ashley Cooper,
third earl of Shaftsbury,
The Moralists

THE STATE AND ESTATE OF NATURE

IT IS A FACT of history that in the eighteenth century, enclosure radically altered the English countryside, suiting it to the needs of the expanding city market. It is a fact of art history that in the eighteenth century, with the "discovery of Britain,"[1] the English saw their landscape as a cultural and aesthetic object. This coincidence of a social transformation of the countryside with the rise of a cultural-aesthetic ideal of the countryside repeats a familiar pattern of actual loss and imaginative recovery. Precisely when the countryside—or at least large portions of it—was becoming unrecognizable, and dramatically marked by historical change, it was offered as the image of the homely, the stable, the ahistorical.

With enclosure, landholders acquired land once held in common or waste land once thought unsuitable for cultivation.[2] Old commons and wastes were divided into fields that were either fenced or hedged with a variety of quick-growing shrubs like hawthorne, sloe, and blackthorn. Trees (typically ash, oak, elm) were usually grown in these hedges to produce timber to pay for the enclosure. Although the process of enclosure dated from the fifteenth century, it was enormously accelerated in the eighteenth century by Parliament's willingness to sponsor private bills of enclosure. Until about 1660 the government, to curb the landowners' feudal powers, strongly opposed enclosure, and its efforts slowed substantial agrarian change. In the context of nascent imperialism and mercantilism in the late seventeenth century, however, the need to fashion an agrarian countryside to serve the expanding markets of the towns and colonies became more obvious. The purpose of enclosure was to augment agricultural production by putting more land under cultivation. Coupled with new scientific and mechanical improvements in farming, enclosure vastly increased agricultural yield, making England the most agriculturally productive country in the world. Enclosing the land, as well as draining and fertilizing it and buying the new equipment, required a considerable outlay of capital. As a result, farms grew larger, with the big landowners buying out the little ones. Farms of twenty to thirty acres disappeared, replaced by farms of three hundred to five hundred acres.[3] Enclosure proceeded rapidly. In the first half of the eighteenth century 74,000 acres of land were enclosed by act of Parliament, and in the second half of the century the figure swelled to 750,000 acres.[4] Even these figures, which do not include acreage enclosed by private consensus among landholders, offer a conservative picture.

Precisely in the period of accelerated enclosure (roughly 1750–1815), there fell the dramatic aesthetic and cultural discovery of the countryside on the part of the middle class. Throughout the period, nature, and the natural, as embodied par excellence by the countryside, became important aesthetic and cultural values. The discovery had its literal forms in the researches of Arthur Young in his *Farmer's Tour through the East of England* and Gilbert White's *Natural History of Selborne*, in the enthusiastic antiquarianism of Horace Walpole, and in the picturesque guidebooks of William Gilpin. In poetry, the lyrics of George Crabbe, along with those of John Clare, Thomas Gray, and William Wordsworth, celebrated the countryside and rural values. More important for this study, during this period the garden was transformed from a small-scale, formal structure to an extensive, natural-looking landscape garden. Amateurs like Henry Hoare at Stourhead and Uvedale Price at Foxley, as well as professional landscape gardeners like Lancelot "Capability" Brown and Humphry Repton, planned these gardens. In the pictorial arts it was the great age of landscape painting, marked by the topographical studies of Paul Sandby, William Pars, and Thomas Girtin, as well as by Richard Wilson's classical landscapes and J. M. W. Turner's sublimities. Within the body of this work, however, primarily as the achievement of Gainsborough and Constable, emerged a significant new genre, the rustic landscape, that is, paintings of rural England typically featuring country lanes, farmlands, and river scenes.[5] Rustic landscapes differ from topographical studies in that their main intention is not to portray a famous spot, view, or monument but instead to evoke the countryside and rural life. The rustic landscape is not easily or satisfactorily assimilated into classical-romantic polarities. Modeled on and inspired by the countryside, the genre demands other terms for its understanding, terms derived from the fortunes of the actual countryside that it represents. Precisely through its apparent claim to a direct, empirical vision of the countryside, the ideological implications of this ideal (and idealizing) perspective show for their most subtle and most interesting.

The contradiction between the social reality of the countryside and its idealized aesthetic representation is my chief concern. I am most interested in the ways in which this contradiction is repeated within the aesthetic realm itself and shall propose a series of readings that will take for their object some of the central moments in the aesthetic idealization of the countryside: the landscape garden, the outdoor conversation piece, the rustic landscapes of Gainsborough, the picturesque aesthetic, and—the burden of my study—Constable. In each case I shall ask how these moments inscribe the loss they are meant to recover. Such an inscription must necessarily be ambivalent. On the one hand, it is a strategy of containment, including its own negation in order to subsume it. On the other, the inscription of loss inevitably betrays the discomfort it would erase. In short, the rustic landscape erases its idealizing signs by naturalizing them and allows what is erased still to stand as an informing presence.

THE LANDSCAPE GARDEN

In the landscape garden art took up the very same raw material as the economic and social process of enclosure. Moreover, because the landscape garden was contiguous with the enclosed landscape, the antithesis between the instrumental and noninstrumental (aesthetic) use of land was pronounced, finally coming to shape the aesthetics of garden composition itself. Throughout the eighteenth century landscape gardens grew more extensive. Not only did they absorb village commons within their boundaries, but occasionally whole villages that stood in the way of a prospect or an improvement were destroyed and rebuilt elsewhere. "Sweet Auburn" in Oliver Goldsmith's "Deserted Village," for example, is believed to have been the village of Nuneham Courtenay, destroyed in 1761 to make a garden for Lord Harcourt.[6] Goldsmith himself endorsed Sir William Chambers's unfashionable "Chinese Garden" because it demonstrated that a "very small extent of ground was enough for an elegant taste."[7]

The change from the smaller Dutch and French models of garden design to a more extensive, informal plan was caused in part by the need to reduce the high cost of maintaining the formal garden. Nevertheless, while the landscape garden was cheaper to maintain, it was not necessarily cheaper to create, usually demanding a considerable initial outlay of capital. In this sense, the rationale and economics of the landscape garden echoed those of the enclosure movement.

As the century progressed, the English landscape garden quickly surpassed the French formal garden in size. In 1709 (translated 1712), A. J. Dézallier d'Argenville in his *Théorie et la pratique du jardinage* recommended that the formal garden take up thirty or forty acres at the most.[8] By mid-century, thirty or forty acres was the norm for the English landscape garden. Forty years after d'Argenville's book, the Honorable Charles Hamilton, youngest son of the earl of Abercorn, completed a thirty-acre ornamental *lake* for his park at Painshill.[9] And Hamilton's lake was a modest predecessor of Lancelot "Capability" Brown's forty-acre lake at Blenheim of about 1764.[10] Landowners after 1750 could afford such extravagant gardens mainly because the land taken out of production for them could be made up for elsewhere by the enclosure of common fields, small farms, and waste lands and because the dispossessed peasants and small landowners could be hired back to rent and work the newly enclosed ground.

Whereas the French formal garden was based on a single axial view from the house, the English garden was a series of multiple oblique views that were meant to be experienced while one walked through it. As early as 1718 Stephen Switzer in his *Ichnographia rustica* argued that the gardener should "buy as many twinings and windings as the villa will allow, . . . diversify his views, always striving that they may be so intermixed, as not to be all discovered at once, but that there should be as much as possible something appearing new and diverting, while the whole should correspond together by the natural error of its natural avenues and meanders."[11] The elaborately planted parterres and terraces that facilitated the single axial view of the formal garden also kept it within certain physical limits. The English landscape garden, with its succeeding multiple views of natural-looking plantings and earthworks, was free to ramble.

The extension of the garden both physically and visually (through the opening up of prospects and views) was accomplished with the ha-ha, a deep narrow trench that allowed the designer to dispense with fences, hedges, and terraced borders. The ha-ha, which served to keep livestock from entering the garden, had been used in France and was mentioned by d'Argenville. The first English designer to exploit it in his garden plans was Charles Bridgeman. Horace Walpole, describing the revolutionary effect of the ha-ha on gardening, noted that it allowed "the contiguous ground of the park without the sunk fence . . . to be harmonized with the lawn within, and the garden in its turn was to be free from its prim regularity, that it might assort with the wilder country without."[12] The ha-ha encouraged not only the expansion of the garden but also its increasingly natural design.

By mid-century, smaller gardens were considered ridiculous, a sign of the tasteless arriviste. Robert Lloyd satirized the small garden of the new gentry in a poem called "The Cit's Country Box" (1757):

A wooden arch is bent astride
A ditch of water, four feet wide,
With angles, curves and zig-zag lines
From Halfpenny's exact designs.
In front a level lawn is seen,
Without a shrub upon the green
Where taste would want its first great law
But for the skulking, sly ha-ha,
By whose miraculous assistance
You gain a prospect of two fields distance.[13]

A description of a garden in *The World* a few years later made the same point: "At your first entrance, the eye is saluted by a yellow serpentine river, stagnating through a beautiful valley, which extends nearly 20 yards in length. Over the river is thrown a bridge partly in the Chinese manner and a little ship with sails spread and streamers flying floats in the middle of it."[14] Such elaborate effects, seen as silly attempts to make up for a want of size, were nowhere to be found in the expansive gardens of Capability Brown and Humphry Repton. The indispensable condition for the true landscape garden was *land*, not simply as the raw material to be worked but as its own ornament and aesthetic effect as well. Uvedale Price reacted to exactly this delight in expansive landscapes when he criticized Brown's and Repton's tendency to "bare and bald" the landscape—to restrict vegetation to smooth-shaven lawns broken only occasionally by small clumps of trees.[15] The landscape garden's aesthetic effect depended on a completely nonfunctional, nonproductive use of land.

Most historians of the landscape garden fail to consider that its size and appearance related directly to the rescaling and redesigning of the real landscape through enclosure.[16] Whereas the garden put a premium on informal and irregular plantings and earthworks, enclosure divided the landscape and regularized its appearance. The first step in the process of enclosure was to survey, measure, and assess the area to be enclosed—usually determined by estate holding, parish, or town lines.[17] Next, the whole area was parceled out so that every landholder received his proportionate share. In the new allocations, the lines of fields were fixed so as to form rectangles. Each new property was bordered, usually by hedges, which also delimited the fields within it. Inevitably, the newly enclosed landscape of neatly hedged fields looked small in scale compared with the unbroken commons and wastes that it replaced. "Extent and freedom" took refuge in the landscape garden that aimed precisely at "disguising or hiding the boundary" and "making the whole appear the production of nature only."[18] As the real landscape began to look increasingly artificial, like a garden, the garden began to look increasingly natural, like the preenclosed landscape.[19] Thus a natural landscape became the prerogative of the estate, allowing for a conveniently ambiguous signification, so that nature was the sign of property and property the sign of nature. It would be only a slight exaggeration to say that the ideological role of nature in the eighteenth century lay in this reversibility of signifier and signified.

During the period of accelerated enclosure, the garden and "common nature" were no longer seen in opposition but in symbiosis. Such a relationship was facilitated by devices like the ha-ha that blurred the boundary between the garden and, in Walpole's words, "the wilder country without." As enclosure proceeded, leaving the "country without" increasingly less wild, professional gardeners refined the planning of prospects to avoid the raw-looking new enclosures.[20] Brown's and Repton's gardens excluded such unpleasant objects from view while allowing real views of the countryside only if they were pleasing and of a piece with the garden. In most cases these views were glimpses of meadows, lakes, or church spires framed by trees. Describing such a garden, whose hillside setting included real views, Arthur Young wrote, "In front of the house and garden, between the hills, an extensive woody valley opens *beautifully variegated*. An old tower, Helmsley Church, and the town scattered with clumps of trees, are seen in the midst of it at those *points of taste which make one think them the effects of design*."[21] The dialectic between *art* (the formal garden) and *common nature* (the real landscape) achieved in the gardens of the first half of the century (for example, Pope's garden at Twickenham) foreshadowed the conflation of the two terms.[22] Whereas the formal garden had stood between art and nature, the landscape garden tended to collapse the distinction altogether. In this sense, it became a *trompe l'oeil*. By conflating nature with the fashionable taste of a new social order, it redefined the natural in terms of this order, and vice versa.

THE OUTDOOR CONVERSATION PIECE

By means of an "art that masks art," the landscape garden collapsed the opposition between nature and the cultural (social, aesthetic) processes that appropriated it. The opposition of nature and culture in the outdoor conversation piece might at first seem less able to be suppressed, for the genre presents a landscape garden with people in it—typically its owners. The figures who take their leisure in the garden give a cultural and historical date to the universal and timeless image of nature. The informality that inspired the figures' gestures, poses, and groupings linked the social and the natural, for in such informality—conceived of as "being oneself"—the class dominating the countryside and directing its transformation could see itself, at the most intimate level, as acting naturally.

Nature, therefore, plays an equivocal role in the outdoor conversation piece—on the one hand, reduced to a sign of its owners' status and privilege and, on the other, rehabilitated as a primary source of value that legitimizes this status and privilege. The outdoor conversation piece exploits such ambiguity and plays off one meaning against the other. The ambiguity of nature and of the figures' relation to nature promotes a necessarily (and conveniently) ambiguous reading. A subjected nature refers to culture because nature is part of a pictorial code that tells the viewer that the subjects of the painting enjoy a certain status, that they possess both property and taste; at the same time, a subordinate culture refers to nature for its ultimate justification: the figures' gestures are signs of the ease and self-identity that nature intrinsically embodies. Thus nature signifies class while class signifies a universal, classless nature. Nature in the outdoor conversation piece is made to "say" bourgeois culture, but bourgeois culture is also made to say nature. This implicit derivation of social convention, practice, and attitudes from the natural structure of the world is what I shall be calling the *naturalization of the sign*.[23]

A typical example of this naturalization can be found in Arthur Devis's portrait *Richard Moreton, Esq., of Tackley*, of about 1757 (Figure 1). Moreton sits in a landscape garden, chatting with his niece and nephew. They have been fishing and interrupt Moreton's reading to show him their catch. Moreton's dress designates him as a man of property, as does the landscape garden behind him. Reading outdoors and fishing from streams imply both conspicuous leisure and the standing of a class exempt from work. At the same time, the landscape garden functions as a sign of transcendent nature (the same double function observed in the landscape garden proper). Its delicately serpentined stream and undulating grassy hills evoke the estate as a state of nature. Moreover, the informality of the figures' gesture, pose, and grouping echoes the naturalness of the landscape. Moreton's glance has turned casually toward the viewer; his legs are crossed and his arm is slung over the back of the chair he sits on; he has improvised a resting place for his hat against a leg of the chair. His nephew absently retains fishing rod in hand. Like the naturalness of the landscape garden, informality operates a confusion between nature and culture. Thus the Moreton group is not simply *in* a state of nature but is consubstantial with it. Nature is recreated in the image of certain class practices and values, which are thereby naturalized.

An even more pointed equivalence between the nature of the estate and the state of nature occurs in John Zoffany's *The Colmore Family*, of about 1775 (Figure 2). As in the Devis portrait, the family is depicted relaxing in a landscape garden.

FIG. 1.   Arthur Devis, *Richard Moreton, Esq., of Tackley*, ca. 1757 (28½ × 36 in.). Present whereabouts unknown.

Three generations are represented: a grandmother, a married couple, and their
children. In the foreground is a mother hen with her chicks. The caesura between
the self-contained group of women and children on the right and the figure of
the father on the left carries over to the landscape background. An oak tree
behind the family divides the background so that the landscape garden of the
estate is visible behind the father while its farmland and henhouse can be seen
behind the women. The social values represented by the family find their transcendent justification by being staged in a nature that they appear merely to
echo. The depiction of generations, for example, gives the family a continuous
history comparable to nature's endless cycles. Like the mother with her children,
the hen with her chicks implies that motherhood is woman's natural condition.
The caesura between the women and children and the father is naturalized by
(as) the division of the landscape into garden and farm. Implicitly, the father's
status equals that of the garden as a representation of absolute intrinsic value

FIG. 2. John Zoffany, *The Colmore Family*, ca. 1775 (39½ × 50 in.). Present whereabouts unknown.

(that is, land) while the women's status, like that of the farm, is related to production. The metaphor is a central, recurring one in the agrarian bourgeoisie's imagination of itself: masculinity is associated with the natural right to inherit and possess the land and femininity with the natural responsibility to (re)produce and maintain a family.[24] For just as the hen's production is ultimately directed toward the agrarian market (as the henhouse discreetly reminds us), the mother's childbearing is also caught up in an economic program: heirs to the estate, off-spring for the marriage market. Both mother hen and henlike mother ensure the survival and perpetuation of the estate.

Both the Devis and Zoffany portraits depict nature and the natural in a social context that is in turn justified by its reference to nature. A key tactic in this justification is informality. The informal dress, pose, gesture, and grouping cor-respond to a middle ground between nature and society, the ground in which their mutual justification is possible. Compared, for instance, to the fancy dress in society portraits by artists like Thomas Hudson, Allan Ramsay, and Joshua Reynolds, the dress of the Moreton and Colmore groups seems relatively unaffected. Similarly, their gestures and poses seem more the effect of chance or narrative incident than of heroic posturing.

This informality, however, does not have a uniform character; even in the two conversation pieces considered here, informality is unevenly pursued, present in different degrees. Devis's figures, for example, appear more self-conscious than Zoffany's, his poses more contrived, his landscape more obviously designed (with its neat lawns and perfectly serpentined stream). But while more relaxed, Zoffany's figures are also more formally dressed. Mr. Colmore wears a gold-embroidered coat with *marinière* cuffs.[25] Mrs. Colmore wears a gown with a train and a ribboned stomacher, and all three adults powder their hair. The Colmores are more dressed up than Moreton and his nephew in their plain cloth frock coats. Clearly, then, while both artists foreground informality, they locate it in different places. To a modern viewer, Zoffany's portrait may seem to realize a more consistent, more evenly distributed informality than Devis's. Yet what is perhaps more important than this distinction is the recognition that in both paintings such informality apparently coexists in harmony with a certain conventionalism. Carried to its extreme, informality would seem to exclude conventional social coding, just as such coding would exclude spontaneous natural ease. But the conversation piece hyphenates the opposing models of signification so that they are no longer fully distinguishable from each other.

In his important study of eighteenth-century English art, Ronald Paulson observed that the indoor conversation piece usually portrayed middle-class families and exact sociopersonal definitions whereas the outdoor conversation piece tended to display aristocratic families, garden imagery, and symbolism relating art to nature.[26] Judging from the Devis portrait and others, this distinction began to blur by mid-century as the outdoor conversation piece became increasingly popular with aristocrats and bourgeoisie alike because of its powerful ability to confer status on its subjects while naturalizing it. According to George Vertue, the outdoor conversation piece was introduced into England via France by Philip Mercier, a follower of Antoine Watteau, who adapted the master's lyrical *fête galante* to the more prosaic needs of the group portrait. Mercier's modifications of the *fête galante* are significant. Typically Watteau placed his figures in the corner of a formal garden, which functioned as a setting or even a "set" for them and their activities. In this sense, the backgrounds relate to contemporary stage design and to the garden plans sometimes derived from it.[27] The lush, enchanted look of Watteau's settings calls up in our imagination the very thing they seem to wish to suppress—the real world—whose total exclusion in the painting sug-

FIG. 3. Philip Mercier, *Viscount Tyrconnel with Members of His Family on the Grounds of Belton House*, ca. 1725–1726 (24 × 29 in.). National Trust, Belton House.

gests its totalizing presence elsewhere, making the garden appear a tenuous and thus precious preserve.[28] By contrast, Mercier in his portrait *Viscount Tyrconnel with Members of His Family on the Grounds of Belton House*, from about 1725–1726 (Figure 3), places his figures in a landscape that is clearly the extension of the estate. The temporal quality of the *fête galante* is lost because here the pleasures abandoned one day can be resumed the next. In fact these pleasures seem to be part of the life of the estate, for the semipermanent objects, like the swing tied to a tree and the removal out of doors of toys and chairs, suggest that such amusements belong to the daily ritual of family life. The landscape has become

an outdoor nursery where informal play is not only allowed but called for. Moreover, the safe play initiated here clarifies proper social pairings rather than obscuring them. Mercier emphasizes the individual pose, in sharp contrast with
Watteau's usual arrangement of his figures into an amorous serpentine. Even
stylistic similarities between the two seem to serve different ends. Thus the rococo delight in surface, in the shimmer of silks and the luster of velvets, and the
aerial softness of the landscape that in Watteau underline the transitory exqui-
siteness of the scene, its illusionary character, in Mercier detail the opulence of
the sitters' lives, a permanent luxuriousness into which they have been born. Its
very permanence is the fact, or better, the essence, of their lives. Mercier erased
the tension Watteau had established between the setting and the figures by substituting permanency for transitoriness, proper social liaisons for dangerous or
questionable ones, the desirable materiality of surface for a quasi-allegorical dis-
trust of surface, and ownership for visitation. Mercier's substitutions formed a
basis for representation on which the outdoor conversation piece built; they
muted the distinctions between nature and the sitters, suggesting that the life
of the estate was an extension of the natural order.

The whole range of eighteenth-century discourse on manners and gestures
was characterized by this same refusal to separate nature from a certain culture,
the informal from a certain formalized social code. The natural was a touchstone
for eminently social behavior, justifying and articulating such behavior in terms
other than social ones. Early in the century Addison observed approvingly: "The
fashionable world is grown free and easy; our manners sit more loose upon us:
nothing is so modish as an agreeable negligence. In a word, good breeding shews
itself most where to an ordinary eye it appears the least."[29] Gentlemanly ease
became the standard of all critics and observers of contemporary manners. Writing to his son, Lord Chesterfield remarked: "Besides being civil, which is abso-
lutely necessary, the perfection of good breeding is, to be civil with ease, and in
a gentlemanlike manner. For this, you should observe the French people, who
excel in it, and whose politeness seems as easy and natural as any other part of
their conversation."[30] Similarly, William Pitt, the first earl of Chatham, warned
his nephew that in fashionable society "bowing, ceremonious, formal compli-
ments, stiff civilities, will never be politeness, that must be: easy, natural, unstudied, manly, noble."[31] The reform even touched dress, and women were cau-
tioned in manuals of decorum against high stays, which "obstruct and change
the position and design of Nature, from an easy, genteel and natural position to
an awkward, ungenteel and unnatural one."[32]

Behind all the admonitions to act naturally was an implicit social referent.
Just as the garden implied an art that hides art to collapse the opposition between

nature and the cultural processes that appropriate it, "natural ease" in the eighteenth-century discussion of manners both affirmed social standing and denied
such standing its class origins. For example, Addison recommended "an agreeable negligence" as a sign of "good breeding" that "shews itself most where to
the ordinary eye it appears least." In both Addison and Chesterfield, "breeding"
is the switchword used to talk of social claims while apparently using the vocabulary of nature. Pitt equated the easy, natural, and unstudied with socially
charged, value-laden terms like *manly* and *noble*. Such discourse effectively
merged the natural and the social to the point where they seemed to make common cause. It permitted the class character of their recommendations to be expressed but not openly acknowledged.

The reflections of Addison and Chesterfield find a less subtle counterpart in
the social manuals or etiquette books that abounded in the period, which typically defined politeness as a balance struck between excessive ceremony and excessive freedom: "Real Politeness is attended with Ease and Freedom, it is a
sworn Enemy to every Thing that is unnatural and affected. But, a proper Deportment, a little Ceremony, is necessary to recommend you, as in Moderation
they are consistent with Politeness; 'tis carrying Ceremony to excess that renders
it odious and blameable. Now to behave genteel is to find a Mean betwixt the
two Extremes."[33] The assumption that such balance is possible stood behind the
seeming contradiction of a characteristic injunction like "stand firm, yet easy
and without Affection."[34] Besides neutralizing the conflict between society and
nature by recommending a "real politeness" that ideally incorporated the terms
of both the social and the natural, the etiquette books' frequent recommendation
of a middle ground reflects the middle rank of society to which they addressed
themselves. Detached from both the ceremony of court and the uncouth omis-
sions of common people, "real politeness" became the preeminent bourgeois
virtue.

Closely tied to the reform of manners is the question of gesture. The art of
polite gesture, or deportment, was widely discussed in etiquette books and became—after the minuet—the most important subject taught by dancing masters. In addition, the theory of gesture had an important bearing on rhetoric,
oratory, and drama. Significantly, gesture was characterized as a natural language. Unlike verbal language, gesture offered a system in which the rudimen-
tary sign and signified were grounded in resemblance. Here is Lord Kames in
his *Elements of Criticism*:

> The external signs of passion are of two kinds, voluntary and involuntary. The vol-
> untary signs are also of two kinds; some are arbitrary and some natural. Words are

arbitrary signs, excepting a few simple sounds expressive of certain internal emotions; and these sounds being the same in all languages, must be the work of nature.
But though words are arbitrary, the manner of employing them is not altogether so;
for each passion has by nature peculiar expressions and tones suited to it. . . . the
other kind of voluntary signs, comprehends certain attitudes and gestures that naturally accompany certain emotions with surprising uniformity. Thus excessive joy is
expressed by leaping, dancing or some elevation of the body, and excessive grief by
sinking or depressing it. Thus prostration and kneeling have been employed by all
nations and in all nations in all ages to signify profound veneration. Another cir-
cumstance, still more than uniformity, demonstrates these gestures to be natural,
viz. their remarkable conformity or resemblance to the passions that produce them.[35]

Thomas Sheridan makes the naturalness of gesture even more radical: "There is
no emotion of the mind, which nature does not make an effort to manifest by
some of those signs (tones, looks, gestures), and therefore a total suppression of
those signs is of all other states apparently the most unnatural."[36] From Sheridan's perspective, gestures are so natural that they are all but inescapable and
Kames's notion of "voluntary" gesture seems almost a contradiction in terms.
Not to employ this transparent language must be an active "suppression" and an
"unnatural state."

Contrary to what one might expect, however, this insistence on the naturalness of gesture did not preclude a counteremphasis on its conventionality. Such
a counteremphasis informs the *Réflexions critiques sur la poésie et sur la peinture* by
the French writer Jean-Baptiste Du Bos.

Or les gestes significatifs sont deux espèces. Les uns sont des gestes naturels, et les
autres sont des gestes artificiels. . . . Mais il est rare que le geste naturel signifie
quelque chose distinctement, quand on le fait sans parler . . . cela arrive lorsque le
geste naturel signifie une affection, comme un mal de tête ou de l'impatience. Mais
le geste naturel ne suffit pas même alors pour donner à connoître les circonstances
de cette affection. . . . homme qui veut exprimer distinctement, sans parler, une
autre chose qu'une affection, est obligé d'avoir recours à ces démonstrations, et à ces
gestes artificiels, que ne tirent pas leur signification de la nature, mais bien de
l'institution des hommes.[37]

Though Du Bos's views found few explicit echoes in England, the whole enterprise of systematizing deportment in etiquette books implies something like it.

The etiquette books regularized bodily movements and encoded them into a
network of social and class meanings. Deportment could facilitate social inter-
course and forestall misunderstandings only if its gestural signs were uniform,
appropriate, and unambiguous. The etiquette books continually reminded their

FIG. 4. Louis Philippe Boitard, *Standing*, ca. 1737. Engraving after Bartholomew Dandridge. From Francis Nivelon's *Rudiments of Genteel Behavior*, 1737.

FIG. 5. *Standing*, ca. 1770. Engraving from Mathew Towle's *The Young Gentleman and Lady's Private Tutor*, 1770.

readers of the unhappy consequences of failing to use the code correctly: "Mary is good and virtuous, but her Dress is gay, her Conversation loose, and by that means she is deemed a Coquette."[38] To be mistaken for what one is not represented an alarming breakdown in the sign system—a breakdown more easily avoided than repaired. That mistakes and misuses are possible at all, however, is a precondition of etiquette books. Despite some claim to be describing a universal norm of deportment, the large number of etiquette books published in

FIG. 6. Louis Philippe Boitard, *To Offer or Receive*, ca. 1737. Engraving after Bartholomew Dandridge. From Francis Nivelon's *Rudiments of Genteel Behavior*, 1737.

FIG. 7. *To Offer or Receive*, ca. 1770. Engraving from Mathew Towle's *The Young Gentleman and Lady's Private Tutor*, 1770.

this period offer contrary evidence that their norm was not universally accepted or fully legible, as it would have been had it been entirely natural. Because the task of etiquette books was to define, disseminate, and preserve the system, it is not surprising to find little change in the art of deportment throughout the century. Illustrations from two etiquette books from the first and last half of the century (Figures 4–7) show the same limited supply of gestures for standing, sitting, walking, dancing, bowing and curtsying, and giving and receiving objects. Moreover, the etiquette books, reflecting the new talk about naturalness, incorporated many admonitions to temper manners with "Ease and Freedom." The etiquette books maintained the social code of deportment intact by describing it under the umbrella of the natural.[39]

Whether from the openly reformist perspective of men like Addison and Sheridan or from the apparently conservative perspective of the etiquette manuals, gesture was generally viewed as forming a highly readable system of representation. In addition, the gestural sign was always read according to two coterminous keys, the natural and the social. These two keys, however, did not enjoy equal status, and the natural key always dominated and subsumed the social one. The effect of this dominance of the natural was to present nature and society as one and the same.

Zoffany and Devis gave two different emphases to the gestural sign in their conversation pieces. Zoffany employed its psychological nuances while Devis preferred a more conventionally legible, even routinized model of the natural. In terms of the eighteenth-century discourse on manners and gesture, gestures in Devis have the same status as illustrations in etiquette books. Nevertheless, these artists are not simply opposites, for even though Zoffany's gestures are less conventional and more thoroughly naturalized than Devis's, they nonetheless refer to the social values that structure them.

Without resorting to extravagant or theatrical gesticulations, Zoffany painted a highly expressive portrait of the Colmore family. The gestures he portrays are subtle, virtually unconscious: slight turnings and inclinations of heads and bodies, relaxed positions of arms and legs, easy placement of hands. These gestures are all unself-conscious, for the figures' attention is directed elsewhere. The husband looks admiringly at the wife, who modestly returns his gaze. The grandmother lovingly regards the child on her knee, who attentively watches an older sibling amuse a baby with a newborn chick. The oldest child, a girl, stands somewhat apart from this play and stares dreamily in front of her. Everyone's attention is distracted by someone or something else. These quasi-narrative distractions justify the figures' "candid" poses, which can then be taken to reveal character. The figures' psychological absorption in one another and their correspondingly relaxed poses comment on the character of the interfamilial ties that knit the Colmores together. Moreover, such naturalization raises the specific portrayal to a level of universality, implying that this is the ideal character of all family ties. Husbands are proud, wives modest, grandmothers doting, and children curious, playful, affectionate, and dreamy. The painting thus implicitly refers to a body of maxims that it exemplifies and reconfirms. These maxims mark the intervention of the cultural—in the form of its most cherished stereotypes—into the natural and of the universal—in the form of social norms—into the empirical study of individual phenomena.

FIG. 8. Arthur Devis, *Mr. and Mrs. Hill*, ca. 1750–1751 (30 × 25 in.). Yale Center for British Art: Paul Mellon Collection, New Haven.

FIG. 9. *Positions for Holding the Fan*, ca. 1770. Engraving from Mathew Towle's *The Young Gentleman and Lady's Private Tutor*, 1770.

In Devis's work, the accommodation of naturalness to underlying social values is more blunt. The "ease" of his gestures is very much like the ease codified and illustrated by the etiquette books. Indeed at times, as Ellen D'Oench has shown, his gestures directly correspond to those illustrated in the manuals.[40] For instance, in the conversation piece *Mr. and Mrs. Hill* (Figure 8) of about 1750, husband and wife strike poses recommended by etiquette books—he for standing, she for sitting (Figures 4, 9). Rarely, however, are all the figures in a Devis conversation piece in such perfect agreement with the etiquette book models as Mr. and Mrs. Hill. In the contemporaneous *Gentleman Presenting a Lady with a Piece of Honeysuckle* (Figure 10), the man occupies the pose prescribed for pre-

FIG. 10 *(left)*. Arthur Devis, *Gentleman Presenting a Lady with a Piece of Honeysuckle*, ca. 1748–1749 (28 × 36 in.). National Trust, Wimpole Hall.

FIG. 11 *(right)*. *To Give or Receive*, ca. 1770. Engraving from Mathew Towle's *The Young Gentleman and Lady's Private Tutor*, 1770.

senting an object (Figure 6) but the woman does not occupy the matching one for receiving an object (Figure 11). But even when (as in the case of the Moreton conversation piece) the poses in Devis are not identical to those of etiquette book illustrations, they resemble the illustration poses insofar as they eschew psychological naturalism in favor of standardized tokens of natural behavior. The crossed legs and drooping arms in Devis are not the spontaneous reflexes that Zoffany portrays but consciously displayed badges of informality.

Devis's figures, although far busier than Zoffany's, appear to use their activities of reading, fishing, or presenting flowers merely as pretexts to strike a pose. The self-consciously posed propriety of Devis's gestures did not pass unnoticed by his contemporaries. The fourth duke of Devonshire satirically anticipated his portrait by Devis: "I am afraid it will be frightful, for I understand his pictures are all of a sort: they are whole lengths of about two feet long; and the person is always represented in a genteel attitude, either leaning against a pillar, or standing by a flowerpot, or leading an Italian greyhound in a string, or in some other such ingenious posture."[41] Granting that "genteel" attitudes and "ingenious" postures hardly suited the taste of an aristocratic class whose pretensions could be better satisfied by Reynolds's Olympian grand manner, one nonetheless senses in the duke's criticism a Sheridan-like distaste for the relatively unmotivated character of Devis's gestures, which, because they signify the natural but fail to embody it, betray their artificial origins in a social code. Both Devis and Zoffany work toward naturalness in their representations, but if their tenor is the same, their vehicles are different. In Devis the tenor is belied by the vehicle; the signs of naturalness are too obviously signs, marked by a discontinuity with what they signify. In Zoffany the tenor and vehicle are consubstantial; signifier and signified seem to occupy common ground. The two artists' treatment of the gestural sign summarizes the ways the period aestheticized the natural: by increasing codification and by increasing naturalism.

The conversation pieces of specialists like Devis and Zoffany foreground the norms of this genre and furnish a context for the more complex and elusive work of Thomas Gainsborough. Gainsborough's outdoor conversation pieces, rustic landscapes, and fancy pictures together provide the richest and most sustained meditation on the English landscape in the eighteenth century. Although the norms exemplified in Devis and Zoffany are relevant to this meditation, they by no means exhaust it. Landscape was given a new centrality in Gainsborough's work. Even in his conversation pieces, unlike Devis and Zoffany, he always depicted the figures out of doors. While Gainsborough worked out of an established tradition in painting his conversation pieces, he also invented a whole new genre, the rustic landscape. Rooted as they were in a familiar set of norms, Gainsborough's conversation pieces offer an inroad into the rustic landscape's complex of ambivalent feelings and attitudes toward nature and the countryside.

Although Gainsborough's portrait *Mr. and Mrs. Robert Andrews* of about 1748–1749 (Plate 1) is often taken to exemplify the genre of the outdoor conversation piece, its atypicality is striking. The figures are not set in a landscape garden but at the edge of a sunny wheat field; they conform neither to the codified gestures of naturalness nor to the psychological ones; moreover, they do not dominate the composition but share it with the landscape elements. Yet by means of these unusual features the work not only exposes the ideological preconditions of the genre, as do the works of Devis and Zoffany, but also uses them to illuminate the economic root of this ideology.

Frances Andrews sits on an iron bench against which her husband casually lounges. She is dressed in a closed robe of blue silk worn over the wide oblong hoop of the 1740s. She wears a "round-ear" cap under her fashionable straw *bergère* hat whose brim has been rolled in imitation of a milkmaid's. The hat came into fashion in the 1730s with the increasing taste for informality and rusticity.[42] This fashionable informality is even more evident in Robert Andrews's comfortable slouch and his sporty shooting jacket. He wears a large cocked hat called the Kevenhuller Cock that, according to the *British Magazine* of 1746, was the rage among the beaux of London.[43] Holding a flintlock and accompanied by a pointer, Andrews is the epitome of elegant leisure and moneyed privilege. Even his informal hunting attire, gun, and dog represent privilege, for at that time only landowners holding property worth £100 or more were allowed to hunt game.[44] Like Devis, Zoffany, and the writers on manners and decorum, Gainsborough makes these signs of informality (Frances's hat, Robert's dress and pose) double for signs of class, wealth, and fashion. Quite simply, the Andrewses can afford to be themselves.

Gainsborough's farm setting is a departure from the norm of the conversation piece, which typically placed figures in a landscape garden.[45] It is as though Gainsborough were deliberately making it hard on himself, refusing as too easy the integration of man and nature in the garden pastoral and taking on the difficult task of recreating that integration in the more inclusive image of a georgic. Unlike the traditional garden setting that naturalizes behavior based on an ideal of nature, the field in this painting reveals the particular economic relationship to the land on which the Andrewses' behavior is based: economic productivity. Even more remarkable than its revelation of the economic base of naturalization is the painting's revelation of the specific myth of economic production that, according to Marx, sustained this first generation of agrarian capitalists—the myth of the Robinsonade.[46] The gun and dog that signal Robert Andrews's economic status also suggest the hunter and provider. The unfinished portion of the painting, the area around Frances Andrews's hands, was meant to be a dead pheasant, shot by Robert and presented to her.[47] The Andrewses are thus presented as producers of a particular sort. His gun, her hat, the field, and the unpainted dead pheasant all point to their individual intervention in nature, their shaping of it to their own needs. Sport and providing, leisure and labor all happily coincide. Andrews's farm is not just a sign of status but also his very life's labor, his physical and moral sustenance. The painting works toward an organicism in which man and nature partake of one another in an equilibrium suggested by even the painting's balanced division of space between the two. Andrews bears the mark of nature, naturalness, and nature bears the mark of human nature, cultivation.

The field is the painting's most obvious image of this mutuality. As several commentators have pointed out, the field symbolizes the prospective fertility of the newlyweds themselves.[48] They are in tune with the natural imperative to "be fruitful and multiply." At the same time, the cultivated field, together with the other aspects of the farm portrayed, yields genially to human organization, so genially, in effect, that the painting shows nature virtually organizing itself according to the will of its owners. The field, paddock, and park, evacuated of laborers, yield directly to the Andrewses themselves. The painting presents the myth of the independent producer, whose productivity, like Robinson Crusoe's, depends solely on his own wit, labor, and capital and not on the productivity of others. On this myth a society of free competition rests; toward this economic end the eighteenth century's naturalization of social codes was directed. As Marx makes clear, the social contract of the eighteenth century posits the individual not as a historical result but as history's starting point. Consequently, the individual appears to be the creation of nature alone, not the recent product of historical and economic circumstances.

Gainsborough's full celebration of a working harmony between man and nature is an anomaly in the conversation piece, which if it depicts farm fields at all relegates them discreetly to the margins. His example was apparently unpopular and never widely followed. An analogy might be drawn between Gainsborough's agrarian conversation piece and what in gardening was called the *ferme ornée*. This unusual garden was created by Phillip Southcote in 1735 when he turned 35 acres at the perimeter of his 150-acre farm into an ornamental walk, whose decorative plantings, seats, alcoves, and inscribed urns all thematized and eulogized farming.[49] The theme was reinforced by views of the farm's actual dairy, pasture, haystacks, and tillage. Whereas the landscape garden of Brown and Repton was designed to hide an estate's farmlands, Southcote's Woburn Farm was literally built around them. The *ferme ornée* was as rare as the agrarian conversation piece, and the landscape garden was generally preferred to it. Often where small gardens retained the name of *ferme ornée*, they largely ignored the farmland they enclosed, on the model of the poet William Shenstone's Leasowes, whose walks were decorated with classical statues and urns and led visitors into the "Lover's Walk" and "Virgil's Grove."[50] Both Gainsborough's agrarian conversation piece and Southcote's *ferme ornée* seem to have gone against the dominant taste. In general, the period made an increasingly rigid distinction between the landscape garden as the natural domain of the landlord and the agrarian landscape as the appropriate province of the laborer. This differentiation, which became increasingly obvious as agrarian capitalism replaced small-scale subsistence farming, was lamented and condemned in the following century by William Cobbett in his *Rural Rides*.

Why by mid-century was the evidence of agricultural labor consistently avoided in the gentry's collective imagination of itself? Most simply, one could say that work was precisely what this class had been freed from, that work characterized a different class with which the gentry had no wish to be identified.

Work was a breach of taste, offering no occasion to display that "Ease and Freedom" so much recommended and in that sense highly unnatural for a gentleman. More seems to have been at stake, however, than the gentry's prideful need to advertise its leisure. After all, in the Andrews portrait, Robert and Frances Andrews are shown at leisure. Indeed, the portrait might have catered to both the gentry's desire to be portrayed at leisure and its equally powerful desire to be portrayed in the midst of all its possessions. The Andrews portrait remained an unpopular anomaly, then, not because work was something the gentry did not do but because any suggestion of labor in the context of a leisured gentry was unacceptable.

The Andrews portrait itself suggests why mixing labor with leisure was disagreeable. For the structure that seems to idealize the organic harmony of the country squire's life may in fact be read *a contrario*. The juxtaposition of leisured gentry and working estate, for instance, that Gainsborough makes stand for an organic totality equally registers the discrepancy, or problematical linkage, between the two. The conceptual harmony of the painting might dissolve into a series of oppositions or contradictions: the owner opposed to his property, his leisure to others' production, and his pseudo-hunting to their real gathering. His space is carefully marked off (by the line of the bench) from the space of the field. Even as the painting celebrates a self-identity of proprietor and property, it betrays an alienation. The painting's unmediated relationship between the landowner and his land paradoxically evokes the real mediations between them in the visible signs of the labor performed by the invisible men and women who work the farm. The miraculous bounty of Robert Andrews's farm becomes a conspicuous fantasy, and the painting reaches a state of radical paradox in calling attention to the irreducibility of the very thing it wishes to sublate. The evocation of mediators subverts the organic relation between Andrews and his farm: the fields do not yield to him naturally but to the labor of those who plow, fertilize, and seed them.

By making his organicism depend on a dream of bountiful production located in a farmland rather than basing it on an abstraction of pure ownership located in a landscape garden, Gainsborough goes against the century's tendency to erase the process of production in the relationship between owner and product. While certainly sharing the concerns of its age with naturalizing social appearances and arrangements, Gainsborough's agrarian conversation piece is in one sense naive and anachronistic and in another sophisticated and modern. It naively ignores the cultural directive to screen out labor from a representation of gentry, and its juxtaposition of owner and farmer harkens back to a less estranged union of the two than had become the case. But its representation of an organic totality seems to backfire, reintroducing the breach or fall from grace that it was meant to repair. The exemplary significance of the painting lies precisely in the ambiguity of its image, a picture of coziness and alienation together.

The ambiguous vision of the Andrews portrait informs Gainsborough's other conversation pieces as well. Though the agrarian landscape disappears or becomes peripheral, Gainsborough attempts to overcome the separation of man and nature. Usually, as Paulson has noted, formal correspondences link the figure and the landscape setting. The best example of such correspondences is in the small portrait *John Plampin* of about 1753–1754 (Figure 12). There is a one-to-one correspondence between Plampin's pose (borrowed from Watteau) and the formation of the tree behind him.[51] The tree mirrors the disposition of his legs and the slant of his body, and even his hidden right arm is echoed by the tree's broken branch directly behind it. The tree is a double of the figure. Similarly, two of the trees depicted in the background of the *Richard Savage Lloyd* conversation

FIG. 12. Thomas Gainsborough, *John Plampin*, ca. 1753–1754 (19¾ × 23¾ in.). National Gallery, London.

piece of 1750 wittily echo the spindly shape of Lloyd's legs. Two entwined trees behind *Heneage Lloyd and His Sister* of 1750 repeat the love-knot tangle of the brother and sister's arms. The tree precariously perched above *Mr. John Brown and Family* of about 1755 seems a splayed and leafy version of Brown himself.[52] One might even point to the oak behind the Andrewses, which miraculously combines her bolt uprightness with his serpentine slouch, as another example of this correspondence between the figures' poses and parts of the landscape.

Like Devis, Gainsborough relied on an accepted stock of poses. Devis's poses indicate a socially given version of the natural sufficient to integrate the figures with the landscape. Gainsborough's conversation pieces inscribe the poses in nature itself. One effect of this inscription is to recreate nature (or at least a small part of it) in the form of social codes, as though nature were their ultimate source and explicit referent. In this sense, Gainsborough's conversation pieces reflect a limited naturalism, one that exists well within the classicizing process of codification. Finally, however, Gainsborough's correspondences are too playful and witty to serve as evidence of a totally organic union between men and nature. Significantly, unlike the usual repetition of shapes that artists use to compose a painting, Gainsborough's local correspondences do not necessarily contribute to an overall compositional scheme. They appear as flashes of wit, humorous analogies, in which the artifice of the artist is evident. The correspondences and the harmonious vision they involve seem feigned, more the product of the artist's ingenuity than an essential characteristic of nature. The vision thus calls attention to its own fictiveness, like a fantastic dream whose conspicuous ideality points to a deficient reality. Again Gainsborough's art seems at once conventional and iconoclastic, masking the profound division between man and nature and then pointing to the mask.

GAINSBOROUGH'S RUSTIC LANDSCAPES

According to his friend William Bate-Dudley, Gainsborough began painting landscapes while still a boy living in his home town of Sudbury in Suffolk.[53] Although no examples of this "schoolboy stile" survive, the painting known as *Gainsborough's Forest* (Figure 13) was, according to the artist himself, at least started before 1740 when he left home for London at thirteen.[54] It is generally believed, however, that the landscape was completed upon his return to Suffolk in 1748.[55] One of the earliest dates attributed to a Gainsborough landscape is 1744–1746 for an unfinished forest study now in the collection of Sir Alfred Beit at Russborough.[56] Like most of the early landscapes, this work has a pronounced

FIG. 13. Thomas Gainsborough, *Gainsborough's Forest*, ca. 1748 (48 × 61 in.). National Gallery, London. Also known as "Conard Wood."

Dutch look. Although Bate-Dudley claimed that "nature was his teacher and the woods of Suffolk his academy," the influence of the Dutch masters on Gainsborough's landscapes at this time was profound.[57] The obituarist of the *London Chronicle* wrote after Gainsborough's death in 1788: "The first manner he studied was Wynants [Wijnants], whose thistles and dockleaves he frequently introduced into his early pictures. The next was Ruysdael [Ruisdael]."[58] This acknowledgment tallies with the remark of Gainsborough's early friend Joshua Kirby that Gainsborough's first oils were in "the manner of Waterloo, whom in his early days he much studied,"[59] and with Gainsborough's own admission that his early landscapes were "imitations of the little Dutch Landskips."[60] One can see the Dutch influence, particularly that of Ruisdael, in the brittle, knotted trees of the Russborough study and in their screenlike arrangement as well.

FIG. 14. Thomas Gainsborough, *Road through a Wood*, dated 1747 (40⅛ × 58 in.). Philadelphia Museum of Art: The W. P. Wilstach Collection, Philadelphia.

This Ruisdaelian screen of trees was a favorite compositional device of Gainsborough's at this time.[61] In both *Gainsborough's Forest* and *Wooded Landscape with a Seated Figure* (Plate 2) from about 1747, the screen of trees serves as a line of demarcation between the overgrown forest and the distant prospect. In a case where Gainsborough opens up a prospect, as in the *Road through a Wood* (Figure 14) of 1747, the view over the meadow must vie for attention with the screen of trees to the left of the composition. The trees have been arranged like a formal *allée* in a garden, and as such they echo the parallel wagon tracks on the road to the right that leads into the distance. The *allée* of trees sets up a powerful but false axial perspective that like the road attracts the eye but unlike it does not lead the eye to the horizon. Similar *allées* can be found in *Gainsborough's Forest*, where they are disposed like a formal garden's *patte-d'oie* and where only the left *allée* leads to the horizon; the others lead deeper into the woods. These screens of trees and *allées* supply a consistent organizing principle in the early landscapes. Unlike Ruisdael's screens, however, they unfocus the composition. Rather than direct the eye through the landscapes, they contain it, delaying or actually frustrating its journey to the horizon.

FIG. 15. Thomas Gainsborough, *Estuary with Church, Cattle, and Figures*, ca. 1753–1754 (32 × 42½ in.). Ipswich Museums and Art Galleries, Ipswich. Also known as "View near the Coast."

By the mid-1750s, Gainsborough had developed additional ways of containing the eye in the foreground. If one compares Gainsborough's *Estuary with Church, Cattle, and Figures* (Figure 15) of the early 1750s with what seems to be its source, Ruisdael's *Waterfall near a Village* (Figure 16), one is struck by the extent to which Gainsborough has compacted Ruisdael's space by pulling everything into the foreground. In contrast to the Dutch baroque practice of distributing the compositional elements over the foreground, middle ground, and distance, Gainsborough's method was to amass them in a shallow space. His painting seems like a condensed version of the Ruisdael. Works like the *Woodcutter Courting a Milkmaid* of 1755 or even the conversation piece *Mr. John Brown and Family* similarly tend to remain all foreground. The tendency is even more

FIG. 16. Jacob van Ruisdael, *Waterfall near a Village*, ca. 1656 (33⅜ × 39⅛ in.). National Gallery, London.

decided in Gainsborough's landscape drawings and remains a pronounced characteristic of them throughout his life.[62]

The screens and *allées* or the details amassed in the foreground make intimate landscapes in which everything is, so to speak, kept within arm's reach. The viewer sees parts rather than the whole, the synecdochic details of landscape— leaves, moss, flowers, trees, sandy banks, and forest pools—rather than a general conceptualization. The palpable materiality of Gainsborough's renderings—the lush detail, for instance, in his drawing of burdock leaves (Figure 17)—became the raison d'être of his large landscape as well. In a revealing letter of the late 1760s about history and landscape painting, Gainsborough wrote to his friend William Jackson:

FIG. 17. Thomas Gainsborough, *Study of Rocks and Plants*, later 1760s (9 × 11⅛ in.). Black chalk and watercolor drawing, heightened with bodycolor and varnished. Yale Center for British Art: Paul Mellon Collection, New Haven.

> Do you really think that a regular Composition in the Landskip way should ever be fill'd with History, or any figures but such as fill a place (I won't say stop a Gap) or create a little business for the Eye to be drawn from the Trees in order to return to them with more glee—I did not know that you admired those *tragicomic* Pictures, because some have thought that a regular History Picture may have too much background and the composition hurt by not considering what ought to be principle [*sic*].[63]

In addition to warning his friend about the dangers of overloading a landscape with allegorical figures, Gainsborough implies that in the ideal landscape composition figures are used only to "stop gaps" and return the eye to the principal elements in the foreground. Just before his death in 1788, he remarked about

Gainsborough's Forest that "though there is very little idea of composition in the picture, the touch and closeness to nature in the study of the parts and *minutiae* are equal to any of my latter productions."[64] One senses that the "*minutiae*" of landscape were the principal objects in these early works and that Gainsborough conceived landscape as a collection of things rather than an expanse of space, as a confined place rather than a prospect.[65]

The intimacy of Gainsborough's early landscapes reflects the small-scale landscape of his native East Suffolk. Rich soil and abundant pasture had made East Suffolk the center of the wool industry since Tudor times, and large parts of it had been enclosed as far back as the sixteenth century. These preparliamentary enclosures were small since areas of twenty to forty acres were found to be too large for good farming and did not allow rapid rotation of pasture for grazing.[66] Because of these early enclosures, only ten parliamentary acts of enclosure were passed for Suffolk between 1727 and 1801, and these for the most part affected towns and parishes in the western and northern parts of the county.[67] The eastern half of Suffolk, like the early-enclosed counties of Essex, Kent, and Sussex, was almost wholly excluded from the eighteenth century's large-scale enclosures.

As a result, the eastern and western halves of Suffolk are noticeably different to this day. In the east the landscape is densely overgrown, with a network of narrow winding lanes, isolated churches, and scattered houses. In the west it is regular, with straight roads and more villages. Whereas the larger-scale enclosures of the eighteenth century shaped the west, the crooked, closely packed enclosures of the east grew up piecemeal over the centuries.[68]

The densely packed, overgrown eastern part of Suffolk is associated with Gainsborough's landscapes and with the genre of the rustic landscape he established. Its small sixteenth-century patchwork pattern of enclosures bordered by crooked hedgerows and lines of trees was becoming anomalous in Gainsborough's time. Irregular like the unenclosed landscape but bounded and fragmented like the newly enclosed landscape, East Suffolk offered Gainsborough a landscape of richly ambiguous connotation. These old Suffolk enclosures must have looked "natural" in comparison with the newly cleared spaces and regularly plotted fields of the parliamentary enclosures, and at the same time they must have seemed more benignly pastoral and variegated than the sweeping, unenclosed commons and wastes. One easily sees why such a landscape lent itself in the eighteenth century to an aesthetic typology of the English countryside: its socially determined design could stand for a naturalness relatively free of social determination. Ironically, an earlier phase of the economic transformation of the countryside was drafted into the representation of untouched nature. The earlier enclosures—once as great an alteration of the countryside as the later—came to signify the "real" or "natural" landscape of rural England.

Gainsborough's depiction of rural existence in these landscapes is altogether sunnier than that of poets like Oliver Goldsmith, George Crabbe, and John Clare, who were quick to stress the painful changes the country was undergoing because of enclosure.[69] Gainsborough's vision of the countryside, however, is no less important and perhaps no less faultfinding, not because it depicts the actual changes in the countryside, but because it depicts its happier past. His idealized vision of an earlier form of enclosure, one more comfortably scaled to the needs of the small cottagers and tenants, implicitly rejects the harsh new order as much as Goldsmith's "Deserted Village." With the rustic landscape, a stick has been fashioned to beat the present.

Even though Gainsborough's landscapes depict and valorize an earlier form of enclosure, their position with regard to the general direction of agrarian change is nonetheless ambiguous. While containing an implicit argument for the relative naturalness of the old order, they also embody the new at the level of form. The bounded and broken spaces of these landscapes, together with their blocking screens of trees, relocate the phenomenon of enclosure in the viewer's visual perception itself. The contemporary parceling of the commons and wastes into pieces of property that is rejected in the subject matter is at the same time reinstated in the form as piecemeal perception of the countryside. Gainsborough's shallow and fragmented landscape is new. It resembles neither the classical landscape with its rhythmic *coulisses* nor the panoramic landscape with its broad horizontal sweeps. Although Gainsborough's rustic landscapes do not actually depict the eighteenth-century enclosures, they enforce a mode of perception that profoundly accommodates them. Gainsborough's landscapes are thus highly ambivalent, on the one hand expressing a nostalgia for the old order, its small scale and relative naturalness, and on the other hand promoting a mode of perception that adjusts to the new.

While Gainsborough's anachronistic landscapes are ambiguously antienclosure, they are more decidedly antiurban. Peopled with woodsmen, haymakers, herdsmen, and milkmaids, these landscapes celebrate a sylvan idyll, exotically remote and far from the noise and bustle of the city. Gainsborough's landscapes are often anonymous, devoid of the usual topographical landmarks (villages, churches, and so forth) that help identify the view. It seems irrelevant to search for the exact site Gainsborough painted. His landscape was "the countryside." Towns, if they appear at all, are barely distinguishable, relegated, as in *Gainsborough's Forest*, to the distant horizon. This visual rejection of the town is even more pronounced in the landscapes Gainsborough painted later in Bath and London. Paintings like the *Woody Landscape with Milkmaid and Drover* of 1766 and

FIG. 18. Thomas Gainsborough, *The Watering Place*, exhibited at the Royal Academy 1777 (58 × 71 in.). National Gallery, London.

The Watering Place (Figure 18) of 1777 are set deep in the heart of a forest that almost totally envelops the figures.[70] In Gainsborough, the simple way of life becomes associated exclusively with the remote, at times almost primordial, countryside and with its humblest inhabitants. In these rustic landscapes, Gainsborough explores more thoroughly than in the conversation piece an unmediated and organic relationship between man and nature, as though isolation from urban culture were an essential prerequisite for such a relationship.

As in the conversation piece, the organic relation between man and nature evident in the rustic landscape seems to depend on work and its productive force. Nevertheless, in landscapes like *Ploughing Stoke Hill near Ipswich*, from the early 1750s, this relationship is less ambiguous than that found in the Andrews portrait.[71] Most of the rustic landscapes skirt the question of ownership, and the figures look as though they belong to the land and not vice versa. Production is referred to not only in the pastures and farmlands depicted but also in the wood-land settings, where country people are shown going to and from market, gath-ering faggots or chopping wood, and herding cattle and sheep. The labor and production alluded to, then, are highly simplified. The life of these country people seems to be their own, for the paintings do not suggest that they work to pay rent or to receive wages; their relation to the land is mediated by nothing more complex than "home economics." They resemble the rustic laborer in Gold-smith's "Deserted Village," for whom

> light labour spread her wholesome store,
> Just gave what life required but gave no more:
> His best companions, innocence and health;
> And his best riches, ignorance of wealth.[72]

The land is the only master in Gainsborough's landscapes and an ideal one at that. Labor and production are organized not according to the demand of an expanding market but according to the simple needs of the laborer.

The rustic landscape's transformation of rural isolation and agrarian labor into an ideal of organicism must be seen as overdetermined by Gainsborough's own frustration with the demands on his labor and production as an artist. Much of Gainsborough's correspondence was given over to professional woes—woes that arose from his having to bend to the demands and expectations of a society with no taste for simple pleasures. "I'm sick of Portraits," he wrote to his friend William Jackson from fashionable Bath, "and wish very much to take my Viol da Gamba and walk off to some sweet Village when I can paint Landskips and enjoy the fag End of Life in quietness and ease."[73] Many impediments stood between Gainsborough and his "sweet Village," not least among them his wife and his two marriageable daughters:

> But these fine Ladies and their Tea drinkings, Dancings, *Husband huntings* and such will fob me out of the last ten years, & I fear miss getting Husbands too—But we can say nothing to these things you know Jackson, we must jogg on and be content with the jingling of Bells, only d—mn it I hate a dust, the Kicking up of a dust, and being confined *in Harness* to follow the track, whilst others ride in the waggon, under cover, stretching their Legs in the straw at Ease, and gazing at Green Trees & Blue skies without half my Taste, that's damn'd hard. My Comfort is, I have 5 Viols da Gamba 3 Jayes and two Barak Normans.[74]

If his family was an impediment, "gentlemen" and the fashionable society they represented were his natural enemies. In an impetuous outburst he warned Jackson:

THE STATE AND ESTATE OF NATURE

> Now damn Gentlemen, there is not such a set of Enemies to a real artist in the world as they are, if not kept at a proper distance. *They* think (and so may you for a while) that they reward your merit by their Company & notice; but I, who blow away all chaff & by G— in their eyes too if they don't stand clear, know that they have but one part worth looking at, and that is their Purse; their Hearts are seldom near enough the right place to get a sight of it.[75]

In a more reflective letter on the subject a week later he attempted to clarify his opinion. "If I meant anything (which God knows if I did) it was this, that many a *real Genius* is lost in the fictitious Character of the Gentleman; and that as many of those creatures are continually courting you, possibly you might forget, what I without any merit to myself remember from mere shyness Namely that they make no part of the Artist."[76] The notion of artistic integrity so pronounced in these letters centers on the artist's ability to paint what best pleases him and suits his genius. Gainsborough's pride in even his earliest landscapes indicates that they represented to him his natural though frustrated inclination, his essential artistic genius. Writing to Henry Bate in 1788 regarding *Gainsborough's Forest*, he said, "It is in some respects a little in the *schoolboy stile*—but I do not reflect on this without a secret gratification; for as an early instance how strong my inclination stood for Landskip."[77] Painfully aware that "a Man may do great things and starve in a Garret if he does not conquer his Passions and conform to the *Common Eye* in chusing that branch which *they* will encourage & pay for,"[78] Gainsborough gave landscape the status of pure painting: private, personal, and unmediated by the demands of society. The idealized organicism of country life and the fulfillment associated with agrarian labor are the direct antitheses of the alienation Gainsborough felt from the fashionable life in Bath and London and from his own labor there as a painter of society portraits. His nostalgia for the simple rural life may have exceeded the truth of that life, but it was nonetheless in direct proportion to his dislike for the urban alternative.

Gainsborough deeply distrusted all artistic pretension as he valued artistic integrity. To the earl of Dartmouth he wrote:

> For my part (however your Lordship may suspect my Genius for Lying) I have that regard for truth, that I hold the finest invention as a mere slave in Comparison, and believe I shall remain an ignorant fellow to the end of my days, because I never could have patience to read Poetical impossibilities, the very food of a Painter; especially, if he intends to be KNIGHTED in this land of Roast Beef, so well do serious people love froth.[79]

The reference to knighthood was an irreverent swipe at Reynolds, who as president of the Royal Academy had been the first artist in the century to be knighted. To Gainsborough's mind, landscape was the complete antithesis of Reynolds's "grand style." It was void of literary and historical subject matter, and unlike portraiture, where one had to please and often flatter a patron, it allowed the artist freely to exercise his imagination and powers of observation. Gainsborough never relinquished his fond dream of abandoning portraiture to paint landscapes in the country. Some twenty years after recounting to William Jackson his desire to retire to a "sweet Village," Gainsborough expressed the same wish to Sir William Chambers in a letter about his *Two Shepherd Boys with Dogs Fighting*, which he exhibited in 1783 at the Royal Academy:

> I sent my fighting dogs to divert you. I believe next exhibition I shall make the boys fighting & the dogs looking on—you know my cunning way of avoiding great subjects in painting & of concealing my ignorance by a flash in the pan. If I can do this while I pick pockets in the portrait way two or three years longer, I intend to turn into a cot & turn a serious fellow; but for the present I must affect a little madness. I know you think me right as a whole, & can look down upon Cock Sparrows as a great man ought to do, with compassion.[80]

That landscape was a "low subject" at the Academy doubtless accounts for some of its appeal for Gainsborough, who took perverse glee in pointing out its "inferiority" to friends. When Jackson urged him to paint more serious subjects, he replied: "Do you consider my dear maggotty Sir, what a deal of work history Pictures require to what little dirty subjects of coal horses & jackasses and such figures as I fill up with."[81] His delight in his "little dirty subjects" was clearly a way to *épater les bourgeois*.

Formally and ideologically, landscape for Gainsborough was a refuge—from the demands of the present, of an urban culture and its society, and of portraiture. His celebration of country life was an implicit rejection of his own and a fantasy recasting of it in terms of an identification with simple country people. Juxtaposed with his remarks to Jackson and Chambers about retiring to the country, landscapes like the "Cottage Door" series seem like idealized autobiographies.[82] The first of these, *The Woodcutter's Return* (Figure 19), in the collection of the duke of Rutland and probably painted about 1773,[83] establishes the basic motifs: sunset; a thatched cottage in a small, deeply shadowed forest clearing; a nursing mother on the doorstep surrounded by children; the husband either returning home or sitting on the stoop having a pipe. While summing up an ideal for Gainsborough, these scenes doubtless had as little to do with the real situation in the country as they did with his own unhappy marriage. They graft Gainsborough's own dream, generated by a specific social predicament, onto a situation that is intrinsically different. This grafting is what Raymond

FIG. 19. Thomas Gainsborough, *The Woodcutter's Return*, ca. 1773 (58 × 48 in.). Duke of Rutland, Belvoir Castle.

Williams has called "negative identification."[84] The organic integrity that Gainsborough wished these landscapes to embody is belied by their status as unattainable dreams. The countryside exists less in its own right than as a fantasy solution to dilemmas formed elsewhere, and to the degree that the organic integrity of the countryside is thus seen as fictitious, the countryside represents less adequately a real place where these dilemmas do not exist. In other words, as the fantasy "irrealizes" the countryside, the countryside becomes less able to "realize" the fantasy.

Gainsborough's images of the landscape characterize his own alienation.[85] The separation between Gainsborough and his subject (the landscape of rural England and the life it bears) resulted in a pattern of alternating identification with and estrangement from it. Metaphorically, this pattern took the form of voyeurism in his work. In the early *Wooded Landscape with a Seated Figure* (Plate 2), a tiny figure with hat and walking stick sits at the edge of a wooded path and gazes at the landscape before him. This contemplative figure was a favorite device of the Dutch landscapists, in whose works it was intended to link the viewer with the landscape through a process of sympathetic identification. But this mediating figure might also embody a recognition that a prior alienation exists to be overcome. In addition to this device, Gainsborough often used hidden figures who, instead of studying the landscape, watch other figures. In his Bath and London landscapes, these figures are more openly voyeuristic. In a landscape of 1774, *Cattle and Sheep at a Pool*, a cowherd stands and watches two courting lovers from behind a thicket of trees.[86] In *The Market Cart* (Figure 20) of 1786, a boy who has been gathering faggots peeps through the trees at the girls in the passing cart. Voyeurism is the main theme of late subject pictures like *The Haymaker and the Sleeping Girl* (Figure 21) of about 1785 and the extraordinary *Diana and Actaeon* that was begun about 1784 and left unfinished at his death.[87] Voyeurism in Gainsborough, as a way of being simultaneously present and detached, suggests an alienated involvement. Moreover, it allows one to see what would normally be concealed by modesty or social convention. It tacitly acknowledges the artificiality of normal appearances and values what is hidden as the more true or real.

Gainsborough was not the first artist of the century to suggest a connection between voyeurism and painting. Hogarth's subscription ticket for *A Harlot's Progress* is a more explicit and satiric example. In this etching, entitled *Boys Peeping at Nature* (Figure 22), "Nature" refers both to the ancient female personification and to the personification's own "nature" that has been modestly veiled. The classical putto seated at an easel paints Nature's official portrait; the satyr, his irreverent curiosity whetted by natural appetites, lifts her skirts. Hogarth

FIG. 20. Thomas Gainsborough, *The Market Cart*, 1786 (72½ × 60¼ in.). Tate Gallery, London.

FIG. 21 *(left)*.   Thomas Gainsborough, *The Haymaker and the Sleeping Girl*, ca. 1785 (89 × 58½ in.). Courtesy Museum of Fine Arts, Boston: Maria T. B. Hopkins and Seth K. Sweetser Residuary Fund.

FIG. 22 *(right)*.   William Hogarth, *Boys Peeping at Nature*, 1731. Etching. Subscription ticket for *A Harlot's Progress*.

meant the putto to stand for the old masters and the satyr to represent himself, a new kind of artist who does not hesitate to investigate the unseemly side of nature (or, as in the case of *A Harlot's Progress*, human nature).[88] Hogarth emblematized here values and presuppositions about the nature of painting that Gainsborough shared and that became increasingly important as the eighteenth century drew to a close. Both the eighteenth century's equation of the painter with the voyeur and the nineteenth century's notion of him as a "natural philosopher" (to use Constable's term) suggest that painting is an investigative art, one

FIG. 23. Thomas Gainsborough, *Mrs. John Douglas*, exhibited at Schomberg House 1784 (92½ × 57¼ in.). National Trust, Waddesdon Manor.

that has nothing to do with conventions and ready-made views of things but looks through the layers of cultural values and conventions to the truth behind them. This independence turned Hogarth away from the examples of the old masters and prevented Gainsborough from accepting Reynolds's "grand style." While hardly as empirical as Constable would claim, the voyeuristic attitude pointed the way from the classical system of codification to the more discreet significations of naturalism. It replaced the old system of highly legible codification with a more subtle and evocative system of connotation.[89]

Although Gainsborough's desire to undercut the established code of painting is best exemplified in his rustic landscapes, it also appears on occasion in his society portraits, as in the portrait of 1784 *Mrs. John Douglas* (Figure 23). While

FIG. 24. Joshua Reynolds, *Sarah Siddons as the Tragic Muse*, exhibited at the Royal Academy 1784 (93 × 51½ in.). Henry E. Huntington Library and Art Gallery, San Marino, California.

it is often noted that Reynolds's portrait of the same year, *Sarah Siddons as the Tragic Muse* (Figure 24), is borrowed from the Sistine *Isaiah*, it is never pointed out that Gainsborough's *Mrs. Douglas* is derived from the same source. In almost every respect (the throne, the accompanying figures of Pity and Terror, and Mrs. Siddons's dress) the Reynolds portrait calls attention to its quotation from the Sistine ceiling. Gainsborough, on the other hand, translated the quotation so thoroughly into his own idiom as to erase the quotation marks. The comparison points up how even when Gainsborough worked well within the code of art-historical cross-referentiality advocated by academics like Reynolds, he managed to lighten and personalize it.

From the late 1740s until his death in 1788, Gainsborough's rustic land-scapes change very little in their overall composition and subject matter. Stylisti-

FIG. 25. Thomas Gainsborough, *A Pool in the Woods with Cottage and Figures*, exhibited at the Royal Academy 1782 (47 × 57 in.). Private collection, Great Britain.

cally they follow the progression of his technique from a delicate, Anglo-French rococo handling to a more summary, robust Rubenism. In the late works Gainsborough gives less attention to details and reduces the elements of landscape to a few convenient symbols. A graceful, feathery brushstroke gives the late works textural unity, and the tonal values (always important for the compositional cohesion of Gainsborough's landscapes) glow with an increasingly ruddy warmth. The abstract, essentializing quality of the late landscapes suggests that they gesture toward the natural world without describing it in detail. One sees behind them an impatience with the concreteness and specificity of landscape and an eagerness to highlight its meaning or value.

Hence it is not altogether surprising to find that, despite the intensity of feeling and richness of color and technique in the late works (for example, *The Watering Place, The Market Cart* [see Figures 18, 20], or *A Pool in the Woods with Cottage and Figures* [Figure 25] of 1782), the rustic landscape loses its central place in Gainsborough's art. In the last decade of his life, he began to paint

FIG. 26. Thomas Gainsborough, *The Wood Gatherers*, later 1780s (58⅛ × 47⅜ in.). Metropolitan Museum of Art: Bequest of Mary Stillman Harkness, 1950, New York.

FIG. 27. Thomas Gainsborough, *The Marsham Children, Charles, Later Second Earl of Romney, and His Three Younger Sisters*, 1787 (94½ × 71 in.). Gemäldegalerie, Staatliche Museen Preussischer Kulturbesitz, Berlin.

"fancy pictures" (pictures of ragged country children) and to augment his landscape repertory with seascapes, Claudian pastorals, sublime mountain scenery, and the "Cottage Door" scenes.[90] In his late works Gainsborough sought out more explicitly sentimental subjects: the snug domesticity of the cottage door, the sublimity of sea and mountain scenery, or the innocence of children.[91] The fancy pictures are especially significant because they are, in effect, the personification of his rustic landscapes. Landscape per se no longer exists in the fancy pictures; figures absorb and reveal its values and meanings. In the fancy pictures, Gainsborough offers the countryside less as an antithesis to bourgeois urban society than as a definition of "naturalness" as a universal truth, its meaning condensed into a romantic vision of childlike innocence (Figure 26). The children in the fancy pictures are portrayed as vulnerable, fragile vessels of innocence,

FIG. 28. George Morland, *The Squire's Door*, ca. 1790 (15⅜ × 13⅜ in.). Yale Center for British Art: Paul Mellon Collection, New Haven.

whose ignorance of the world depends as much on their youth as on their rural existence. So strong was Gainsborough's tendency to portray innocence as childhood at this time that he seemed able to dispense with the rural coefficient of innocence altogether, and one makes a surprisingly easy transition from the fancy pictures to the contemporaneous society portraits of children (Figure 27). The fancy pictures signify an innocence that, while most congenial in a rural setting, is no longer exclusively associated with it. The fancy pictures make only abstract, conventional references to the countryside. Whereas the rustic landscape embodied the tensions and contradictions of both the English countryside itself and Gainsborough's relationship to it, the fancy pictures reduce the countryside to a simplified *topos*, a ready-made pastoral reference. Rather like the etiquette book gestures in the conversation piece, the fancy pictures refer to a number of shared opinions (or perhaps clichés) not only about naturalness but also about childhood and rural existence. Seeking legibility in a preestablished cultural code, they mark a retreat from Gainsborough's previous iconoclasm.

Eminently accessible, these late works of the 1780s found a number of imitators. But Gainsborough's brooding melancholy is absent from the work of artists like George Morland, Thomas Barker, William Hamilton, and the artist's own nephew, Gainsborough Dupont, whose treatment of the countryside is less personal and introspective. And whereas Gainsborough continued to place the countryside in opposition to modern society and its values, these artists often depicted the country as a mere backdrop for bourgeois paternalism.[92] Gainsborough's "Cottage Doors," for example, become Morland's *Squire's Door* (Figure 28), in which Gainsborough's dreamlike utopia is redefined in terms of the bourgeois reality he chose to ignore.[93] One might say that Gainsborough's followers merely extended the implications of his own development. For Gainsborough's late works reveal that his earlier attempt to contest the "naturalness" of eighteenth-century bourgeois society and to relocate nature in "little dirty subjects" was ultimately consonant with the dominant cultural strategy that identified its own values and practices with nature. To sentimentalize the countryside as Gainsborough came to do is to reconfirm the countryside as the ultimate locus of value and thus to comply with other, more ideologically loaded, views of it. The step from the "Cottage Door" to *The Squire's Door* is shorter than it looks. In the decade following Gainsborough's death this new sentimentalizing of the rustic landscape was codified in an aesthetic of the "picturesque." Gainsborough's late landscapes and fancy pictures anticipate such an aesthetic, resolving the earlier ambivalence toward landscape into sympathetic feeling and *sensibilité*.

Is there a place, save one the poet sees,
A land of love, of liberty and ease;
Where labour wearies not, nor cares suppress
Th' eternal flow of rustic happiness;
Where no proud mansion frowns in awful state,
Or keeps the sunshine from the cottage gate;
Where Young and Old, intent on pleasure, throng,
And half man's life is holiday and song?

George Crabbe,
The Parish Register

2

THE PICTURESQUE DECADE

THE EIGHTEENTH-CENTURY TASTE for nature and the natural reached an apogee during the 1790s in the cult of the picturesque. Significantly, the "picturesque" is a category of both landscape and painting. The landscape that was supposed to embody it (as the Campagna embodied the beautiful or the Alps the sublime) was the native English landscape itself—especially in such humble aspects as woodland scenery and winding country lanes. Applied to landscape, the term *picturesque* referred to its fitness to make a picture; applied to pictures, the term referred to the fidelity with which they copied the picturesque landscape. If the highest praise for nature was to say that it looked like a painting, the highest praise for a painting was to say that it resembled a painterly nature. The picturesque extended the ideal of naturalness to the very techniques of painting. The naturalness that surfaced in the conversation piece was mainly a result of the subject matter portrayed: it was conveyed in such social codes as gesture, dress, and gardening. For the most part, however, the "nature" exhibited by picturesque artists relied on a purely pictorial code that covered not only the subject matter but its treatment as well. The picturesque, then, because it linked art and nature with particular closeness, is central to this study of the aestheticization of the English countryside and the "naturalism" of English landscape painting.

As already suggested, Gainsborough was the most important precursor of the picturesque and natural painting. While theorists of the picturesque continued to praise Claude as the greatest landscape painter, they most often found the essential qualities of the picturesque in the rustic landscapes of Gainsborough. I shall first consider, then, how the theorists and practitioners of the picturesque aesthetic "read" Gainsborough as they assimilated and appropriated his legacy. I shall then consider both the picturesque aesthetic itself and its relation to the political and economic development of the countryside contemporary with it. Finally, I shall examine the popular dissemination of the picturesque that provided the context for the early aesthetic efforts of Constable.

THE EXAMPLE OF GAINSBOROUGH

In the decade following his death, Gainsborough emerged as, next to Richard Wilson, the most significant landscape painter of the century. Whereas the work of Wilson, the "English Claude," could be accommodated within the familiar art-historical tradition of landscape painting, Gainsborough's art inspired insights that ran counter to the academic notions of paintings such as Reynolds prescribed. Reynolds himself was the first to address this difficulty a year after Gainsborough's death, in his fourteenth Discourse. While commending Gainsborough's "portrait-like representation of nature, such as we see in the works of Rubens, Ruisdael and others of these schools,"[1] Reynolds stressed that "this excellence was his own, the result of his particular observation and taste; for this he was certainly not indebted to the Flemish School, nor indeed to any school; for his grace was not academical, or antique, but selected by himself from the great school of nature."[2] Although Reynolds saw Gainsborough as working in a "lower rank of art," he preferred his "humble attempts" to "the works of those regular graduates in the great style."[3] Reynolds admitted, "I take more interest in, and am more captivated with, the powerful impression of nature, which Gainsborough exhibited in his portraits and in his landscapes, and the interesting simplicity and elegance of his little ordinary beggar children, than with any works of that [Roman seventeenth-century] school."[4] Reynolds also contributed to the tradition of seeing Gainsborough's work as a direct response to nature. Gainsborough did not need to "go out of his own country" for the objects of his study; "they were everywhere about him; he found them in the streets, and in the fields."[5]

The myth of Gainsborough as a natural painter, however, preceded even these remarks by Reynolds. In the first biography of Gainsborough, published immediately after his death in 1788, Philip Thicknesse reminisced:

> Mr. G like the best was born a Painter, for he told me, that during his Boyhood, though he had no idea of becoming a Painter then, yet there was not a Picturesque clump of trees, nor even a single tree of beauty, no, nor hedge row, stone, or post,

at the corner of the lanes, for some miles round about the place of his nativity, that he had not so perfectly in his mind's eye, that had he known he *could use* a pencil, he could have perfectly delineated.[6]

"Madam Nature," says Thicknesse, "not Man, was then his only study, and he seemed intimately acquainted with the Beautiful Old Lady."[7] Gainsborough's art is the very portrait of nature:

> Friendship there was between him and dame NATURE, for I may justly say;— Nature sat to *Mr. G* in all her attractive attitudes of beauty, and his pencil traced with peculiar and matchless felicity, her finest and most delicate lineaments; whether from the sturdy oak; the twisted eglantine; the mower wetting his scythe; the whistling plough boy; or the shepherd under the haw-thorn in the dale; all came forth equally chaste from his inimitable and fantastic pencil.[8]

Like Reynolds and Thicknesse, writers on the picturesque derived Gainsborough's landscapes not from schools of landscape painting but from the English countryside itself. Hence real scenes and views are described in picturesque travel books as Gainsborough-like. J. Hassell's *Tour of the Isle of Wight* (1790), for instance, includes this description:

> At the entrance of Newton we are met with one of those subjects so often touched by the pencil of Mr. Gainsborough; a cottage overshadowed with trees; while a glimmer of light, just breaking through the branches, caught one corner of the stone and flint fabric, and forcibly expressed the conception of that great master. A few faggots, with a cart under a shed, formed the shadow part of the foreground; and the New Forest, rearing its leafy tenants above the proudly swelling waves, closed the distance.[9]

And again:

> Many old stumps of trees lay scattered near the road, that, with a team of horses, formed a fine group.—The horses belonged to a farmer, who was loading felled timber on one of those picturesque long carriages, just suited to the romantic appearance of the foreground; and which produced as complete a composition as could be desired for such a scene.—A well-known favorite subject of the late Mr. Gainsborough.[10]

Gainsborough's affinity with the picturesque was established not only by travel books like Hassell's but also by the picturesque theorist Uvedale Price. As a young man Price had known Gainsborough, who visited his family estate in Herefordshire during the 1760s. Gainsborough befriended the young Price and took him on walks and sketching excursions in the local countryside, forays Price mentioned in one of his essays on the picturesque:

When he lived at Bath, I made frequent excursions with him into the country; he was a man of eager and irritable mind, though warmly attached to those he loved; of a lively and playful imagination, yet at times severe and sarcastic. But when we came to cottage or village scenes, to groups of children, or to any objects of that kind which struck his fancy, I have often remarked in his countenance an expression of particular gentleness and complacency.[11]

No doubt Gainsborough and his art awakened Price's love of rustic scenery. A landscape beloved by Gainsborough quite often seems to stand behind Price's descriptions of picturesque scenery:

A little way further, but in sight from the entrance, stood a cottage, which was placed in a dip of the bank near the top. Some rude steps led from it into the lane, and a few paces from the bottom of these steps, the rill which ran on the same side of the lane, had washed away the soil, and formed a small pool under the hollow of the bank. At the edge of the water, some large flat stones had been placed, on which a woman and a girl were beating some clothes; a little boy stood looking on; some other children sat upon the steps, and an old woman was leaning over the wicket of the cottage porch, while her dog and cat lay basking in the sun before it.[12]

Such a passage powerfully calls to mind Gainsborough's "Cottage Doors" and late landscapes like *A Pool in the Woods* (see Figures 19, 25) and suggests that the formal connection between Gainsborough and the picturesque was drawn almost unconsciously. In Richard Payne Knight's poem *The Landscape* (1794), for instance, Thomas Hearne's illustration of the ideal picturesque garden borrows heavily from the typical Gainsborough landscape (Figure 29). Hearne uses Gainsborough's blocking screen of trees for the foreground and crowds bushy plants and moldering mossy banks close to the picture plane in true Gainsborough fashion. Significantly, Capability Brown's follower Humphry Repton criticized this illustration for its "wild neglect" and its "ridiculous affectation of rural simplicity."[13]

More than the mirroring of a new aesthetic taste is at stake in these eighteenth-century evaluations of Gainsborough's landscapes. The accounts of Reynolds, Thicknesse, Hassell, and Price all stress the formative influence of "dame NATURE" on Gainsborough's art. Moreover, William Bate-Dudley's claim that "nature was his teacher and the woods of Suffolk his academy" locates his naturalism in the landscape of his youth. By emphasizing the importance of place rather than the study of past art in their assessments of Gainsborough's achievement, these writers extended the period's model of naturalization to the field of art criticism. Thus Gainsborough's early encounter with a specific locale and his sympathetic response to it were seen to be as important as his mastery of the

FIG. 29. Thomas Hearne, *Gothic House Landscaped in a Picturesque Manner*, ca. 1794. Etching for Richard Payne Knight's *The Landscape*, 1794.

techniques of painting. As a result, these accounts transformed Gainsborough the artist into Gainsborough the artistic personality, whose personal response to a particular place determined his character *and* his achievement. This new art criticism took as its starting point not the art of Gainsborough but rather its environmental (and, by extension, biographical) origin.[14] The example of Gainsborough was critical to the development of John Constable. For now, however, it is enough to compare Thicknesse's statement about Gainsborough with a statement by Constable about himself. Here is Thicknesse: "There was not a Picturesque clump of trees, . . . hedge row, stone, or post . . . for some miles round about the place of his nativity, that he had not so perfectly in his mind's eye, that had he known he *could use* a pencil, he could have perfectly delineated." And here is Constable in 1821, in an often-quoted letter to his friend John Fisher: "The sound of water escaping from Mill dams . . . Willows, Old rotten Banks, slimy posts and brickwork. I love such things. . . . I should paint my own places best. . . . They made me a painter (and I am grateful) that is I had often thought of pictures of them before I had ever touched a pencil."[15] The echo of Thicknesse's account of Gainsborough's eye for picturesque detail, the importance of his local attachment, and his preformalized, pictorial visualization of native scenes rings clearly in Constable's explanation of his own development.

The picturesque aesthetic thoroughly reshaped the perception of Gainsborough's oeuvre. In the decade after his death critics increasingly valued the landscapes over the portraits. By the time of the 1814 retrospective exhibition at the British Institution, where Gainsborough's works were shown along with those of Hogarth, Wilson, and Zoffany, the change of taste was complete.[16] The critic of the *New Monthly Magazine* reflected the change. He praised Gainsborough's landscapes: "We are lost in the multitude of his beauties and scarcely know which to enumerate where all are so excellent"; and he slighted the portraits, which, he noted, proved Gainsborough "a respectable portrait painter."[17] Writing about the same exhibition to his friend Perry Nursey, the Scottish painter David Wilkie preferred Gainsborough to Wilson, complaining that the latter's landscapes "want variety, and seem to have rather a flat and common appearance."[18]

Nineteenth-century criticism of Gainsborough continued to stress the naturalism of his landscapes and enlarged its scope. In *Etchings of Rustic Figures for the Embellishment of Landscape* (1814–1815), W. H. Pyne remarked that Gainsborough's landscapes "possessed no other characteristics than those which the woods, copses, hamlets, heaths, lanes, and such places, unadorned by art, offered for his imitation."[19] Similarly, in his important *Lives of the Most Eminent British Painters* (1829–1833), Allen Cunningham presented Gainsborough as an indefatigable naturalist: "No fine clump of trees, no picturesque stream, nor romantic glade—no cattle grazing, nor flocks reposing, nor peasants pursuing their rural or pastoral occupations—escaped his diligent pencil."[20] Cunningham defined more explicitly than any writer before him the quintessentially English character of Gainsborough's landscapes. "A deep human sympathy unites us with his pencil, and this is not lessened because all its works are stamped with the image of old England. His paintings have a national look. He belongs to no school; he is not reflected from the glass of man, but from that of nature. . . . No academy schooled down into uniformity and imitation the truly English and intrepid spirit of Gainsborough."[21] Finally, in the first full-length, scholarly biography of Gainsborough, in 1856, George William Fulcher described the artist sketching out of doors as painstakingly as any Pre-Raphaelite. "Gainsborough now began to study landscape, where only faultless painting can be found, in the woods and fields. The Suffolk ploughman often saw him in the early morning, sketchbook in hand, brushing with hasty steps the dews away; and lingering in the golden light of evening; taking lessons from the sun-set clouds floating in changeful beauty, as if an angel's hand had traced the scene."[22] Fulcher claimed that Gainsborough made sketches of trees "drawn and coloured in the open air" and that "in one of them, a young oak is painted leaf for leaf, whilst ferns and grasses are portrayed with microscopic fidelity."[23] Such an account no doubt owed as much to Ruskin's defense of Turner and the Pre-Raphaelites as to Gainsborough's Suffolk landscapes, but it left substantially unchanged the legend of Gainsborough the nature painter.

Gainsborough played a seminal role in the subtle transition from the picturesque to the naturalistic rustic landscape. Artists of the 1790s imitated his work, and younger men, like Constable, saw in it an inspiring fidelity to nature and to place.[24] The theory of the picturesque encouraged this turning to nature in a crucial way. As the first theory to set "common nature" above the productions of art, the picturesque stands at the origin of the nonacademic landscapes of Constable and Turner, and many of its basic assumptions find their ripest expressions in Ruskin's *Modern Painters*.

THEORIES OF THE PICTURESQUE

The first real theorist of the picturesque was the Reverend William Gilpin (1724–1804), who from 1782 on published accounts of picturesque tours to various parts of Britain. His theory of the picturesque, however, was not set forth until 1792, when he published *Three Essays: On Picturesque Beauty, On Picturesque Travel, and On Sketching Landscape*. Though Gilpin had completed a draft of the *Three Essays* as early as 1776, Reynolds's criticisms discouraged him from publishing it. Gilpin's first draft came only a few years after Gainsborough's first "Cottage Door," *The Woodcutter's Return* (see Figure 19), and, like it, suggests a sensibility quite apart from Burke's aesthetic of sublimity and beauty. Gilpin's method, nevertheless, was inspired by Burke, and Gilpin, like Burke, based his definitions on the analysis of physical characteristics and sensations. Gilpin enlarged Burke's category of beauty to include the species "picturesque" in addition to the "beautiful." "Disputes about beauty might perhaps be involved in less confusion, if a distinction were established, which certainly exists, between such objects as are *beautiful* and such as are *picturesque*—between those, which please the eye in their *natural state*; and those, which please from some quality, capable of being illustrated by *painting*."[25] By virtue of their roughness, irregularity, and variousness, picturesque objects were better suited for painting than beautiful ones, whose smooth, neat qualities lacked pictorial definition. To illustrate this rule, Gilpin compared a landscape drawn on Burke's principles of the beautiful with the same landscape enriched with irregular mountains, shaggy

FIG. 30.   William Gilpin, *Scene without Picturesque Adornment*, ca. 1792. Etching and aquatint from his *Three Essays*, 1792.

trees, and a zigzagging road (Figures 30, 31). Gilpin's point was that a beautiful scene, to be represented to advantage in painting, must be mixed with elements of the picturesque—formally derived from Claude and Gainsborough.

What was for Reynolds "common nature" became for Gilpin a standard for judging works of art. "If we are unable to embody our ideas even in a humble sketch," he wrote, "yet still a strong *impression of nature* will enable us to judge of the *works of art*. Nature is the archetype. The stronger therefore the impression, the better the judgement."[26] This reverencing of nature as the "archetype" led Gilpin to advise the artist against working his "adorned sketch" on top of his original one. "His first sketch is the standard, to which, in the absence of nature, he must at least recur for his general ideas."[27] Gilpin's advice departed from academic tradition, which treated the first sketch not as a "standard" but as a body of notations to be corrected and enlarged by the student's stock of general formal ideals. Although Gilpin professed to look at nature as though it were a painting, he came quickly to propose looking at paintings as though they

FIG. 31. William Gilpin, *Scene with Picturesque Adornment*, ca. 1792. Etching and aquatint from his *Three Essays*, 1792.

were nature. In doing so, he reoriented the concepts of nature and naturalness away from their exemplification in the academic landscape and the landscape garden toward the countryside itself. In the process Gilpin reoriented the formal objective of landscape painting away from creating ideal beauty to depicting the "real landscape." This orientation stressed less the methods of selecting and abstracting in art than the processes of observing and recording. Gilpin's unabashed "study of nature" replaced Hogarth's "peeping at nature."

Gilpin's notion that "nature is the archetype" had some interesting consequences. If nature prefigures the picturesque, then there must exist in nature a purely picturesque landscape, one that is all roughness, irregularity, and variousness. Yet if there were such a landscape, the hand of art, unable to improve it, would become secondary and even superfluous. In the essay "On Picturesque Travel," Gilpin wrote: "The more refined our taste grows from the study of nature, the more insipid are works of art. Few of its efforts please. The idea of the great original is so strong, that the copy must be pure, if it do not disgust."[28]

And again: "But although the picturesque traveller is seldom disappointed with *pure nature*, however rude, yet we cannot deny, but he is often offended with the production of art."[29] This theme became perennial in succeeding decades as the art that depended on nature for its validity and purpose grappled with the problem of its possible superfluousness. It was precisely this problem, for instance, that Ruskin took up in later volumes of *Modern Painters*.[30] As landscape painting came to derive its value from nature, nature became increasingly charged with significance. As a guarantor of value, nature subsumed the authority of art, which began to act only in a deputy capacity.

The picturesque vision of landscape represents an ideological as well as aesthetic commitment. The relationship between ideology and aesthetics is perhaps best seen in the work of the second theorist of the picturesque, Uvedale Price. Whereas Gilpin was mainly concerned with itemizing picturesque effects, Price, a gentleman of wealth and landed property, offered an integrated account of them from the perspective of an agrarian paternalism. Price was a Whig member of Parliament, and his interest in the new agrarian improvements led him to contribute to Arthur Young's *Annals of Agriculture*. Price's involvement with the landscape may seem contradictory: as a gentleman farmer, he was concerned to increase production by maximal use of land, improved machinery, and so forth; as a theorist of the picturesque, however, he preferred an irregular, overgrown landscape dotted with dilapidated cottages and peopled with gypsies and beggars. The aesthetically pleasing landscape was not the economically productive one. Yet this double, even split, involvement in the landscape is itself a significant gloss on the picturesque and on the transformation of the countryside to which it was a compensatory response. The picturesque landscape was precisely the opposite of the landscape produced by the agricultural revolution, and therein lay a primary aspect of its value.

Unlike Gilpin, who sought the picturesque in natural scenes throughout Great Britain, Price was concerned with the picturesque in the form of the estate garden. The previous chapter observed of the garden of Brown and Repton that as the real landscape looked increasingly artificial, the garden aspired to look increasingly natural. Price attacked the landscape garden of Brown and Repton because it did not seem natural enough. While Repton felt that the "extent and freedom" of his garden made "the whole appear the production of nature only," Price saw the extensive prospects of this garden as signs of an all-too-human intervention. The moment the "mechanical and commonplace operation, by which Mr. Brown and his followers have gained so much credit, is begun," he claimed, "adieu to all that the painter admires. . . . in a few hours, the rash hand of false taste completely demolishes what time only, and a thousand lucky accidents can mature, so as to make it become the admiration and study of a Ruisdael or a Gainsborough and reduces it to such a thing as an oilman in Thames Street may at times contract for by the yard at Islington or Mile End."[31] Price described the horrendous operation as the efficient ("in a few hours") workings of a "mechanical" process that resulted in uniformity and duplication. Far from being a counterpoise to the transformed agricultural landscape, this landscape garden reflected a similar process of mechanization and standardization. Price saw the Brownian garden as a rape of nature, the "open, licentious display of beauties" in place of "nature's modesty."[32] But the worst crime of which Price could convict this garden was apparently its association with commerce, as the scornful reference to the oilman in Thames Street shows. The value of the picturesque landscape was that no amount of money could bring it about; it was the work of time and accident. The vocabulary of economics and commerce recurs frequently in Price's satire of the Brownian garden as the conspicuous consumption of *nouveaux riches*:

> Extensive prospects are the most popular of all views, and their respective superiority is generally decided by the number of churches and counties. Distinctness is therefore the great point. A painter may wish several hills of bad shapes, and thousands of uninteresting acres to be covered with one general shade; but to him who is to reckon up his counties, the loss of a black or white spot, of a clump or gazebo, is the loss of a voucher.
>
> Then, again, as the prospect-shower has great pleasure and vanity in pointing out these vouchers, so the improver, on his side, has full as much in being pointed at; we therefore cannot wonder that so many churches have been converted into beacons of taste, or that so many hills have been marked with them.[33]

So opposed was Price to the creation of extensive views in the garden that he found "something despotic in the general system of improvement—all must be laid open—all that obstructs levelled to the ground—houses, orchard, gardens, all swept away."[34] And he condemned such tyranny: "He who destroys dwellings, gardens and enclosures, for the sake of mere extent and parade of property, only extends the bounds of monotony, and of dreary selfish pride; but contracts those of variety, amusement and humanity."[35] Price's anger, however, was no libertarian's outrage at the injustices that attended enclosure and the creation of extensive gardens. The old aesthetic of the landscape garden was disreputable not because it throve on these injustices but because it made them too obvious at a time when such injustices were being met with popular force in France. In discussing an uncle who wisely took the local inhabitants into consideration in his gardening plans, Price showed his hand: "Such attentive kindnesses are amply repaid by affectionate regard and reverence; and were they general throughout the kingdom, they would do much more towards guarding us against democratic opinions 'Than twenty thousand soldiers, arm'd in proof.'"[36] The "attentive kindnesses" were a tactic in a general anti-Jacobin strategy. Price's language suggests that the Brownian landscape garden not only alluded to the forces of despotism but also evoked the malice of democracy in the "leveling" and "sweeping away" that brought it into being.

Price's plan for the picturesque garden initially depended on the examples of the great landscape painters. He advised landowners to consider "experiments in the different ways in which trees, buildings, water, etc. may be disposed, grouped and accompanied."[37] Nevertheless, as he developed his category of the picturesque and suggested specific picturesque effects landowners might use in their gardens, he relied on examples from nature as much as art. Price's argument, then, tended to displace the source of the picturesque away from the picturesque in painting to the picturesque in nature. Like the landscape sketch for Gilpin, the picturesque garden referred back to its pattern in nature. And just as the picturesque sketch promoted naturalism in landscape painting, the picturesque garden fostered a new naturalism in gardening. Price directed many of his barbs against the Brownian landscape garden at its contrived effects. Brown's innovations, once seen to embody a new naturalism—clumps of trees in place of formal *allées*, belts of trees instead of masonry walls—struck Price as ludicrously artificial. "Clumps, placed like beacons on the summits of hills, alarm the picturesque traveller many miles off, and warn him of his approach to the enemy;—the belt lies more in ambuscade; and the wretch who falls into it, and is obliged to walk the whole round in company with the improver, will allow that a snake with its tail in its mouth, is comparatively but a faint emblem of eternity."[38] For all the artificiality of the Brownian garden, it could still be contracted for by the yard. The picturesque garden, precisely because it depended on the maturing effects of time and on not entirely calculable accidents, was fated to remain little more than an impractical ideal.[39] It never substantially affected the practices of gardening, which after Waterloo reverted to pre-Brownian designs. In fact, Price's essay was one of the last aesthetic speculations on the garden. Less bound to the real landscape than the picturesque garden, landscape painting became the focus for the naturalism that developed in the visual arts in nineteenth-century England.

Though the picturesque idealized a nature that was in fact rapidly vanishing, its perspective was not simply nostalgic or backward-looking. If the picturesque was a refuge from the agricultural revolution, it was also an aesthetic response to some of its effects. For example, Price found "hovels, cottages, mills and the insides of old barns" picturesque.[40] Similarly picturesque objects were "to be

found among the wandering tribes of gypsies and beggars, who in all the qualities which give them that character, bear a close analogy to the wild forester and
worn-out cart horse, and again to the old mills, hovels and other inanimate
objects of the same kind."[41] In comments like these, the aesthetic effect of the
picturesque seems to be calculated precisely on poverty and misery.[42] An appropriately elegiac background for the laborer dispossessed by the agrarian revolution was the picturesque landscape, whose preindustrialized character demodern-
ized his plight and whose charms compensated him for it. The derelict
habitations, mills, and so forth established the picturesque landscape as a largely
abandoned one. The pathos of such a landscape cut two ways. On the one hand,
the picturesque landscape celebrated a rural way of life as that which had been,
or was being, lost. On the other hand, the manifest desolation of the landscape
could work as a justification for transforming it to a more efficient, vital one.

The distance essential to perceiving the picturesque was not exclusively aesthetic. Price wrote of a natural repulsion toward rough and irregular objects that,
though charming the eye with their intricacy, offered no temptation to the touch.
"I have read, indeed, in some fairy tale, of a country, where age and wrinkles
were loved and caressed, and youth and freshness neglected; but in real life, I
fancy, the most picturesque old woman, however her admirer may ogle her on
that account, is perfectly safe from his caresses."[43] If one multiplies Price's "picturesque old woman" into the gypsies, beggars, foresters, and other members of
the rural poor, who were in his opinion also "picturesque," one sees that this
"natural repulsion" barely disguised a social disdain. The systematic grouping
of "picturesque objects" by Gilpin and Price, the systematic analyses of these
"objects," and the systematic disposal of these "objects" into an aesthetic system
were the aesthetic counterparts to the increasingly bureaucratic system of rural
poor relief.

The literature that itemized picturesque objects also expressed in its discussion of the picturesque effects of time a particular class attitude toward agrarian
change. Price conferred on the picturesque a transitional character: with time,
all things become picturesque, and with more time, picturesque things become
"deformed."[44] Unlike Burke's static categories of the beautiful and sublime, the
picturesque allowed for, depended on, and was finally undone by time and its
changes. Gilpin, too, acknowledged the crucial role of time in determining the
picturesque, even suggesting that the painter prematurely age the objects of his
vision to secure a picturesque effect.

A piece of Palladian architecture may be elegant in the last degree. The proportion
of its parts—the propriety of its ornaments—and the symmetry of the whole may
be highly pleasing. But if we introduce it in a picture, it immediately becomes a

formal object, and ceases to please. . . . Should we wish to give it picturesque beauty, we must use the mallet instead of the chisel: we must beat down one half of it, deface the other and throw the mutilated members around in heaps. In short, from a smooth building, we must turn it into a rough ruin.[45]

The picturesque love of the ruined and the dilapidated was in keeping with the period's general elegiac mood and graveyard melancholy. Coming at the height of the agricultural transformation of the countryside, the picturesque was suited to express the complexity of the historical moment. In its celebration of the irregular, preenclosed landscape, the picturesque harkened back nostalgically to an old order of rural paternalism. In its portrayal of dilapidation and ruin, the picturesque sentimentalized the loss of this old order. And in its emphasis on the erosions of time, it not only doomed the old order but also obliquely recognized the precariously temporal nature of the new order that replaced it.

A profound pessimism lay at the root of picturesque theory, a spirit very different from that of Burke and Reynolds, who earlier in the century believed in universal qualities of beauty and an unchanging human nature capable of admiring them. The picturesque, according to Price, was an exclusive taste shared only by those sensitive enough to appreciate the priceless and irreproducible. Whereas Burke's beautiful and sublime were most often described as categories, the picturesque was usually spoken of as a "cult" or "taste." Both the emphasis on taste and the curiosity about its origin, development, and significance were unparalleled at this time. For the most part, the discussion originated during the Scottish Enlightenment, in the work of Thomas Reid and especially Archibald Alison. Alison's *Essay on the Nature and Principles of Taste* (1790) was the first full-scale investigation of the subject. Emotions of taste were felt, Alison thought, "When the imagination is employed in the prosecution of a regular train of ideas of emotion."[46] Over this issue of taste and its role in the perception of the picturesque, Price quarreled with his friend Richard Payne Knight. Their quarrel has been sufficiently aired not to need rehearsal here in detail.[47] Suffice it to say that Knight used Alison's ideas to criticize Price's theory, claiming that any distinction between the beautiful and the picturesque is "an imaginary one" and that the picturesque is merely that kind of beauty "which belongs exclusively to the sense of vision—or to the imagination, guided by that sense." Notions of beauty, sublimity, and picturesqueness are all derived "from the minds of the spectators; whose pre-existing trains of ideas are revived, refreshed and reassociated by new, but correspondent impressions on the organs of sense; and the great fundamental error, which prevails throughout the otherwise able and elegant *Essays on the Picturesque* [*sic*], is seeking for distinctions in external objects, which only exist in the modes and habits of viewing and considering them."[48] These differences aside, it is significant that both Price and Knight saw the picturesque primarily as a taste granted to only a few and inaccessible to vulgar minds.

Alison's and Knight's ideas reflected a growing interest in the role of memory and emotions in perception and moved away from the mechanical notions of sensation in the theories of Hogarth, Burke, Gilpin, and Price. By stressing the role of the perceiving subject in the act of perception, Alison and Knight anticipated the romantic sensibility of Constable's art. By applying Alison's theories to the picturesque, Knight tied the picturesque as closely to the new theories of perception and romantic sensibility as Gilpin and Price had tied it to a nonacademic naturalism. The picturesque, then, emerged at the end of the eighteenth century as a major alternative to the hierarchical, mechanical, and idealistic systems of Burke and Reynolds, and its various internal polarities (for example, objectivity/subjectivity, naturalism/romanticism) oriented early nineteenth-century art.

Knight published his ideas in their most complete form in *An Analytical Inquiry into the Principles of Taste* (1805). The *Inquiry* is significant because, as it discusses Alison's ideas in relation to picturesque theory, it provides (unlike the merely snobbish comments of Price) the theoretical grounds for establishing the picturesque as an exclusive taste available to only a few. Knight attributed to a single class the preconditions required to spark the chain of imaginative associations that led to aesthetic appreciation. One precondition, for instance, was ownership of property.

> Love may be extinct, and friendship buried in the grave with deceased contemporaries: but, nevertheless, both will be replaced by habitual attachment to inanimate objects:—to the trees, that we have planted or protected:—to the lands, that we have purchased or improved:—to the books, that we have studied or admired:—to the curiosities, that we have collected or valued:—and even to the money, that we have amassed.[49]

The openly materialistic perspective of Knight's associationism, different from the emphasis on optical sensation in Gilpin and Price, manifested Knight's tendency to personalize experience by locating it in a specific environment. The class-bound prejudices of Knight's theory dispossessed the poor of human sympathy and imagination so that the population deprived of the benefits of the agrarian revolution were also denied aesthetic sensibility, the lack of which confirmed their brutal condition. In discussing inheritance Knight made explicit this double *dis*inheritance:

> In the lower orders of society, where there are no such objects of habitual attach-
> ment, but where
>
>> The modest wants of every day
>> The toil of every day supplies—
>
> the parental affections generally die away, as in the brute creation, with the neces-
> sities for their exertion, and the habits of continued intercourse, which those neces-
> sities produced.[50]

Lacking property, the poor become an inferior species of humanity. Moreover,
Knight—evidently sensitive to the attacks on property by the Jacobins and some
democratic industrialists—made a point of defending the owning of property
against accusations of selfishness.

> Though this habitual attachment to objects of property or possession may with
> propriety be ranked among our selfish attachments, as it arises, in a great degree,
> from selfish affection; it is, nevertheless, much less purely or sordidly selfish than
> many of those gratifications of vanity or sensuality, which pass, in the general es-
> timation of mankind, for social, liberal and generous pleasures. The dissipated rake,
> and the voracious glutton, who spend their property in the unlimited indulgence of
> their passions and appetites, are surely more thoroughly selfish than any of those,
> who, through parsimony or frugality, do not spend at all.[51]

While one doubts that lust and gluttony were considered "social, liberal and
generous pleasures" in Knight's day, his argument shows that miserliness was
not only tolerated by the property-owning class but also defended by it as a
social, economic, and moral good.

In the last analysis, perhaps, "the association of ideas" outlined in Knight's
essay was no more than the imaginative appropriation of the countryside by a
class already responsible for its territorial appropriation. The association of ideas
referred all that was seen to the values of the viewer; as a result, nature merely
mirrored personal and social values. Whereas the previous generation had considered "common nature" an inadequate reflection of themselves and hence had
sought to correct it by means of the landscape garden, the men of the 1790s
needed no such mediation. Their romantic naturalism issued forth from an introspective subjectivity that found in nature a direct expression of the human
spirit. To this extent, Knight's theory of associationism gave back to landscape
painting something of the purpose denied it by Gilpin's and Price's naturalism
and sensationism. For Knight, the purpose of landscape was to arouse the emotions, to stir the imagination, and to delight the eye with its naturalness.

Knight's arguments shifted emphasis away from the familiar signs of nature
and the natural in landscape painting to more personal and less codified expressions of the terms. The quarrel between Price and Knight is indicative of the

alternative directions artists took in responding to the picturesque. One approach involved the mechanical picturesque—the arrangements of gypsies, beggars, cart horses, and donkeys before ruined cottages in overgrown rustic landscapes; the second involved natural-looking landscapes so represented that they would—given their truthful recording of nature's optical and structural qualities—operate upon the senses and sensibilities just like the scenes themselves. As with the conversation pieces of Devis and Zoffany, both directions are symptomatic of the move to aestheticize nature and the natural. Whereas the generation reaching artistic maturity in the 1780s and early 1790s (George Morland, Thomas Barker, Francis Wheatley, Thomas Hearne, Julius Caesar Ibbetson, Sir Francis Bourgeois, and, to some extent, John Crome) remained tied to the picturesque as a mere code of rustic naturalness, younger men like Thomas Girtin, Turner, and, of course, Constable came to value natural scenery not for its picturesque clichés, but for its optical, formal, and poetic possibilities.

THE POLITICS OF THE PICTURESQUE

The period 1790–1825 is an important one in the history of the English countryside. From 1790 to 1815 (the period coinciding with the taste for the picturesque) the countryside experienced a great agricultural boom brought about by the wars with France. As the price of wheat and other raw commodities soared, two million new acres of land were brought into cultivation by enclosure.[52] Large wartime profits increased not only rents and tithes but taxation as well, the burden of which was almost wholly carried by the farming community. The number of loans and mortgages increased dramatically as farmers accelerated the enclosure and improvement of land. The value of land itself rose as high agricultural prices and the territorial aspirations of the newly rich industrial class created competition for it. Thus when prices fell after Waterloo, the countryside found itself economically overextended, that is to say, left with very little liquid capital and saddled with commitments it could no longer meet. While postwar taxation remained high, agricultural profits and the value of land dramatically declined. Large numbers of landowners and farmers went bankrupt and the majority of agricultural laborers were left jobless. The result was a steady depopulation of rural areas. Whereas in 1815 the majority of Englishmen still worked in agriculture, just twenty years later nearly half the population was employed in industry and lived under urban conditions.[53] As cities and towns began to swell, the countryside around them became more and more suburban.

The postwar depression that brought about striking economic and demographic changes in rural England dramatically sustained the mode of organizing social and economic relationships begun about twenty-five years before Waterloo. During the period of the picturesque, as agriculture boomed, the relationship between landowners and their dependents shifted from a paternalistic, quasi-feudal system of reciprocal rights and duties to an industrial employer-employee relationship, bonded only by a cash nexus. Evidence of this shift can be found in the increasingly wide and rigid class divisions that developed at this time between landowner, farmer, and laborer. In his *Memoir*, the artist Thomas Bewick recalled that during the war years

> the gentry whirled about in aristocratic pomposity; they forgot what their demeanour and good, kind behaviour used to be to those in inferior stations of life, and seemed now far too often to look upon them like dirt. The character of the richer class of farmers was also changed. They acted the gentleman very awkwardly, and many of them could not, in these times, drink anything but wine, and even that was called "humble port." When these upstart gentlemen left the market, they were ready to ride over all they met or overtook on the way.[54]

In a similar vein, William Cobbett was particularly outraged by the new bourgeois style of life embraced by the farmers who had become rich during the wars. Describing the dwelling of one such farmer in Reigate, Cobbett wrote:

> One end of the front of this once plain and substantial house had been moulded into a *"parlour;"* and there was the mahogany table, and the fine chairs, and the fine glass, and all as bare-faced upstart as any stock-jobber in the kingdom can boast of. . . . And I dare say it has been *Squire* Charington and the *Miss* Charingtons; and not plain Master Charington, and his son Hodge, and his daughter, Betty Charington, all of whom this accursed system has, in all likelihood, transmuted into a species of mock gentlefolks, while it has ground labourers down to real slaves.[55]

In addition to a segregation of classes, there was a marked tension between the old established country families and the new industrialists who were creating rural estates and setting themselves up as country squires. Much of Price's snobbery toward the tastes of the new industrial class was a response to this invasion of the countryside by the *nouveaux riches*. Nevertheless, one might argue that it was precisely the social cachet of the picturesque that led to the invasion in the first place. Whereas early manufacturers like Josiah Wedgwood built their estates close to their factories so as to command a view of them from the house and grounds, after 1795 these self-made men were careful to live far away from such unpicturesque sights.[56] The values expressed by Price in his picturesque theory parallel the social practices of the time in another way. The picturesque emphasis on age is echoed in the increasing stress old country families placed on their ancestry to distinguish themselves from the new squires.

Even as they maintained their distinction from the new squires, the old established landowners were generally complicit with the forces of industrial capitalism. As a result, the older paternalistic relationships between landowner, farmer, and laborers deteriorated, to be replaced by wage-mediated relationships. The picturesque embodied an early ideological response to this decline of rural paternalism during the war years. Although the picturesque celebrated the old order—by depicting a pastoral, preenclosed landscape—some of its features—the class snobbery, the distancing of the spectator from the picturesque object, and the aestheticization of rural poverty—suggest that at a deeper level the picturesque endorsed the results of agricultural industrialization. Picturesque theory complemented the policies behind such schemes as the Speenhamland system of poor relief. Moreover, the picturesque, like the political debates of the period about the problem of rural poverty, mystified the agency of social change so that fate, and not the economic decisions of the landowning classes, seemed responsible. In this respect, the picturesque represented an attempt to wipe out the fact of enclosure and to minimize its consequences.

After Waterloo, as the countryside sank in economic power and prestige, the gentry, many of them new industrialists with little commitment to its way of life or its survival as a political and economic force, withdrew from personal participation in rural affairs and left the management of their estates to bailiffs and overseers. In 1821, Cobbett outlined the difference between

> a resident native gentry, attached to the soil known to every farmer and labourer from their childhood, frequently mixing with them in those pursuits where all artificial distinctions are lost, practicing hospitality without ceremony, from habit and not on calculation; and the gentry only now-and-then residing at all, having no relish for country-delights, foreign in their manners, distant and haughty in their behavior, looking to the soil only for its rents, viewing it as a mere object of speculation, unacquainted with its cultivators, despising them and their pursuits, and relying for influence, not upon the good will of the vicinage, but upon the dread of their power.[57]

Even the older families who had a longer tradition of participation in country affairs were dividing their time between their estates, London, and the continent. Wintering in London became the common practice of such families, with the result that when they did return to the country, they brought with them urban ideas and values. William Howitt noted in 1838 that "one of the chief features of the life of the nobility and gentry of England is their annual visit to the metropolis, and it is one which has a most essential influence upon the general character of rural life itself."[58]

The importation of urban ideas, it is often noted, had some salutary effects. For instance, there was a steady improvement in the habits of the gentry—increasing sobriety and a revulsion against the crueler blood sports.[59] Nevertheless, as E. P. Thompson has shown, urban influences often alienated landowners from the personal responsibilities of running their estates and made them increasingly indifferent to the lot of those who worked them. In addition, the urbanization of rural life led to a suppression of native folk festivals and customs. The forces of a capitalistic gentry and a puritanical Methodism combined to discipline the agricultural laborer and to make him an efficient worker in the new industrialized agriculture.[60]

Although changes in the countryside were brought into particular relief during the postwar depression, they either were anticipated by events of the 1790s or were well under way during the decade. One of the clearest depictions of rural England in the last decade of the century is the Board of Agriculture's *Annals of Agriculture*, compiled and edited by Arthur Young. Two important economic trends can be abstracted from the *Annals*. The first is that farmers in the southern and eastern counties were turning from dairying to growing wheat. This conversion largely resulted from the wars, which drove up the demand for and the cost of wheat while giving farmers a protected market. In the southern counties especially, farmers quickly and easily converted their rich dairy lands into wheat fields. Although they grew wealthy during the war years, they were left vulnerable after Waterloo when grain prices fell. John Constable's father, Golding Constable, was a prominent Suffolk miller, wheat factor and wheat transporter. The fortunes of the Constable family in East Bergholt were closely tied to the production of wheat in Suffolk and the fluctuation of wheat prices.[61]

A second trend the *Annals* suggest is that in every parish the number of destitute families was rapidly increasing, and parish poor rates (the taxation levied by each parish on farmers and/or landowners to support the local poor) were rising.[62] Young and several other contributors to the *Annals* saw the poor rate as a direct result of enclosure, which left poor families without rights of common.[63] Young's own solution was to establish a minimum wage regulated by the cost of wheat and to set aside £20 million to provide a half million dispossessed families with land allotments and cottages. While Young's solution acknowledged that enclosure was the root of the problem, it missed the real economic significance of this fact. Because the solution, for instance, took no account of the change in agriculture from a labor-intensive to a capital-intensive pursuit, it failed to recognize that the land could not absorb any increase in or even stabilization of the labor force. Furthermore, agricultural laborers receiving a "bread wage" could never raise their standard of living above subsistence and would be devastated if the price of wheat fell in proportion to the cost of other raw and manufactured necessities.

Even though Young's proposals aspired, in a limited way, to re-create the living conditions of the rural poor before enclosure, they were primarily meant to maintain the profits gained by the landowners from enclosure and wartime demand by keeping the poor rate and the cost of labor low. Instead of simply attempting to turn back the clock, such solutions borrowed on nostalgia for the old order to maintain the new. One correspondent's comments to the *Commercial and Agricultural Magazine* made this tactic explicit. After admitting that "a quarter of an acre of garden ground will go a great way towards rendering the peasant independent of any assistance," he went on to warn that "in this beneficent intention, moderation must be observed or we may chance to transform the laborer into a petty farmer."[64] To many landowners and improvers of the 1790s, a "bread wage" and a carefully controlled land allotment program were ways to lower the poor rate without either unduly threatening the supply of cheap labor or necessitating the payment of a living wage. This strong commitment to the economic order of the present expressed as a nostalgia for the past had its aesthetic counterpart in the picturesque.

In 1795 concern over the rising poor rate became associated with open fear of insurrection among the poor. A severe winter, subsequent crop failures, and a bad harvest in 1794–1795 caused the price of wheat to soar on the London corn exchange.[65] The resulting food riots lasted from May to December. Although the rioting was serious everywhere, it was particularly intense in the southern counties of Wiltshire, Norfolk, and Suffolk. Wheat destined for export was stopped by rioting bands in Cambridge, Burford, Bath, and Wells. By July 1795 the Privy Council could no longer guarantee the transport of supplies from one county to another. Millers were popularly believed to be buying up wheat to raise its price; their mills were attacked, and in London the great Albion Flour Mill was burned. The culmination of the food rioting came on October 29 when George III, on his way to open Parliament, was hooted and his carriage attacked by a mob of two hundred thousand brandishing small bread loaves on sticks. The carriage window was smashed and the king believed himself shot at. Official reaction to the riot was swift. On the following day when the king attended the theater, the streets were cleared and he was accompanied by nearly one thousand soldiers and constables. A royal proclamation was issued against assemblies, and on November 10 Pitt introduced the Treason and Sedition Acts, which were passed into law on November 18.[66]

As a result of the riots, a new antirevolutionary conservatism silenced the debate over enclosure, and anti-Jacobin fear overrode sympathy for the poor in agricultural circles. Many in the upper classes agreed with Fredrick Morton Eden, whose monumental analysis *The State of the Poor* (1797) began with the thesis that "the miseries of the labouring poor arose, less from the scantiness of their income (however much the philanthropist might wish it to be increased) than from their own improvidence and unthriftiness."[67] After the riots proposals for a minimum wage based on the cost of bread became less popular as a solution to the rising poor rate, and land allotment schemes were criticized as encouraging insurrection. Land in the hands of the poor, especially common land, was seen as a threat to national security. In 1799, pressing for full enclosure, Young wrote: "I know nothing better calculated to fill a country with barbarians ready for any mischief than extensive commons and divine service only once a month. . . . Do French principles make so slow a progress that you should lend them such helping hands?"[68] A Mr. Bishton expressed similar sentiments in the *Agricultural Report for Shropshire*, arguing that enclosing the commons ensured "that the laborers will work every day in the year, their children will be put out to work early and that subordination of the lower ranks of society which in the present times is so much wanted would be thereby considerably secured."[69]

In response to the riots and the rising poor rate, the justices of the town of Speenhamland, Berkshire, in May 1795 passed a proposal to supplement wages out of the poor rate. The parish made up the difference between the wage a master paid the laborer in private employment and the current price of bread. Unlike Young's plan, which was meant to be a minimum *wage* paid by the employer, the Speenhamland supplement was meant as charity. Laborers who could not find private employment were either maintained by the parish rate-payers or employed in the old "roundsman system" whereby their labor was sold by the parish to employers at a low rate.[70] The Speenhamland tables for the rates and payments, passed from county to county, were easily incorporated into earlier relief systems. While the Speenhamland plan temporarily eased distress in the southern counties, in the long run it did great harm, for it relieved large land-owners and manufacturers of the responsibility to pay fair wages, and it forced less prosperous ratepayers to supplement these wealthy men's wage bills.[71]

Because it depended on the traditional paternalism of the poor rates for its mechanism rather than the new forces of wages and capital, landowners saw in the Speenhamland system a familiar and acceptable solution to their problems. By disguising employment as relief, Speenhamland implied that the rural poor were small farmers fallen on hard times, not an agrarian proletariat dependent on wages. Although the system attempted to set the economy of the countryside apart from that of industrial capitalism, the traditional paternalistic mode of relief merely masked the common interest of large landowners and manufacturers in keeping the cost of labor low. Moreover, through this structure of paternalistic relief (that is, the poor rates, leasing of roundsmen, and controlling bills of settlement) the landowners, particularly in the northern counties, had the power to regulate the cost and supply of labor to the industrialists. While making a sentimental gesture of paternalistic protection of the poor, Speenhamland in fact functioned to protect the landowners against a loss of power and prestige to the new industrial class.

Throughout the 1790s rural resistance to industrial capitalism often involved capitalistic practices and institutions masquerading as older paternalistic ones. The parish workhouse or "school of industry," for instance, was modeled on and functioned like a factory.[72] Unemployed poor people were sent to the workhouse where they made articles to be sold by the parish. The products of workhouses like those in Suffolk, which spun top cloth for Norwich textile manufacturers, found ready markets in industrial towns.[73] The war, however, closed off foreign markets, raised the cost of materials, depressed domestic manufacture, and sharpened the competition between the parish and private industries. Hence it is not unusual to find in reports written by countrymen on the problem of the poor rate glowing descriptions of clean and cheerful "houses of industry" juxtaposed with visions of dark satanic mills.[74] Similarly, agricultural work was contrasted favorably to factory work, which was seen as promoting moral laxity. The Reverend David Davies, a regular contributor to the *Annals of Agriculture*, noted that

> by living in towns, and associating at public houses, factory workers are habitually improvident and mind nothing but present enjoyment; and when flung out of work, they are immediately in want. They also, from their sedentary occupations and habitual intemperance, are more short-lived than day-labourers; and leaving families behind them unable wholly to maintain themselves, these, as the men die off, fall on the parishes.[75]

By the end of the century, rural objections to the new industrial forces were expressed not only by the politics and practices of the countryside but by the aesthetic of the picturesque as well. For instance, there was a shift in aesthetic response toward factories and the industrial landscape they created. The change is evident when we compare Arthur Young's 1785 description of Coalbrookdale with Uvedale Price's 1794 account of the cotton mills in Derbyshire. Young wrote:

> Coalbrookdale itself is a very romantic spot, it is a winding glen between two immense hills which break into various forms, and all thickly covered with wood, forming the most beautiful sheets of hanging wood. Indeed too beautiful to be much in unison with that variety of horrors art has spread at the bottom: the noise of the

forges, mills, &c. with all their vast machinery, the flames bursting from the furnaces with the burning of the coal and the smoak of the lime kilns, are altogether
sublime, and would unite well with craggy and bare rocks, like St. Vincent's at
Bristol.[76]

Price observed:

When I consider the striking natural beauties of such a river as that at Matlock, and
the effect of the seven-story buildings that have been raised there, and on other
beautiful streams, for cotton manufactories, I am inclined to think that nothing can
equal them for the purpose of disbeautifying an enchanting piece of scenery, and
that economy had produced, what the greatest ingenuity if a prize were given for
ugliness, could not surpass. They are so placed, that they contaminate the most
interesting views; and so tall, that there is no escaping from them in any part; and
in that respect they have the same unfortunate advantage over a squat building, that
a stripped elm has over a pollard willow.[77]

Postdating Young's statement by about ten years, Price's statement represented
a significant shift in attitude. Though Young, relying upon the opposition between the beautiful and the sublime, suggested that the factories were too sublime to be consonant with the gentle beauty of their surroundings, he did not
dismiss them as totally unaesthetic. Price, however, condemned the industrial
buildings as ugly, unwanted intrusions into picturesque nature. The rejection of
the industrial scene was so pronounced in picturesque theory that it extended to
the depiction of staffage figures. Discussing the inclusion of such figures in a
landscape, Gilpin wrote, "In a moral view, the industrious mechanic is a more
pleasing object than the loitering peasant. But in the picturesque light, it is
otherwise. The arts of industry are rejected; and even idleness . . . adds dignity
to a character."[78]

Such anti-industrialism may be said partly to account for the development
of a new "industrial" genre of landscape. A comparison of Joseph Wright of
Derby's *Joseph Arkwright's Mill, View of Cromford, near Matlock* (Figure 32) of
1783 with John Sell Cotman's 1802 watercolor *Bedlam Furnace, near Madeley*
(Figure 33) suggests a decided change in the portrayal of industrial sites.[79]
Whereas for Wright, as for Young, nature sustains its integrity in the presence
of industry, for Cotman, as for Price, industry overpowers nature. The Georgian
domestic architecture of Arkwright's mill intrudes on the scene no more than
might a brightly lit country house. Cotman's furnaces, however, with their
strange smoky silhouette, have taken possession of the site, befouling and dead-
ening the residual natural vegetation. The picturesque decade that intervened
between Wright's view and Cotman's condemned manufacturing and divided

FIG. 32. Joseph Wright of Derby, *Joseph Arkwright's Mill, View of Cromford, near Matlock*, 1783 (36 × 45 in.). Private collection, Great Britain. Photograph: Courtauld Institute of Art.

industry from nature, resulting in a separate genre of landscape: the industrial site.

Analogous to the politics of the poor rate, which borrowed its ideological trappings from an earlier mode of production, the picturesque aesthetic celebrated anachronistic or disappearing industries. Picturesque genre paintings by Francis Wheatley, George Morland, John Opie, Julius Caesar Ibbetson, and others all commemorate the virtues of an older rural life and labor. Wheatley's *Industrious Cottager* (1786), for example, shows a girl, presumably living in the countryside along the coast, making and mending nets for local fishermen.[80] Wheatley's famous series *The Rustic Hours* (1798–1799) portrays milkmaids and field laborers going about their daily tasks of maintaining a small farm.[81] As portrayed in these works, homely activities bear both moral and material fruit. Such picturesque genre paintings fail to suggest, however, that small cottage

FIG. 33.   John Sell Cotman, *Bedlam Furnace, near Madeley*, 1802 (10¼ × 18½ in.). Watercolor. Private collection, Great Britain. Photograph: Courtauld Institute of Art.

industries and domestic farms had been rapidly disappearing since enclosure. When it appears in these paintings, poverty is portrayed as a failure of moral nerve caused by sloth, improvidence, and intemperance. Morland's contrasting pendants, *Comforts of Industry* and *Misery of Idleness* (1790), offer a typical example.[82] In the first painting a husband returns to his well-furnished cottage and tosses a coin into the lap of his wife sewing at the fireside. In the second a drunken husband and wife, surrounded by their offspring, sprawl on the hearth of their barren and untidy cottage. Another typical treatment of poverty is found in the numerous depictions of "rustic benevolence" that show cottagers giving food to beggars. Wheatley especially was drawn to such scenes, and his *Rustic Benevolence* of about 1797, in which a woman at her cottage door offers food to a poor mother and her children, embodies the standard formula.[83] Depictions of such benevolence suggested that the rural poor could still be cared for within a self-sufficient system of individual acts of charity. They implicitly reject the actual mechanism through which the rural poor received care: the new bureaucratic systems like Speenhamland or institutions like the parish workhouse. While all these genre paintings depict the old order of small farms, cottage industries, and yeoman charity, they embody the new industrial ethics of hard work, thrift, and sobriety. Like the politics of the poor rate, they express a nostalgia for the old way of life while endorsing the values that facilitate the new.

The picturesque decade attached new supremacy to the values of nature. Its socioaesthetic character is reflected in the discovery of Gainsborough's landscapes, in the cult of the picturesque, and in the emphasis on the "truth" of painting over the manipulation of nature in the landscape garden. The picturesque is seminal in the history of rustic landscape painting. As a result of the writings of Gilpin and Price, nature became a standard by which landscape would be judged throughout the nineteenth century. The next chapter will examine the formative effects of the picturesque aesthetic on the second great painter of rustic landscapes, John Constable. In the social history of the English countryside, too, the picturesque represents no less important a development. Picturesque nature, as defined by Price and Knight, embodied the values and worldview of the wealthy landowning class. Knight's critique of Price, in which property was almost an ontological condition for the picturesque association of ideas, only reaffirmed the class bias of Price's picturesque aesthetic. Like the politics of the poor rate, the picturesque aesthetic muted the problems caused by enclosure and the agricultural revolution and harkened back to a golden age. Such problems as appeared were seen to come, not from within the countryside, but from changes and developments existing elsewhere. The anti-industrialism implicit in the picturesque grew out of the split between agrarian and industrial capitalism, which would widen considerably after the Napoleonic wars, and the nostalgia of the picturesque anticipated and compensated for the resulting shift of power away from the countryside after Waterloo. Where power was, there beauty shall reside.

THE POPULARIZATION OF THE PICTURESQUE

The picturesque as a practice or way of viewing nature was popularized largely by the guidebooks of Gilpin. The rage for these books peaked in the 1790s and influenced the touring habits of several generations of Englishmen. Picturesque tours to the lakes of Cumberland, the Devonshire coast, or the Isle of Wight were undertaken by hundreds of tourists armed with sketchbooks, diaries, and Claude glasses. Such popularity clashed with the exclusiveness written into the picturesque by Price and Knight. What they defined as the delicate and sophisticated taste of a select few became the popular pastime of the bourgeois. "I'll prose it here, I'll verse it there / And picturesque it everywhere," says the ridiculous hero of William Combe's burlesque, *The Tour of Dr. Syntax* (1812), illustrated by Thomas Rowlandson,[84] indicating that the picturesque was a fad popular enough to be satirized. In a similar spirit, Jane Austen directed her barbs against the picturesque in *Northanger Abbey* (1798–1799): "[Henry Tilney]

talked of foregrounds, distances, and second distances; side-screens and perspectives; lights and shades; and Catherine was so hopeful a scholar, that when they
gained the top of Beechen Cliff, she voluntarily rejected the whole city of Bath,
as unworthy to make part of a landscape."[85] The humor of the passage cuts as
much against the clichés of the picturesque as against the picturesque per se. By
the turn of the century the word *picturesque* had become so overused that it had
become virtually meaningless.[86]

As Catherine Morland's rejection of the city of Bath shows, the picturesque
was as committed as traditional landscape gardening to "improving" the landscape according to preconceived schemes.[87] The unique, unconventionally beautiful landscape that Price encouraged adherents of the picturesque to seek became, when in increasing numbers they sought it, as standardized and
predictable as the gardening plans of Brown and Repton. One might argue that
every aesthetic theory finally makes banal the very thing that it was meant to
enshrine. George Kubler has spoken of a tendency for major works of art—or
what he calls "prime objects"—to generate popular and less inventive replicas of
themselves.[88] An analogous tendency no doubt accounts for the popularization of
the picturesque sensibility. Yet the process of standardization was particularly
rapid and diffuse in the case of the picturesque and appertains to historical conditions that Kubler's general theory cannot account for. More to the point would
be Jean Baudrillard's observations on the ambivalent status of the object in industrial society.[89] The industrial object is valued both for its singularity and for
its mass reproducibility. On the one hand, the means of industrial production
guarantee the standardization of objects, all copies of a nonexistent model. On
the other hand, such objects become consumer goods only by virtue of acquiring
a unique, individual, and even personalized aura. The popularization of the picturesque was one of the first instances in which the emerging dialectic of the
industrial object determined the dynamic of the aesthetic field. The popular
picturesque provided a context in which the experience of uniqueness and indi-
viduality co-existed with an experience of conventionality and conformity.[90]

Though theoretically the picturesque was supposed to resist artistic codification, its popularization as an aesthetic threatened such resistance. The paradox
was dramatized in such picturesque practices and fads as outdoor sketching and
the cult of ruins, where nature in a playful or somber spirit was seen to resist or
circumvent the shaping of art. As Martin Price has noted, the sketch that pre-
cedes formal perfection and the ruin that follows it both allude to a dramatic
contest between imagination and nature.[91] The sketch at once demonstrates the
shaping power of art and acknowledges by its unfinished status nature's ability
to resist such power; the ruin at once concedes the victory of nature over art and

claims for art the power to transform waste into beauty. The concerns brought into play by the sketch and the ruin both seem far enough from the dark satanic mills of the industrial revolution. This remoteness, no doubt, made part of their popularity. Yet to the extent that the sketch and the ruin both laid stress on the value of process, they administered to a sensibility that was perfectly consonant with the relentless forces of productivity unleashed by the industrial revolution.

The play of imagination and nature that characterized the popular picturesque informs the overall structure of picturesque landscape painting. In general, the picturesque landscape aspires to the condition of a vignette—that is, a centralized composition in a shallow space whose boundaries are undefined or shade off. The landscapes of Morland, Crome, and Bewick provide numerous examples. The vignette typically focuses attention in the middle of the composition, on an object or scene rendered in naturalistic detail. The details—token bits of nature—relieve the artificiality of the composition. The emphasis on detail was recognized as a distinguishing feature of the picturesque in its own day, and it is not surprising that the picturesque opened the way to a close study of nature. The detail was never an end in itself, however, but always a stimulus to the imagination. For Gilpin, the detail gave rise to the larger pictorial idea: "From this correct knowledge of objects arises another amusement; that of representing, by a few strokes in a sketch, those ideas which have made the most impression upon us."[92] For Coleridge, the picturesque occurred "where parts only are seen and distinguished, but the whole is felt."[93] The vignette was well fitted to satisfy the double requirements of nature and imagination: its centralized composition focuses on objects and natural details at the same time that its undefined borders suggest an indefinite extension of the imagination.

The picturesque landscape, as popularized in guidebooks, and the practice of painting and sketching out of doors represented a "democratic" landscape. The topographical landscape developed out of the mapping of country estates and hence was tied to aristocratic patterns of ownership. The landscapes of the great seventeenth-century masters depicted exotic Italian scenery with mythological overtones. The picturesque, by restricting itself to humble English rural scenery, represented a landscape both familiar and accessible. It thus could be widely *consumed*, and with all the more enthusiasm in that the landscape it celebrated was beginning to vanish.

The early landscapes of John Constable can be studied in light of the popular picturesque. The young Constable was torn between his own feelings for rural scenery and the dominant conventions of the picturesque available to express them. The drama of his earliest encounters with landscape resulted from his inability to reconcile the two.

Though I am here in the midst of the world, I am out of it—and am happy—and endeavour to keep myself unspoiled. I have a kingdom of my own both fertile and populous—my landscape and my children.

John Constable,
Letter to John Fisher, May 9, 1823

MAPPING THE SELF: CONSTABLE / COUNTRY

Produced at the intersection of a personal obsession with landscape and a general social crisis of the countryside, the art of John Constable gives the tradition of rustic landscape painting its most celebrated and historically consequential example. Constable was born and raised in the countryside, and his attachment to it never ceased. Whereas landscape claimed the attention of Gainsborough only occasionally, it engrossed Constable throughout his career. In contrast to the picturesque artists who were also centrally committed to discovering the countryside, Constable brought to his own commitment all the sustained formal reflection of a major painter. Few other artists' work is so closely tied to a specific place as Constable's is to his native village of East Bergholt and to the nearby Stour Valley. "I should paint my own places best,"[1] he wrote to his friend John Fisher, and indeed the paintings and drawings for which Constable is best known take these places for their subjects over and over again. As he was fond of reminding his correspondents, his landscapes originated in the place of his own origin, and they resonate accordingly with a whole biography. No other painter of this period insisted so strongly on the personal significance of his art. "Painting is but another word for feeling," he wrote to Fisher; "I am fond of being an Egoist in whatever relates to painting."[2] As part of this "egoism," Constable called his sketchbooks "journals" and carefully noted in them not only places but dates and times of day as well.[3] Often explicitly, the journals aspire to the condition of autobiography. In one of them Constable wrote below a sketch of his father's house, "House in which I was born,"[4] as if the identification were somehow necessary even though the sketch would never be exhibited or sold. The same autobiographical impulse is revealed in Constable's correspondence, no less by its sheer quantity (seven volumes) than by the personal remarks the artist makes there.[5] Primarily on the basis of the correspondence, Constable's friend Charles Leslie was able to produce a reliable first biography.

The historical moment in which Constable's personal obsession with landscape unfolded was one of the most eventful periods in the history of the English countryside, spanning the agricultural boom years of the Napoleonic wars, the post-Waterloo depression, and the passage of the great Reform Bill of 1832. During Constable's lifetime England was transformed from an agricultural economy to an industrial one and experienced a corresponding shift in political power. The countryside was depopulated as men and women sought factory work in the newly industrialized cities of Manchester, Liverpool, Leeds, and Birmingham. The impact of industrialism on English life, however, was not immediately visible. Until about 1825 factory areas were contained, and most villages were unchanged. The landscape still bore the stamp of enclosure, with nearly all open fields hedged and drained, and it continued substantially unchanged until after Waterloo.[6] The high wartime price of wheat encouraged farmers not only to continue enclosing but also to convert more and more land into wheat fields. In Constable's county of Suffolk, for instance, the costliness of wheat led to the conversion of dairy land to farmland, a move that continued even after the war when Suffolk farmers found they could not undersell the dairy products imported from Ireland and Holland.[7]

The French wars, however, changed life in the countryside considerably. The class consciousness that had begun to be noticed at the end of the eighteenth century grew stronger. As their standard of living improved, farmers closed their farmhouses to the laborer, and unmarried field hands no longer ate at the farmer's table. "When farmers become gentlemen, their laborers become slaves," William Cobbett warned;[8] for the often easy familiarity between the farmer's and the laborers' children ceased as more farmers sent their children away to be educated. And more than the relations between farmer and laborer changed. During the wars the aristocracy and gentry spent more time away from their estates and were less tolerant of country ways when at home, often electing not to participate in local festivals or simply to suppress them.[9] After the wars heavy taxation and the crash in agricultural prices increased the cost of managing estates. As a result much land changed hands, often falling to industrialists who had never managed an estate before and who had little patience for the genteel paternalism of their predecessors. The landowner's wage bills (still disguised as poor relief) rose, yet nowhere did wages keep pace with the cost of living.[10] During the 1820s the standard of living fell so low that the laborer on relief got less bread than the

prisoner in jail. Conditions were aggravated by a serious fuel shortage. By re-
ducing the wastes that had always supplied cottagers with their fuel (turf, gorse,
reeds, or sedge), enclosure forced on them the hardship of buying their fuel as
well as their food. As a consequence, there were outbreaks of social disorder
ranging from increased pilfering and poaching to the food riots and machine
breaking that swept the countryside (particularly East Anglia) in 1816, 1822,
and 1829–1830.[11]

Because Constable's landscapes belong simultaneously to the biography of a
countryman and to the social history of the countryside, one must understand
them in both contexts. Constable scholarship since Leslie's biography has repeatedly attended to the details of his personal life; critics have typically identified
Constable's views in the actual landscape, pinpointed the spot from which they
were made, and linked them to extra-artistic events in Constable's life.[12] It is
not, of course, a question of repudiating all that we have learned from such
studies, but merely of noting certain limitations they all share. Paradoxically, by
adhering so minutely to the life, they prevent any understanding of it. The
wealth of biographical detail proliferates in the absence of any wider social mediations; as a result, what are supposedly the richest and most concrete studies
of Constable end up by being the most impoverished and abstract, unmediated
by anything more than stylistic analysis. No less paradoxically, one effect of thus
taking the autobiographical aspect of Constable's work for granted as the undis-
puted "key" to his achievement has been to prevent the question of autobiography from ever properly emerging *as a question*: to be accounted for, understood,
"answered."[13]

Both John Barrell's study, *The Dark Side of the Landscape*, and Michael Rosenthal's *Constable: The Painter and His Landscape* are welcome exceptions to the
biographical pointillism that has characterized Constable scholarship.[14] These
studies situate Constable in the landscape that he paints by connecting his art
with the agrarian and social landscape of East Anglia. Concerned with the tradition of depicting the rural poor in English landscape painting, Barrell illuminates Constable's contribution to the ideology of rural poverty, and touches
usefully, if also provocatively, on many of my own concerns. In Barrell's thus
forgoing the biographical conditions (except insofar as they ground what he sees
as the artist's distaste for rural laborers in a general rural-Tory class bias) to deal
directly with the general social history, he impressively enlarges both the scope
of meaning of Constable's art and the questions that can be raised about it. At
the same time, however, he overwhelms the specificity of Constable's landscapes
in the play of social generalities. He profitably suggests that for Constable the
"ideal of the close rural community has replaced the experience of it."[15] But at

the heart of this ideal he places a class fear of the laborer, who must be depersonalized so that he merges "insignificantly with the landscape."[16] To understand Constable's rich ambivalence toward the landscape of East Bergholt as merely exemplifying a class project of dominating the laborer seems unnecessarily reductive and illustrates the dangers of ignoring the personal biography—or, to choose other terms, the formation of the subject. Rosenthal's study provides a more textured account of Constable's art, one that is sensitive to both the social and psychological aspects of Constable's response to the landscape of the Stour Valley. My own approach and analysis coincide with Rosenthal's at many points; however, where he is tempted to see direct connections between political developments in the 1820s and changes in Constable's style, I see such changes as more complexly motivated.[17]

Constable's feelings about landscape, while class-bound, were rooted not in his feelings about interclass relationships but in his own sense of place in a landscape that constantly reminded him of external authorities (his father, the community, artistic tradition, the public, God). His painting of landscape was a way both to challenge these figures and to reinstate their power at a more acceptable level. As this analysis suggests, Constable's mode of personalizing the social and agrarian landscape of his youth was a way to repress questions of larger social meaning by naturalizing them as part of a private struggle for domination and control. Thus Constable's autobiographical project becomes the key to understanding how he transformed the previous century's naturalization of social codes and practices by extending it to his own involvement with nature and landscape.

Constable was a conservative Tory but hardly a political animal. Writing to Fisher about the food riots and machine breaking that swept East Anglia in 1822, Constable reported: "My brother is uncomfortable about the state of things in Suffolk. They are as bad as Ireland—'never a night without seeing fires near or at a distance,' The *Rector* & his brother the *Squire* (Rowley & Godfrey) have forsaken the village—no abatement of tithes or rents—four of Sir Wm. Rush's tenants distrained next parish—these things are ill timed."[18] Juxtaposed with his brother's alarms, Constable's assessment of the situation ("these things are ill timed") strikes a curiously cool note. What, one might ask, was ill-timed—the riots? the tithes and rents? things generally? This detachment typifies Constable's response to the fortunes of the kingdom. He rarely mentioned current political events, and his few statements about them, like the one just quoted, came in response to another's inquiry. Nor did he ever seem to bother soliciting someone's opinion in his turn. Unlike his brother Abram or his friend Fisher, Constable seems to have been little exercised by historical events, the one exception being the passage of the great Reform Bill that he feared would rob his children of their inheritance.[19] As his violent response to it indicates, Constable proved to be political only when politics directly threatened him or his loved ones. Otherwise he was not so much apolitical as antipolitical. In the midst of the political, economic, and social upheavals of the postwar period, he founded "a kingdom of [his] own" ("my landscape and my children"), a counter-kingdom where antipolitics reigned. Constable's antipolitics thus extended to his painting. He believed he was creating an art that was as "universal" in its meanings as it was "natural" in its style. By looking critically at Constable's biography I wish to demonstrate the ideological nature of this universality and naturalness and to discuss both as the extension of the process of naturalization.

To do justice to Constable's autobiographical project as well as to its social and historical moment, an analysis must occupy the middle distance between the accumulation of anecdotes in the foreground and the social generalities in the background. But what occupies this middle distance? What concepts or levels can be said to determine it? Analysis requires a structure that mediates between the personal and the social, and such a structure, in Constable's day as now, is the family.[20] The family—together with the conceptualization of its dynamic in psychoanalysis—both unifies the data of the biographical field and provides the means of internalizing social categories in a personal history. As recent histories of the nuclear family have shown, rather than serving as a haven from capitalist structures of power and authority, the family has been thoroughly invaded by the spirit of economic rationality. Parental authority rests on the provision of material services, and parents who have no property to pass on to their children can exact obedience only by appealing to a sense of duty, deference, filial piety— principles out of place in a society based on rational self-interest. Constable rejected his father's legacy out of a primal ambivalence toward parental control. He can be seen at one level as resisting capitalist structures of power (by rejecting the provision of material services) and at another as embracing them (by acting in the capitalist mode of self-interest). Similarly, his antipolitics were not the negation of capitalist modes of thought and feeling but, as in the case of his original rejection of parental authority, their unconscious acceptance and sublation. The result was a personal dichotomy: Constable the rebellious son/Constable the dutiful son, father, and husband; Constable the romantic/Constable the conservative Tory; Constable the artistic nonconformist/Constable the academician; Constable the indifferent maverick/Constable the anxious autobiographer.[21]

The psychological emphasis in this chapter marks a detour from the sociocultural perspective brought to bear on the rustic landscape so far, and I shall rejoin the concerns of this perspective in the following chapter. However, as I have tried to suggest, the division of interest is only apparent.[22] For if I appear to be substituting a psychological determinism for an economic one, my premise is that the psychological factors pertinent to Constable's landscapes were grounded in a relationship to specific economic structures (the family, the community, the art market). Specifically, my argument assumes that because of the naturalization of capitalist property relationships as conditions of fact and not the result of social activity, rebellion against authority (even in the family) is discouraged by the "reality principle," by the "way things are." In such a situation one rebels only to learn better how to submit. I am ultimately concerned with reading Constable's landscapes in their general social context, but Constable himself first absorbed this context as it was reproduced in the immediate conditions of country life in his own family.

THE PATRIA

At the time of Constable's birth, East Bergholt was a village of about one thousand people and represented six ancient manorial holdings that over the centuries had been leased or sold in parcels to local inhabitants. Reading the Constable family letters with their accounts of neighborly visits, dances, and card parties, one is reminded of the rural society of Jane Austen's novels. Raymond Williams has said of that world that "to be face to face . . . is already to belong to a class."[23] Austen stretched her web of propertied families over the countryside, obscuring from view its humbler denizens. The letters present this same class of propertied families in the community of East Bergholt, with the countryside reduced to a place of business or a backdrop for the amusements of middle-class life. "Sad weather for your Father's & everyone's clover & hay that is sever'd & spread upon the ground," Constable's mother wrote; "—but these matters must be endured."[24] Or again: "We have had before this snow & frost, almost constant rains, and great floods, which has greatly impeded navigation & dispatch of business."[25]

Constable's own participation in this eminently sociable business community, however, seems always to have been marked by estrangement. At the most banal level of psychology, it emerges as a social shyness in the persistent reserve with which he regarded the East Bergholt inhabitants. "I believe it is thought," his mother admonished him, "you avoid notice too much, which damps the ardour even of the best friendship."[26] The retiring nature she complained of is evident in his letters to his future wife, Maria Bicknell. He could not give her "many particulars" about recent balls "as I do not join in these things."[27] "I am quite unable to give you any news of this village. . . . I am very civil to all but continue to make my escape from all but the Godfreys."[28] When he gave reports of the village, he cast them in ironic terms: "The bear is dead and Mr. Eyre is inconsolable, he loved it dearly though he has the marks of its teeth in many parts of his body."[29]

This withdrawal from society finds its companion gesture in a retreat to nature. If Constable's correspondence offers little information about the inhabitants of East Bergholt, it amply and affectionately evokes the natural beauties there: "Nothing can exceed the beautifull appearance of the country at this time, its freshness, its amenity—the very breeze that passes the window is delightfull, it has the voice of Nature."[30] He seemed to feel affection for the landscape in direct proportion to his social alienation: "The village is now in great beauty. I think I never saw the foliage more promising—and as I love the trees, and feilds [sic], better than I do the people, I can tell you [little] about our 'new neighbours.' "[31] Constable's rapturous response to the natural beauties of East Bergholt was always more than an artist's native visual sensitivity; or rather, precisely as such, it registered a covert dissent from the values shared by his family and the community represented in the letters.

Constable formulated his self-consciousness in this community most suggestively in a letter written to Maria from East Bergholt after their marriage: "All here who meet me inquire kindly after you—but I am a *shy cock*—especially on this ground."[32] Where cocks proverbially crow—on their own ground—there this cock turned shy. The paradox is worth investigating and is sharpened by the ambiguity of "this ground" meaning not just the topic of his marriage but also, and more important, the East Bergholt community itself. Why should the cock have been shy? What did the young son of a well-placed, eminently respected merchant and landowner have to be shy *about* in this society of landowners? Why did he not, when at home, feel entirely at home? If Constable was a shy cock in East Bergholt, it may be that he did not feel that this ground *was* his own. In such a case, to whom did he think it belonged?

Such questions lead to a consideration of Constable's ambivalence toward his father Golding and toward his own role as heir apparent of Golding's property. Golding Constable was a wealthy mill owner and merchant who supervised the work of his mills. At the time John was born he owned a large house with thirty-seven acres and rights of commons, Flatford water mill and a share in Dedham water mill, a windmill in East Bergholt, several cottages, a warehouse at Mistley, a granary and kilns, a dry dock, several river barges, and the sailing ship *Telegraph*. The flour ground at his mills was transported down the Stour River to

Mistley harbor; from there the *Telegraph* carried it to London to be sold on the corn exchange.[33] Because his first son, also named Golding, was apparently mentally defective, Golding senior had decided that the responsibilities of the firstborn should fall to John. Much as Golding had inherited the business from his uncle, so John would gradually inherit the task of managing it from Golding. The scenario was already in operation by 1792, when Constable was tending his father's windmill on the commons. It was planned that when Golding died, the annual income from the business would be divided among his six children but that the business itself would remain a single concern directed by John, who would thereby assume his father's role as provider for the family.

Constable's choice of art as a profession, then, was an act of refusing this ideally projected line of inheritance, and it was perceived as such by his family. Constable's interest in art awakened precisely during his apprenticeship in the family business,[34] and the Constable who first emerges in the letters and in Leslie's biography was thoroughly caught up in a domestic contention over the choice of a career. Throughout the period from 1795 to 1799, Golding continually discouraged his son from the calling he found increasingly attractive.

By the fall of 1797 Constable's resistance to his father's will probably produced a crisis. He left East Bergholt for London to visit John Thomas Smith, an accomplished practitioner of etching and mezzotint with whom he had become acquainted (ironically enough) while on family business at Edmonton the previous year. Smith, the first professional artist Constable met, did more than anyone to set him on a professional artist's career. Though Smith had originally advised Constable to accede to his father's wishes, he now changed his mind and wrote to Constable's parents to plead his case. The letter does not survive, but Constable's mother's reply, dated October 2, indicates how strongly the Constables opposed their son's desire to become an artist.

> We are anticipating the satisfaction of seeing John at home in the course of a week or ten days, to which I look forward with hope that he will attend to business—by which means he will please his Father, and ensure his own respectability, comfort & accommodation. His Sister Whalley, & every Friend to whom he has been a welcome visitor, all speak well of him & his conduct which gives me an idea—far—far different from that, of having our Grey Hairs brought down with Sorrow to the Grave.[35]

The tone of his mother's letter suggests that tactics of emotional blackmail were common in the parents' attempts to dissuade their son from a career as a painter. Constable's distress at having, as he put it, to "walk through life in a path contrary to that which my inclination would lead me" was no doubt counterbalanced by his fears of disappointing his father and bringing his parents' "Grey Hairs . . . down with Sorrow to the Grave."[36]

Golding Constable finally relented in the fall of 1798 when he allowed his son to study art in London and provided him with an allowance. Even then, however, he was not reconciled to Constable's vocation. Remembering a visit to East Bergholt in December 1799, Ann Taylor recalled:

> There were . . . rumors afloat which conferred upon [John Constable] something of the character of a hero in distress, for it was understood that his father greatly objected to his prosecution of painting as a profession, and wished to confine him to the drudgery of his own business—that of a miller. To us this seemed unspeakably barbarous, though in Essex and Suffolk a miller was commonly a man of considerable property, and lived as Mr. Constable did, in genteel style.[37]

Even Constable's mother could accept his career only in conventional terms, imagining him becoming a great portrait painter or history painter like Reynolds or Benjamin West.[38] Her letters wax enthusiastic over his commission to copy some of Reynolds's portraits and over the prospect of his painting an altarpiece for Brantham Church, but on the subject of landscape they are silent.

Constable's relationship to his family and to the East Bergholt community was further complicated by his seven-year courtship (1809–1816) of Maria Bicknell. As the granddaughter of Dr. Rhudde, the wealthy pastor of East Bergholt and Brantham churches, Maria would have been a socially acceptable choice, except that Dr. Rhudde appears to have had a serious falling-out with Golding Constable some years before John began his courting.[39] Although the disagreement had been patched over, Rhudde violently opposed the young couple's marriage, threatening to disown Maria—and even her brothers and sisters—if it took place. Ostensibly he objected to Constable's unsettled career and finances, but the old quarrel, as well as a bias against families "in trade," may have contributed to his displeasure. Responding to the social slight that Rhudde's opposition implied, the Constables rallied to their son's side, and Constable's mother in particular made every effort to placate the crotchety Rhudde.[40] This was the stuff of which novels were made, and the plot, as it thickened, was too good to be ignored by the village at large. "Our enemies," Constable lamented to Maria, "are busy and vigilant and unprincipled."[41] But even those friendly or indifferent followed the matter with interest.[42] Constable was made the subject of talk and legend such as Ann Taylor reports, and he became warier than ever of the East Bergholt community.

In choosing to marry the granddaughter of his father's old (and perhaps only) adversary in East Bergholt, Constable again chose a contrary path, making his father doubly anxious for him. Though he approved of Maria personally, Golding Constable was as unhappy with his son's plans for marriage as he was with his plans for a career. In one of his few surviving letters he advised his son "to defer all thought of a [marriage] connection until some removals here take place & your expectations [are] certainly known."[43] Constable did not marry Maria until a few months after Golding's death in 1816, when he inherited a sixth of his father's estate (managed at that time by Constable's younger brother Abram).

It is not enough to say that the most important dramas of Constable's first forty years unfolded in the landscape of East Bergholt. One needs to add that by dint of association these experiences were *en*folded there as well. Tending Golding's windmill on the East Bergholt commons, Constable had gone about his father's business; but in the adjacent fields he had also courted Maria. From the back windows of his father's house he saw the windmill as well as his father's fields and the rectory of Dr. Rhudde. The landscape thus came to Constable charged with ambivalence. Insofar as it was marked by culture (his father's business, Dr. Rhudde, his "enemies," the East Bergholt community), this landscape oppressed him; but insofar as it could be seen as nature (in "the beautiful appearance of the country" or in Maria herself), it offered him a refuge from this oppression.[44]

In this context, what did it mean for Constable to paint landscape—to paint *this* landscape? Constable's turning to the landscape involved him in several kinds of retreat. It allowed him to abandon his father's business and to withdraw from both the East Bergholt community and the enemies of his happiness with Maria. Yet as Constable turned to the landscape, I would suggest, his rebellious retreats became symbolic recoveries as well. As a landscape artist he continued to "work" his father's land; as the celebrant of the beauties of East Bergholt, he continued to belong there; and by painting the "dear scenes" of his frustrating courtship, he achieved the intimacy with Maria denied to him by Dr. Rhudde and her family. Of course, if Constable's landscapes mirror his ambivalence toward his father and the East Bergholt community, they do so only by displacing it. Instead of the dramas of his early life, Constable painted their stage, and instead of the East Bergholt inhabitants, he concentrated on their environment. The advantage of the metonymy (substitution by contiguity) was not only that it made the autobiographical interpretation of landscape possible but also that it made it invisible. The mute, "objective" character of landscape veiled the painting subject, of whom it could thereby speak in complete safety.[45] Constable thus continued to "avoid notice" in his landscapes, but the shy self-effacement camouflaged and facilitated a sly self-assertion. Though the landscapes represent his *looking back at* the community whose scrutinous gaze intimidated him, it is a looking back that need never be seen as such. And though, formerly the object

FIG. 34. John Constable, *Dedham Church and Vale, Suffolk,* 1800 (15⅝ × 20¾ in.). Pen, ink, and watercolor drawing. Whitworth Art Gallery, University of Manchester, Manchester.

of village legend, Constable now told his own story, it was told in a code that the public could not decipher.

Though it would be possible to show that this ambivalence, whose poles are retreat and recovery, left its mark on all Constable's early landscapes, it is most visible in its diachronic dimension, that is, in the historical progress made by Constable's work from one pole to the other. At one end of this progress, in 1800, are the Hurlock drawings (Figures 34–37) and the Downing College *View from Golding Constable's House* (Figure 38), the first occasions of Constable's treating the Stour Valley comprehensively. At the other, in 1810–1811, are the oil sketches of Flatford Mill (see Figures 56–60), in which Constable's art first reached maturity. Separated by almost ten years (during which Constable nearly abandoned the East Bergholt landscape entirely), the two groups stand for the separate moments of a dialectic in which Constable's work is always implicated.

In the Hurlock drawings, Constable for the first time portrayed local scenery in large inclusive views.[46] The four drawings were done as a wedding present for a friend and neighbor, Lucy Hurlock. Her father was the curate of Langham church and introduced Constable to Dr. John Fisher, titular head of Langham and later bishop of Salisbury, whose nephew John Fisher became Constable's

FIG. 35. John Constable, *The Valley of the Stour, with Langham Church in the Distance*, 1800 (13⅝ × 21 in.). Pen, ink, and watercolor drawing. Victoria and Albert Museum, London.

closest friend. The four drawings of the Stour Valley around Dedham and Langham were meant to recall familiar sights to Lucy after she moved with her new husband to Norfolk. The fact that the drawings were intended to commemorate the Stour Valley may account for their compositional factualness.[47] Commemoration proved one of the strongest impulses in Constable's recovery of his native ground: here, *in ovo*, it seems to have made him shy of overtampering with appearances: Lucy's memory was not to be coerced. It is as though Constable put down every detail of the landscape in the hope of producing an objective record devoid of any conceptual or affective interpretation on his part. While the uniform treatment of detail partakes of a topographical tradition, the awkward profusion of detail recalls the picturesque predilection for bits and pieces. No doubt the confusion of stylistic aim had to do with Constable's artistic immaturity at this point in his career. Yet the immaturity arose specifically in connection with a landscape that Constable had experienced long before he experienced the artistic models available for representing it. It is as though Constable's profound sense of the "reality" of this landscape could not be rendered except by throwing his artistic models into a certain dislocation.

FIG. 36. John Constable, *The Valley of the Stour, with Stratford St. Mary in the Distance*, 1800 (13½ × 20½ in.). Pen, ink, and watercolor drawing. Victoria and Albert Museum, London.

The timidity of the Hurlock drawings suggests Constable's unwillingness to mark the landscape in any way as his own possession. The other face of this retreat, however, is the aggressive appropriation of the landscape that emerges in the Downing College *View from Golding Constable's House*.[48] The painting represents a view from the back windows of the family house across Golding's fields toward the East Bergholt commons. But though the distant view is represented exactly, with its fields, cottages, the family windmill, and (to the right) Dr. Rhudde's rectory, the Constable property has been curiously transformed. In the place of the farm buildings and the family gardens, Constable put a winding track along which a picturesque cowherd leads his cows.[49]

In what the painting (like a sin) both omits and commits, one may read a repetition of the original act of filial disobedience on which Constable's artistic career was founded. It is not too much to suggest that the view was invested for Constable with Oedipal meanings. If only by virtue of Golding Constable's extensive holdings, the land literally became a *patria*, inspiring all the ambivalence that the authority of fathers induces in their sons. When, under the circumstances, to paint at all was to resist paternal domination, to paint the very domain

FIG. 37. John Constable, *The Valley of the Stour, Looking towards East Bergholt*, 1800 (13⅜ × 20⅛ in.). Pen, ink, and watercolor drawing. Victoria and Albert Museum, London.

of this domination must have been fraught with even greater filial anxiety. Later in life, Constable equated his art with the ownership of land: "Whatever may be thought of my art, it is my own: and I would rather possess a freehold, though but a cottage, than live in a place belonging to another."[50] Accordingly, the flight from the *patria* engendered a desire to return to it in full possession. Such a return is anticipated even here, in a work that performs a decided act of retreat. In the aggressive transformation of the family property and in his aesthetic improvement of it, Constable reappropriated it for himself. He made it conform to the order of his art, an order of which he, not his father, was master.

Yet the order of art resembled the order of the father that it replaced in at least this respect: it imposed an authority that, preceding Constable's work, threatened to preempt its development. From 1800 to 1809 Constable's career can be understood as a response to both tyrannies. On the one hand, he virtually ceased to paint not only his father's property but even (with a few exceptions) the whole East Bergholt landscape.[51] On the other hand, he engaged in a vigorously critical apprenticeship in his art. During this period, he sketched in long-canonized picturesque areas, such as Derbyshire and the Lake District, devoid of personal associations. He even tried his hand at portraiture and history

FIG. 38. John Constable, *View from Golding Constable's House*, ca. 1800–1802 (13 × 29½ in.). The Masters, Fellows, and Scholars of Downing College, Cambridge.

painting.[52] His art continually experimented—eclectically and often chaotically—with a medley of representational modes. At different times he relied on Claude, on Richard Wilson, on Thomas Girtin, and on Gainsborough. In sketching and copying the works of other landscape artists, Constable followed the wisdom of the Royal Academy (where for most of this period he was a student) and of his mentors Joseph Farington and Sir George Beaumont. Constable followed the conventional course of wisdom, however, because it ministered to his need to lay secure foundations for the "cottage" that would be his own.

It is a commonplace of Constable scholarship to note the coincidence in 1809 of Constable's falling in love with Maria Bicknell and the emergence of his mature artistic style.[53] It seems certain that Maria's love had a profound effect on Constable's art, an effect best understood as a reversal of his original retreat from his native ground. It was precisely during a long stay in East Bergholt in 1809 that Constable first began to court Maria. During the tedious trials and long separations he had to undergo before marrying her in 1816, the landscape appears to have acquired a new meaning for him. In a letter to Maria in 1812 Constable described the view that he had altered so drastically in the Downing College painting: "From the window where I am now writing, I see all those sweet fields where we have passed so many happy hours together."[54] What Constable saw from the window was not the scene of his prospective submission but the scene of his own courtship—that is, of his own attempt to found a patrimony.

Even in this case, however, landscape retained the value of a compensation: it bespoke Maria's absence and Constable's loss. In the same letter he went on to say, "It is with a melancholy pleasure that I revisit those scenes that once saw us so happy—yet it is gratifying to me to think that the scenes of my boyish days should have witnessed by far the most affecting event of my life."[55] In a similar vein Constable wrote to her from London that same year, "I long to see the country again, but I cannot go to Bergholt without being at least sixty miles farther from you and seeing a thousand objects to remind me of those happy hours when we *could* meet."[56] Two years later, in 1814, he wrote Maria again of the view from the back windows of the house, "I can hardly tell you what I feel at the sight from the window where I am now writing of the fields in which we have so often walked. A beautifull calm autumnal setting sun is glowing upon the gardens of the Rectory and on adjacent fields where some of the happiest hours of my life were passed."[57] The landscape that "once" saw him and Maria

FIG. 39. John Constable, *Golding Constable's Flower Garden*, 1815 (13 × 20 in.). Ipswich Museums and Art Galleries, Ipswich.

happy, as it once had witnessed his boyish days, became a positive value for Constable only in retrospect.

As this interpretation of his letter already suggests, Constable's old alienation from the landscape was not wholly overcome in his new association of it with Maria. In 1815 he painted a panoramic view, in two pendants, from the windows of his father's house. The one pendant, *Golding Constable's Flower Garden* (Figure 39),[58] depicts Golding's farm buildings and the village of East Bergholt directly behind them. The other pendant, *Golding Constable's Kitchen Garden* (Figure 40), represents the view Constable described in his letters to Maria, where he associated it with their courtship. Overlooking the kitchen gardens to the fields beyond and to Dr. Rhudde's rectory, the view is a visual metonymy for Constable's desire and longing for Maria. Together forming a single panorama, the two paintings thematize the division in Constable's consciousness. The associations with Maria did not expel prior associations. Rather, Constable's vision of landscape was informed by both sets of associations in dialectical relation to each other. The dialectic ensured Constable's distance from the landscape and his attachment to it as well. The tense conjunction of these two perspectives was

FIG. 40. John Constable, *Golding Constable's Kitchen Garden*, 1815 (13 × 20 in.). Ipswich Museums and Art Galleries, Ipswich.

precisely the condition for the great change in Constable's art in 1809–1810.

Significantly, the change was first registered in the small oil sketches of Golding Constable's mill at Flatford (see Figures 56–60).[59] The subject, which Constable treated in these sketches for the first time, preoccupied him intensely until 1817, when his large *Scene on a Navigable River* ("Flatford Mill") (Figure 41) was exhibited at the Royal Academy. His fascination with Flatford Mill even became a joke between him and Maria. "I am sure you will laugh," he wrote to her in 1812, "when I tell you I have found another very promising subject at Flatford Mill."[60] The 1810–1811 Flatford sketches mark the beginning of Constable's attempt to clarify his feelings about the *patria*. For the first time since the Downing College *View*, he painted his father's property. By this time, however, Flatford Mill had other associations for him besides those connected with his father's business. In a letter of 1811 he recalled to Maria the time she had

FIG. 41. John Constable, *Scene on a Navigable River*, begun in 1816, exhibited at the Royal Academy 1817 (40 × 50 in.). Tate Gallery, London. Also known as "Flatford Mill."

sketched there: "I have tried Flatford Mill again, from the lock (whence you once made a drawing)."[61] It is exactly this view from the lock that Constable most frequently represented in the sketches. By associating the scene with Maria, Constable, it seems, began to recover the landscape of East Bergholt. Flatford no longer represented a culture that Constable did not want to possess; it embodied a nature that was his own.

The metonymy linking the mill to Maria became complete in Constable's mind. When in the summer of 1816 the two lovers at last decided to marry regardless of the consequences, Constable wrote to Maria about his disappointment that the *Scene on a Navigable River* was not "forwarder."[62] Writing back, Maria was hurt to see implied in his regret a desire to postpone their nuptials. "How sorry I am my dearest Love," he hurriedly replied, "that anything should have escaped me that could have caused you one moment's uneasiness at such a time as this. . . . My only object was to gain as much of the time here as I could for my business."[63] As the exchange makes clear, not only had Flatford temporarily displaced Maria in Constable's mind, but also the habit of substitution had become virtually unconscious. And this unconscious substitution permitted another: "My only object was to gain as much of the time here as I could for my business." By 1816 Flatford Mill had become as much Constable's business as his father's.

THE PICTURESQUE LEGACY

For the paternal authority that Constable denied to his father, he substituted the paternal authority of his artistic mentors (John Thomas Smith, Joseph Farington, Sir George Beaumont, Thomas Stothard) and models (Gainsborough and Reynolds). Constable's deference to their opinions and examples is a striking feature of his early artistic life and clashes sharply with the picture we today have of him as a maverick or rebel.

This displacement of his father began even before Constable had definitely decided on an artistic career. J. T. Smith's intercession for him with his parents in 1797 was the culmination of an intense year-long friendship between the engraver and the young miller. When Constable first met Smith—on a business visit to his uncle in Edmonton—Smith was preparing to leave for London to work on an essay on picturesque cottage scenery. No doubt a pleasant change from the routine of business, the acquaintance with Smith seems to have inspired Constable with the desire to follow him to London. Constable must have communicated this desire to his father, who evidently rebuked him with the charge of ingratitude. The only surviving letter in this exchange is Constable's apology, dated August 1796, Edmonton:

> I must own upon first reading your letter I was rather confused, but upon recollecting myself I soon found that I deserved all the reproof you was so good as to give me. . . . I find you mistake the matter if you think it was my own intention or wish to get a situation in town, (any more than this) that if I could have been somewhere for a year or two, to have got some knowledge of a business which had some affinity to your own, it might have been of service to you now and to myself hereafter.[64]

Constable's pretext for wanting to work in town was the corn market, but it seems clear from subsequent developments that his deeper motive was to be near Smith and to share in his artistic activities.

After the Edmonton visit, Constable began to serve two masters, working as conscientiously for Smith as for Golding. Not only did he enthusiastically recruit subscribers for Smith's book from among his family and friends, but he also made some sketches of local cottages that he sent to Smith for possible inclusion in the book. "I have in my walks," he wrote to Smith in October 1796, "pick'd up several cottages and peradventure I may have been fortunate enough to hit upon one, or two, might please."[65] Although Smith found one or two of the sketches worthy of his own needle, none of the ten surviving sketches appears in Smith's publication.[66]

The purpose of Smith's book was to call attention to the beauties of cottage scenery. "Of all the picturesque subjects," he wrote in his essay, "the English cottage seems to have obtained the least share of particular notice and appropriate discriminations by modern *tourists*."[67] As one might expect, the example of Gainsborough provided Smith's enterprise with an important precedent.

> [Gainsborough] appears to have been the first English master that had courage to quit the dull unvarying routine in rural painting, and from more profound and accurate observations of Nature, to give distinct characteristics and original varieties to his cottagery, and to the furniture and circumstances with which his best works are so eminently enriched: His woodsmen, shepherds, dairy-maids, cottage-children, pigs, dogs, fallen timber, leafless stumps, thorny and bramble fences, and other incidents of rural economy, have the full merit of originality, both in the selection and in the combination.[68]

Smith repeated the high praise accorded by Thicknesse and others to Gainsborough's laborious naturalism. "His earliest essays, of which I have had the pleasure of examining a great number, appear to have been exactly imitative as possible, and to have been executed with the most careful and laborious precision: the

consequence of which was—a rapid advancement to that stile of broad and simple dashes—an effect which those never can accomplish who begin with broad
pencilling."[69] Following in the tradition he thus established for himself, Smith
noted that his own illustrations for the essay were "all from nature and indeed
some of them were etched on the spot."[70]

In the cottages that he drew for Smith—his earliest extant landscape subjects—Constable attempted to see his native ground picturesquely. All were
done, probably during the fall of 1796, in pen and ink on rough paper that
appears to have made up a single pocket sketch book, and all but one are inscribed with their locations (Figures 42, 43). Constable's intention in the
sketches was clearly to produce cottage studies like Smith's. He went so far as to
imitate Smith's vignette style of composition as well as his scratchy line and
zigzag foliage (Figure 44). Yet a comparison of Constable's cottages with Smith's
reveals a significant difference. While he paid attention to such picturesque details as moldering plaster, overgrown thatch, and crooked casements, Constable
did not seem to understand the role they played in Smith's work. Rather than
dramatizing the details with chiaroscuro in the manner of his friend, Constable

FIG. 42. John Constable, *Cottage at Capel, Suffolk*, 1796 (7⅛ × 11¾ in.). Pen and ink drawing.
Victoria and Albert Museum, London.

FIG. 43.   John Constable, *Cottage at East Bergholt*, 1796 (7⅛ × 11¾ in.). Pen and ink drawing. Victoria and Albert Museum, London.

merely registered them along with the rest of the cottage. The end effect was that, unlike Smith, who drew picturesque cottages, Constable drew cottages that only incidentally happened to be picturesque.

One senses strongly in these works that Constable could not relinquish his native pride in East Bergholt in order to be properly picturesque. For Smith, the picturesque depended crucially on poverty and neglect:

> In poverty nothing will more easily, or more universally excite the attentions of benevolence, than the appearance of neatness and cleanliness. . . . But it is nothing to the artist. . . . [T]he neglected fast-ruinating cottage . . . the weather-beaten thatch—the fissures and crevices of the inclining wall—the roof of various angles and inclinations—the tiles of different hue—the fence of bungling workmanship— the wild unrestrained vine . . . the slatternry of tubs and dishes scattered about the door—the intrusion of pigs . . . offer far greater allurements to the painter's eye.[71]

Although city artists like Smith or even estate owners like Price and Knight could indulge in the picturesque aestheticization of rural poverty, the practice was unfamiliar to Constable, who, as the descendent of hardworking yeoman

near EDMONTON CHURCH.

FIG. 44. John Thomas Smith, *Near Edmonton Church*, ca. 1796. Etching from his *Remarks on Rural Scenery*, 1797. Photograph: The British Library.

stock, probably saw local poverty as a disgraceful drain on the finances of the parish ratepayers.[72] If the picturesqueness that his sketches display is so muted and even tentative, it is perhaps because Constable was too close to the consequences of rural poverty to enjoy the spectacle of it. Behind his hesitant rejection of the picturesque aestheticization of poverty stood his parents' values of hard work, neatness, and cleanliness. His attempt to follow Smith's artistic style was disrupted by Golding Constable's moral sense.

An interesting example of Constable's discomfort at this time with the picturesque mode can be found in a drawing entitled *A Fisherman's Cottage in Brantham, Suffolk, with a View of Mistley Hall, Lately the Seat of Lord Viscount Galway* (Figure 45). The bowl-shaped foreground containing the cottage focuses our eyes on the center of the composition, occupied by the distant Mistley Hall. The spatial tension between the foreground and distance echoes a thematic tension between the rustic cottage and the country house. Is the drawing a study of a picturesque cottage or a topographical view of a country seat? Once we become conscious of Mistley Hall, the cottage and its rustic wilderness are transformed into an extension of the estate. The cottage area could almost be the corner of a picturesque garden, a contrived wilderness like the one illustrated by Thomas Hearne for Knight's poem *The Landscape* (see Figure 29). Reduced to the status of a garden folly, the cottage implies its parasitical relation to the estate, and the picturesque representation, by virtue of its sheer naïveté, becomes an unintended commentary on the picturesque itself, underlining the privilege inherent in such an aesthetic.

Smith's model of picturesque picture making was soon displaced for Constable by Gainsborough's. As early as 1798 Constable was imitating Gainsboroughesque motifs in a small drawing of a dozing shepherd (Figure 46).[73] The

FIG. 45. John Constable, *A Fisherman's Cottage in Brantham, Suffolk, with a View of Mistley Hall,* 1796 (7⅛ × 11¾ in.). Pen and ink drawing. Victoria and Albert Museum, London.

style is still Smith's, but the overall mood and specific details—the blasted tree, the forest glade, the shepherd—recall Gainsborough. A year later, Constable was in Gainsborough's home town of Ipswich and writing to Smith, "Tis a most delightful country for a landscape painter, I fancy I see Gainsborough in every hedge and hollow tree."[74] A wash drawing of a cottage from that year (Figure 47) shows how far Constable had come in his imitation of Gainsborough.[75] In a scene reminiscent of Gainsborough's late "Cottage Doors," the elegant loops and swirls of Constable's outline as well as the free yet delicate handling of the wash attest to both Constable's increasing understanding of Gainsborough's style and his facility in imitating it. Although both these drawings allude to the pointedly artificial pastoral mode of Gainsborough's late style, Constable soon repudiated this phase of Gainsborough's work in favor of his earlier naturalistic style. After his first meeting with Constable in 1799, Farington noted that Constable

FIG. 46. John Constable, *Figure Resting beside a Wooded Track*, ca. 1798 (6⁵⁄₁₆ × 8¹⁄₁₆ in.). Pen, ink, and wash drawing. Private collection, Great Britain.

thought the "first pictures of Gainsborough his best, [the] latter so wide of nature."[76]

Constable's exposure to the early naturalism of Gainsborough's art came through an acquaintance with George Frost, Samuel Kilderbee, and Benjamin Strutt, all of whom collected Gainsborough's early landscapes and two of whom—Kilderbee and Strutt—had known the artist personally. Constable met these men on his trips to Ipswich and Colchester, where he went to collect information about Gainsborough for Smith's book.[77] The context of his discovery of early Gainsborough places Constable's naturalistic drawing of a copse of trees from about 1799 (Figure 48), which clearly shows Constable's effort to emulate Gainsborough's early practice of making careful studies of trees from nature (Figure 49).[78] Under the tutelage of George Frost, a clever imitator of this kind of Gainsborough drawing, Constable did a number of drawings of trees and forest scenery, many of which were subsequently confused with the work of Frost.[79] Constable sketched with Frost in and around Ipswich and from him presumably

FIG. 47. John Constable, *A Cottage among Trees*, dated 1799 (9½ × 13 in.). Pencil and gray wash drawing. Yale Center for British Art: Paul Mellon Collection, New Haven.

learned the Gainsboroughesque style of hatching that he later transmuted into his own chiaroscuro technique for rendering both broken natural light and the mass and texture of the objects thus illuminated. In one of these drawings (Figure 50) this method of hatching led Constable to rely less on outline and to develop a dense, thoroughly integrated style of drawing. If one compares this drawing to the Gainsborough (see Figure 49) or to one by Frost (Figure 51), one can see how Constable, much less interested in the decorative function of the hatching technique than in its ability to render light, was already transforming it into a tool of naturalistic representation. By about 1806, the presumed date of this drawing,[80] Constable had gone beyond imitating the picturesque conceits of Smith, Frost, and Gainsborough and was subjecting all their stylistic methods to a new criterion of naturalism.

Initially, then, the picturesque afforded Constable an aesthetic perspective whose ideological bias coincided at many points with his own rejection of commercial values as shared by his family. Furthermore, the picturesque focus on the specific appearances of objects and the power of these appearances to evoke strong

FIG. 48. John Constable, *A Copse*, 1799 (8⅞ × 12⅞₆ in.). Pencil, pen, and brown ink drawing. Private collection, Great Britain.

imaginative associations encouraged Constable's own propensity to infuse particular views and objects with affective significance. Yet the picturesque was also a
formation from which Constable from the start had taken his distance. Specifically, he distanced himself from distance: the hierarchical, aestheticizing remoteness the picturesque interposed between beholder and countryside. As a
result, Constable's attempts at the picturesque, even at the height of his picturesque phase, tended toward a naturalism that, while certainly a dimension of the
picturesque aesthetic, was never central to it. As his somewhat unorthodox pref-
erence for early rather than late Gainsborough shows, Constable's surpassing of
the picturesque was, in the last analysis, a redistribution of its properties according to a new pattern of emphasis. Even when Constable's naturalism became
an apparently independent style, it was never severed from its picturesque
origins. Many features of Constable's naturalism—roughness, irregularity, frag-
mentation, the use of the vignette, the focus on objects and their expressive
possibilities—were rooted in the picturesque legacy, for in the end Constable
treated that legacy as he treated any legacy, abandoning it after internalizing
many of its imperatives.

FIG. 49. Thomas Gainsborough, *Study of Wooded Landscape with Figures*, mid to late 1740s
(4⅝ × 7¼ in.). Pencil drawing. Courtauld Institute of Art: Witt Collection, London.

FIG. 50. John Constable, *Figure on a Roadway*, ca. 1806 (8½ × 7½ in.). Pencil drawing. Public Archives of Canada, Ottawa (C–93167).

FIG. 51.   George Frost, *Track through Trees*, ca. 1800 (7⁷⁄₁₆ × 9 in.). Black chalk and stump drawing. Ipswich Museums and Art Galleries, Ipswich.

"A NATURAL PAINTURE"

During his first years in London, much as he had previously done with Smith, Constable submitted himself to the authority of older artists like Farington, West, Beaumont, and Stothard. He studied and copied the old masters under their influence, and he rejected the companionship of fellow students, whose approach to landscape he found superficial.[81] His dedication to artistic excellence was severely tried. His father persisted in believing him to be "pursuing a shadow" and in wishing to see him "employed."[82] In the spring of 1802 opportunity for employment came in the form of an invitation from Dr. John Fisher

to apply for the post of drawing master at the Military Academy at Great Mar-
low. At twenty-six—much older than the other students at the Royal Academy—Constable must have felt the plausibility of his father's fears, for he applied for the post and went to be interviewed for it. With economic prudence
and artistic ambition once again in contest, Constable, after seeking the advice
of Farington and West, decided once again in favor of ambition and withdrew
his application. Although siding with his new fathers, Constable went on—in
the compensatory pattern already noted—to commit himself with even greater
urgency to his father's ethic of diligence and hard work. His extraordinary letter
to his friend John Dunthorne on May 29, 1802, clearly set forth the commitment:

> For these last few weeks, I believe I have thought more seriously on my profession
> than at any other time of my life—that is, which is the shurest way to real excel-
> lence. And this morning I am more inclined to mention the subject having just
> returned from a visit to Sir G. Beaumont's pictures.—I am returned with a deep
> conviction of the truth of Sir Joshua Reynold's [sic] observation that "there is no
> easy way of becoming a good painter." It can only be obtained by long contempla-
> tion and incessant labor in the executive part.
>
> And however one's mind may be elevated, and kept up to what is excellent, by
> the works of the Great Masters—still Nature is the fountain's head, the source from
> whence all originality must spring—and should an artist continue his practice with-
> out referring to nature he must soon form a *manner*, & be reduced to the same
> deplorable situation as the French painter mentioned by Sir J. Reynolds, who told
> him that he had long ceased to look at nature for she only put him out.
>
> For these two years past I have been running after pictures and seeking the truth
> at second hand. I have not endeavoured to represent nature with the same elevation
> of mind—but have neither endeavoured to make my performances look as if really
> *executed* by other men.
>
> I am come to a determination to make no idle visits this summer or to give up
> my time to common place people. I shall shortly return to Bergholt where I shall
> make some laborious studies from nature—and I shall endeavour to get a pure and
> unaffected representation of the scenes that may employ me with respect to colour
> particularly and anything else—drawing I am pretty well master of.
>
> There is little or nothing in the exhibition worth looking up to—there is room
> enough for a natural painture. The great vice of the present day is *bravura*, an
> attempt at something beyond the truth. In endeavouring to do something better
> than well they do what in reality is good for nothing. *Fashion* always had, & will
> have its day—but *Truth* (in all things) only will last and can have just claims on
> posterity.
>
> I have received considerable benefit from exhibiting—it shows me where I am,
> and in fact tells me what no body else could. There are in the exhibition fine pictures

that bring nature to mind—and represent it with that truth that unprejudiced minds require.[83]

Though this letter is commonly adduced as evidence of Constable's espousal of "a natural painture," the moral values he attached to the term have gone unnoticed.[84] Adopting "a natural painture" meant condemning dishonesty and expediency and embracing integrity and hard work. Constable's romance with landscape had turned into a labor of love. His determination to make "laborious studies from nature" strikes a note different from that of his affectionate evocation of "every stile, and stump, every lane in the village."[85] More than a little of Golding Constable's work ethic had evidently been absorbed by his son, who as a result refused to be set up either by Dr. Fisher or by Golding himself. It is as though Constable, in rejecting family and paternal values, only assigned them a higher place.

This pattern of simultaneously subverting and sublating established authority shaped not only Constable's psychology but also his conception of art. In a sense, the program that Constable laid out for himself in this letter to Dunthorne was a traditional one that in all essentials followed the recommendations Reynolds made to aspiring artists in his *Discourses*. There Reynolds urged that the student of art first develop a facility in drawing; that he then amass a stock of ideas through the study of pictures; and that he finally examine art against the standard of nature so that he might correct "what is erroneous," supply "what is scanty," and add "by his own observations what the industry of his predecessors may have left wanting to perfection."[86] In his letter to Dunthorne, as though in reply, Constable declared that he had mastered drawing, spent two years studying the masters, and was prepared to take the decisive last step, a step, moreover, sanctioned by Farington, who less than a month before had advised Constable "to study nature and *particular* art less."[87] Implicitly, then, in the middle of what was supposed to be his artistic declaration of independence, Constable put himself under the protection of traditional authority.

Yet Constable's adherence to Reynolds was ultimately more qualified than this statement implies, and his reservations arose precisely in connection with the charged subject of nature. For Reynolds nature was a threatening and mysterious chaos that could not be artistically comprehended without the cultural preconditioning of past masterworks. For Constable, however, nature was not so much a force of chaos as a source of liberation. Hence, unlike Reynolds, he emphasized the artist's heroic struggle to portray nature's truth rather than the task of working nature to perfection. Thus though the natural landscape came to Constable as, in different ways, the property of his father and of the old masters, this paternal inheritance was perpetually unsettled by his quest for the truth of nature.

This theme of truth to nature regularly recurred throughout Constable's career whenever he gave an account of his artistic endeavors.[88] One cannot, of course, accept this truth as ontological, as though Constable were (or could be) uniquely free from the artistic and ideological biases with which other artists' representations of nature are fraught. Still, tradition, extending from Constable's own day to the twentieth century, forcefully asserts that Constable's art is not only true to nature but also much truer to it than the work of his predecessors and contemporaries. Without mistaking the effects of Constable's work for nature itself, one must recognize in his work the existence of a powerful formal rhetoric that might make such a mistake possible.

One can see the beginnings of this naturalist rhetoric in the series of small oil sketches Constable did in the summer of 1802. The sketches were all painted in and around East Bergholt, and some of their subjects—Dedham Vale, Willy Lott's house, and the view from West Lodge—became after 1810 familiar items in Constable's Stour Valley repertory. Though Constable was still relying heavily on the established traditions of landscape, he began to alter them to give an increased effect of reality. The small upright *Dedham Vale* (Plate 3),[89] for instance, has long been recognized as deriving from Claude's *Hagar and the Angel* in Sir George Beaumont's collection, and even many of Constable's "improvements" on Claude are couched in terms already made familiar by the art of Gainsborough.[90] Constable's elaborate treatment of the foreground, the wealth of naturalistic detail there, and the color and tonality all suggest that he borrowed as much from early Gainsborough as from Claude. Nonetheless, an important difference from Gainsborough's work in Constable's boldly individuated handling of trees announces Constable's new conception of nature. If one compares two roughly similar works—Gainsborough's *Wooded Landscape with a Seated Figure* (Plate 2) and Constable's *View of Dedham* (Figure 52)[91]—one sees that for Gainsborough it was enough to make generic distinctions between trees, to differentiate the oaks from the ashes, whereas for Constable it was necessary to tell one ash from another. By means of a generalizing notation of loops and zigzags, Gainsborough's trees exist as ideal examples of their kind. Constable's deliberately varied notation, distinguishing one tree from another, renders them irreducibly individual.

This emphasis on specifics inevitably undermines a strongly hierarchical organization of the whole. Traditionally, when viewing landscape painting, we expect the organization of light and color to highlight what is important and to lead the eye in stages into the distance. We also expect objects to be arranged in

FIG. 52. John Constable, *View of Dedham*, 1802 (13⅛ × 16⅜ in.). Yale Center for British Art: Paul Mellon Collection, New Haven.

a way that facilitates this movement. In all the 1802 sketches, however, Constable's individualizing produces a landscape in which all objects stand out with equal force. No one formal element—color, tone, handling, notation—is allowed to dominate these landscapes. What results in each case is a formal deadpan that frustrates our received expectations.[92] The "artlessness" thus artfully managed in such landscapes convinces us of the realism of the representation, and their impenetrability imposes on us a feeling of nature's mysteriousness. Nevertheless, the naturalism that emerges in these works is still limited in scope. It overlays the compositional structures borrowed from Claude and others without itself determining them. Restricted to the depiction of detail, this naturalism seems at once timid and intrusive. Constable seems to have wanted to rec-

FIG. 53. John Constable, *Man Resting in a Lane*, 1809 (12 × 12½ in.). Private collection, Great Britain. Photograph: Thomas Agnew and Sons, Ltd.

oncile the naturalism of the "study" with the formal artistry of the "scene," but he could not yet abandon the distinction itself, which was inherent in both picturesque and academic theory.[93] These early works vacillate uneasily between the different and contradictory demands of the study and the scene. The full development of Constable's "natural painture" consists precisely in an emancipation of the naturalistic detail so that it no longer serves the local function of conveying perceptual stimuli or, as in the 1802 *Dedham Vale*, naturalizing the formal structure, but comes instead to determine a whole series of overall compositional choices.

A good early example of Constable's developed naturalism is a small 1809 oil sketch, *Man Resting in a Lane* (Figure 53).[94] This work depicts the junction

FIG. 54. John Constable, *Dedham Vale: Morning*, exhibited at the Royal Academy 1811 (31 × 51 in.). Elton Hall, Great Britain. Photograph: Courtauld Institute of Art.

of Fen Lane with the Bergholt-to-Flatford road, a spot Constable painted again many times, notably in his first full-scale exhibition picture *Dedham Vale: Morning* (1811) (Figure 54). The junction commanded a panorama of Dedham Vale, with views of Dedham Church, Langham Church, and Stratford St. Mary Church, the last of which is visible in the sketch. Yet the sketch in no way exploits the panoramic opportunities of the junction. No clear architectonic sense of the whole links the various spots on which our eyes come to rest. The composition is pulled sharply to the right by the lane, but the lane leads out of the painting, not into the distance. Not Claudian *coulisses* but the whiteness of the distant church tower leads the eye to the horizon. In the classical landscape the eye moves along the path the feet might travel if the landscape were truly the three-dimensional space of which it gives the illusion. In Constable's sketch the eye cannot trace a pedestrian itinerary; it focuses on charged spots—the figures, the tall golden trees, the white church, the post in the left foreground—that combine not as the map of a logical progression but as the effects of formal contrast. Unlike the 1802 sketches whose naturalism was uninflected by any contrasts, the 1809 sketch is full of oppositional elements. Verticals stand out against strong horizontals, lights against darks, and bright colors against somber ones. Thus by virtue of his dark tonality and counterdiagonal position, the man stands out from the light-colored foreground and opposes the diagonal pull of the road. Similarly, the verticality of the trees breaks through the strong even line of the horizon; and the brilliant highlighting of both the post and the church brings them into relief against the dark tones surrounding them. The landscape appears to compose itself dialectically.

As this sketch shows, the profusion of dialectically charged spots organizes Constable's landscapes. Whereas the solitude of the mountains in the Lake District, as he admitted to Leslie, "oppressed his spirits,"[95] the places that he cherished for their inspiration were characteristically filled with varied detail. "The sound of water escaping from Mill dams . . . Willows, Old rotten Banks, slimy posts, & brickwork. I love such things. . . . As long as I do paint I shall never cease to paint such Places. They have always been my delight."[96] Constable's multiple focus on numerous vignettelike details goes beyond mere picturesqueness. Nowhere is this more evident than in the large exhibition painting *Dedham Vale: Morning*, begun in the summer of 1810. As in the previous year's sketch of the same scene, certain spots of powerfully realized naturalistic detail stand out: the milestone, the puddle, the donkey, the farmer with his horse, the cows, the woman going to market, the man on the road behind her, the three poplar trees in the distance, and the several white churches and houses scattered over the landscape. All these objects seem discontinuous in relation to one another, like so many unlinked vignettes. The first impression is one of fragments, but these fragments are ultimately meant to suggest and participate in a vast whole. A powerful horizontal sweep of bountiful cultivation grounds the details of both foreground and distance in a continuum that seems to extend far beyond the lateral boundaries of the canvas. Thus grounded, the apparent disorder of these details is retrieved in a greater order, of which the entire painting seems only a random sample. This greater order, gesturing toward the divine, guarantees the stability of the composition, which can thus afford to flaunt its seeming randomness and disorder.[97] Once again, this time on the level of composition itself, one finds a pattern of *Aufhebung*: nature provides both a release *from* order and authority and—in a higher, transcendent dimension—a release *into* them.

FIG. 55. John Constable, *Willy Lott's Cottage*, 1812–1813 (7⅞ × 11¾₁₆ in.). Pencil drawing. Courtauld Institute of Art: Witt Collection, London.

Constable's decentralized composition did not come naturally to him. Rather, as one can see in the pencil sketch *Willy Lott's Cottage* (Figure 55),[98] it probably developed in reaction to his more fundamental tendency to focus his landscapes on a single vignette. The sketch was done on three sheets of paper, apparently at two different times. The middle sheet (depicting the cottage) appears to date from 1812 and the sheet to the left of it as well as the thin strip pasted on its right seem to have been added a year later. The later additions decentralize the composition by giving it more lateral interest; but if one thinks them away, the remaining sketch is a vignette composition reminiscent of Smith's cottage etchings. Indeed, though most of Constable's mature landscapes deemphasize the center, they rarely leave it empty.[99] Even when, as usual, it is occupied by unimportant objects, it never ceases to be marked—typically with a vertical accent (a tree or a spire) that stands out by virtue of its difference from the rest of the scene. This marked center seems to be the vestige of Constable's tendency to centralize his compositions. His artistic progress did not consist in abandoning the central vignette so much as in multiplying it all over the landscape, thereby giving his scenes a seemingly random order and a richness of incident.

The several spots of interest in Constable's landscapes thus result from his attraction and resistance to one spot, which, as in the sketch, is ontologically prior to the others. One may ask, not just of the sketch but more generally of Constable's entire oeuvre: what was the primordial spot from which the landscapes derived? Constable himself supplied an answer in the frontispiece of *English Landscape Scenery*, the collection of his mezzotints first published in 1830. Under a representation of his family home in East Bergholt, Constable placed this Latin inscription:

> Hic locus aetatis primordia novit
> Annos felices laetitiaeque dies:
> Hic locus ingenuis pueriles imbuit annos
> Artibus et nostrae laudies origo fuit.[100]

And here is the translation by John Fisher, which Constable kept in one of his sketchbooks:

> This spot saw the day-spring of my life,
> Hours of Joy and years of Happiness;
> This place first tinged my boyish fancy with a love of the Art,
> This place was the origin of my Fame.[101]

The house at East Bergholt, the inscription suggests, was not merely his birthplace but the origin of his art and fame as well; here, in an important sense, all his landscapes "begin." Some of them, like the Downing College view, taken from the actual windows of the house, began here quite literally. The family house, moreover, defines Constable's landscapes at levels other than the merely anecdotal. It embodies the values that Constable had both to reject and to introject to become a painter of natural landscapes. Constable's attraction and resistance to a central spot in his compositions stemmed from and doubled for his attraction and resistance to *this* spot, which was the origin of his fame because it was also the locus of a power he wanted to disperse and retrieve.

The house is problematic as the place of origin for both his personal history and his artistic career because the demands of the two were originally far from coinciding. The attempt to reconcile both "under one roof" gave rise to two kinds of landscape oriented by the house: views of the house from the landscape and views of the landscape from the house. When the house is viewed from the landscape, Constable almost always gives a back view of it, in which, seen from the fields and laneways, the house becomes part of a panoramic landscape. As the few frontal views of the house that Constable attempted show, this landscape can be rendered only from the back. Constable's tendency, then, was to situate the place of his origin squarely in the midst of the landscape he painted, as though to suggest that like his art he too sprang from this land.

Constable's many sketches of the house filled two functions for him. By making the house part of a landscape, they affirmed his legitimacy as the rightful celebrant of local scenery; and by singling out the house, isolating it from the landscape, they also preserved his difference (alienation) from the world he portrayed. The sketches are thus symptomatic of the ways Constable's art both united him to and divided him from the landscape and life of East Bergholt. Implied in Constable's need to identify the house both with and against the landscape is his imaginative identification with the house itself. This becomes quite explicit in his views of the landscape from the house.[102] The series of these views that begins with the Downing College view reaches its culmination—and receives its most exemplary development—in the two panoramic landscapes of 1815: *Golding Constable's Flower Garden* and *Golding Constable's Kitchen Garden* (see Figures 39, 40). Unlike the Downing College view, in which Constable included certain features of the view and dispensed with others, in these works he represented the view exactly and in great detail. As Charles Rhyne has shown, the situation of the house and the placement of its windows were in every way responsible for the landscape Constable represented.[103] Such is the intense objectivity of this realism that one almost imagines that the windows have taken over the task of perceiving and presenting the landscape. Without the strong metonymic connection between the artist's eyes and the windows of the house, it would be almost as if the house and not Constable were the beholder of this landscape. In a sense, the house—paradoxically, both barrier and access to the world outside it—became a metaphor for Constable's self-conscious alienation from the landscape he painted. On the one hand, the windows licensed him to be "objective"; on the other, they located that objectivity in a subjective framework. Just as in the views of the house Constable had to insist on his origin in the landscape and his difference from it, so in these views he had to proffer his art as a true representation of the landscape but also as one necessarily originating in a specific psychological and cultural milieu. The house thus stands for both the origin and the limitation of his "natural painture."

NATURE AND THE OIL SKETCH

At the core of Constable's natural painture was a dichotomy: the impulse to record with naturalistic objectivity the scenes of his boyhood and an equally powerful desire to infuse these scenes with personal associative meaning. While still connected to this landscape through yearly visits to East Bergholt, Constable managed to balance both tendencies, but after his marriage and settlement in London (and later in Hampstead) the tension between them dissolved and a retrospective nostalgia overtook the Stour Valley scenes. The assured, luminous natural painture of the teens gave way to the expressionistic naturalism of the sixfooters and the later landscapes. This stylistic shift that began in the early 1820s has been attributed to the impact of the East Anglian agrarian riots (1821–1822), which destroyed forever Constable's sense of place in the landscape of his youth.[104] While suggestive, I do not think this account finally explains the change in Constable's art at this time. His connection to such political events as the riots was mediated by his brother Abram's letters and, perhaps more important, by his own ambivalence toward the rural society of East Bergholt. Moreover, the changes in his style were anticipated by his natural painture of the teens and came about as the result of a new purpose he gave his art.

After his marriage, the landscape of the Stour Valley remained accessible to Constable's imagination largely through memory and association. Coupling the fact of his marriage, the death of his parents, and the removal of the rest of his family from the house of his birth to Flatford, one could argue that nothing was left of the landscape of his youth but ghosts and memories. To continue to paint such scenes as he had before would—in the terms of his own understanding of his art—have verged on a heartless denial of all the things that had first impelled him to pick up a brush. In an already familiar pattern, actual loss for Constable had to result in an imaginative recovery. Hence as the landscape became less and less accessible as a vehicle for private metonymy, it became more and more publicly retrospective and autobiographical. This desire to personalize the landscape in a public way accounts for the change of style. At this time (1821) he began in his letters to John Fisher to construct an autobiographical explanation for his personal and artistic relationship to the landscape, using Philip Thicknesse's account of Gainsborough's early development.[105] Constable's need to interpret his work to his friend (and to himself) in these terms stands behind his development of the six-foot Academy landscapes that detail the picturesque economy of the Stour River around his father's mills at Dedham and Flatford. Taken in conjunction with the six-footers, the explanation Constable offered Fisher suggests not the old pattern of a recovery of the landscape through a private system of meaning but a new form of recovery in a public autobiographical identification of himself with these scenes. While in his letters to Fisher he worked out these biographical connections, he struggled in his painting to forge a stylistic equivalent for the emotions stirred by memories and associations.

In this context his discussion of a biography of Nicolas Poussin is revealing. Constable told Fisher how Poussin's life amply proved "how much dignity &

elevation of character was the result of such patient, persevering and rational study—no circumstances, however, impropitious could turn him to the right or left—because he knew what he was about."[106] At a time when he was embarking on the six-footers and anticipating criticism of his work, Constable himself had to know "what he was about." This imperative led him to locate his art in an emotionally sustaining autobiographical project.

To begin making his painting of the landscape an autobiographical project, Constable had to cast its associations into a retrospective mode. The agrarian riots would confirm, and then only in a secondary way, what Constable had already realized: that the landscape of his youth was forever lost to him. This consciousness of loss provoked him to recover retrospectively something of the landscape's original significance; because of his removal from the Stour Valley, this significance could no longer fully depend on the continuation of his natural painture of the teens. Moreover, the Stour Valley scenes, now viewed retrospectively, had to continue to repress politics and society if they were to recall autobiographically their original power to liberate Constable from his unwanted legacy and his ambivalent place in the society of East Bergholt. The time had come, it would seem, for Constable to attempt to fuse himself and the landscape into "Constable Country."

The formal model for this fusion in the 1820s was the *plein air* oil sketch. Its importance escalated in Constable's oeuvre from 1802, when it formed the basis of his natural painture (those "laborious studies from nature"), through the 1820s, when he constructed his six-footers from both *plein air* and preparatory sketches, to the 1830s, when they made an even more significant public debut in his mezzotint series *English Landscape Scenery* (accounting for almost half the examples of landscape). Finally, the oil sketch came to determine the formal language of Constable's late style, in which the difference between a sketch and a finished exhibition piece is almost nonexistent. By 1809, the year that Constable's natural painture came into its own, he had begun sketching extensively in oils and relying on oil sketches for the construction of his exhibition pieces.[107] In these finished works, he transformed the emotional appearance of the sketch into a more detached, naturalistic description of the scene. As the basic record of his immediate response to the landscape, the *plein air* oil sketch embodied both the appearance of the landscape and the emotions aroused by it. In this sense, the *plein air* oil sketch is implicitly retrospective and autobiographical, becoming, as Leslie was to remark of Constable's sketch books, "a history of his affections."[108]

Traditionally, the preparatory oil sketch has been valued and judged on its relationship to the finished work, a relationship seen as a binary opposition between unfinished and finished, rough and smooth, realistic and idealistic, atomistic and synthetic, and so forth. This tendency to see the differences between sketch and finished work as a simple formal opposition, however, prevents one's understanding the role of the sketch in Constable's art and its importance for his later style.[109] Even the most casual observer of Constable's oeuvre is aware that his oil sketches fall outside the territory mapped out for them by the academic tradition.[110] Many of them serve no preparatory purpose, and those that do connect to finished works have no consistent rationale, as they would if they really were *études*. Their relationship to the final work is not logical or programmatic but eccentric and coincidental. This paradox of Constable's preparatory oil sketch, the preparatory sketch that appears to do almost no preparatory work, suggests that for Constable the relationship between the sketch and the finished work was never a simple case, as it was for the academic artist, of process and product, of analysis and synthesis, or of finished and unfinished. Instead, the relationship of the sketch to the final work often appears to be overdetermined by a dense and complex web of things external to the technical and mechanical process of image making. The sketch, I would argue, functioned for Constable primarily as a way for him to collect his feelings and associations with regard to a particular subject. For this reason it forms an important link between his original natural painture of the teens and his later style. By examining the way the sketch can be said to produce meaning, one comes to understand the ideological assumptions of Constable's natural painture that allowed this later style to come into being.

The sketch played a central role in the process of associationism that enabled Constable to take possession of the *patria* through his art. Just as Knight's associationism rested on a materialistic base (property), so too did Constable's (his father's possessions). Yet in Constable's case this base could never be fully acknowledged because such recognition would have brought with it an unwanted Oedipal legacy. Substituting for this materialism something else, something "better," he concealed the material base with feeling and sentiment. Through this veil of emotion, embodied in the formal language of the oil sketch, the viewer originally perceives the landscape. This style of the sketch allowed Constable to suggest a completely personal fusion with the landscape, a fusion exclusive of meaning other than the most personal. Hence through the sketch he sought ultimately to control the production of meaning in his landscapes. The process first emerged in all its complexity in what appears to be the most complete extant set of preparatory sketches made by Constable, the 1810–1811 studies of Flatford Mill and Lock (Figures 56–60) that he used for his 1812 exhibition piece, *A Water-Mill: Flatford Mill, Suffolk* (Plate 4).[111] Ian Fleming-Williams has established the probable chronological order of the five preparatory sketches: the first (Figure 56) was done on the spot in 1810; the next three

FIG. 56. John Constable, *Flatford Mill from the Lock*, ca. 1810 (7¼ × 9¼ in.). By kind permission of His Grace the Duke of Westminster. D.L.

(Figures 57–59) were done out of doors in the late summer and early fall of 1811, the first two (Figures 57, 58) during haymaking and the third (Figure 59) shortly after; the fifth and last sketch (Figure 60), done in the studio, is a composite of the others that Constable used for the final composition.[112]

In the final work are five charged spots: the lock in the left foreground, the mill behind it, the twin poplars in the central distance, the hayfield to the left of them, and the wooden pilings in the right foreground. These points of interest receive different emphasis in the various sketches, and such compositional differences between the sketches are much more pronounced than (with the exception perhaps of Figure 60) any stylistic differences. As with the views of the house, all the changes in the composition result from Constable's changing point of view, here his switching ground from right to left of the lock and back again, which initiated a series of gains and losses in the charged spots. The hayfield lost in the first sketch is retrieved in the second, which must, however, sacrifice

FIG. 57. John Constable, *Flatford Mill from the Lock*, ca. 1811 (10¼ × 14 in.). Royal Academy of Arts, London.

something of Flatford Mill. The third sketch rectifies this omission by including both the mill and the field, but at the cost of part of the lock. Dissatisfied, it would seem, with these solutions, Constable tried the view from the left side of the lock; in this composition, with its diagonal tension between the lock and the mill, the hayfield and pilings disappear. In the final sketch and finished version, he returned again to the right side of the lock and managed to include all the charged spots by taking the position he held in the second sketch and extending the field of vision further left to include more of the lock and mill.[113] Constable's letter to Maria Bicknell in November 1811 in connection with this series of sketches helps explain why his position with regard to the lock determined his ordering of all the charged spots: "I have tried Flatford Mill again, from the lock (whence you once made a drawing)."[114] Hence the lock and the view from it were associated with Maria, with her drawing, with her view of Flatford. The sketches are in this sense retrospective and allowed Constable in Maria's absence to imagine what she had once seen and to infuse that vision with the emotion stirred by

FIG. 58.   John Constable, *Flatford Mill from the Lock*, ca. 1811 (10 × 12 in.). Henry E. Huntington Library and Art Gallery, San Marino, California.

this process of imagining. In this way the sketches' various orderings of the charged spots suggest a superimposition of present retrospective meaning on the past. The desire for fusion prevented Constable from simply repeating the view Maria had made. Instead, he continually shifted ground, seeking a view that would merge what he saw as significant in the landscape with what she had seen, what he felt in the process of imagining with what she had felt, what he experienced in the process of remembering with what she had experienced in the process of drawing. As Karl Kroeber has acutely observed, this fusion of past and present, memory and experience, emotion and sensation links Constable's art to the poetry of Wordsworth.[115]

The collapse of past into present conflates two distinct historical moments into one moment, a moment, moreover, that as the result of the fusion must

FIG. 59. John Constable, *Flatford Mill from the Lock*, ca. 1811 (6 × 8¼ in.). Private collection, Great Britain.

always remain an ideal. Thus Constable's art mimics memory in permitting what time never allows. Only through his art was he able to realize his desires by superimposing his present longing for Maria on the past, specifically the summer of 1809 when he first fell in love with her, the summer, presumably, when she made her drawing of the mill from the lock. This series of sketches and the process of memory they represent recall the lines from Wordsworth's *Prelude*:

> but that the soul,
> Remembering how she felt, but what she felt
> Remembering not, retains an obscure sense
> Of possible sublimity.[116]

The sublimity of memory, the possibility of a profound and infinite emotional sympathy with the past long after its meanings have vanished, is at stake in the oil sketches. In them the past becomes the presence to consciousness of consciousness itself.[117] The style of the oil sketch perfectly embodies consciousness's

FIG. 60. John Constable, *Flatford Mill from the Lock*, ca. 1811 (9¾ × 11¾ in.). Victoria and Albert Museum, London.

awareness of itself, for it signals both the present sensuous reality of the landscape and Constable's emotionally charged perception of it. The palpable emotion of Constable's perception that viewers of the sketches feel they must understand if they are to comprehend the landscape is at the same time something they feel at some deeper level they have already understood.

In 1809 when Constable came to depend on the oil sketch for the construction of his finished works, he inscribed into his natural painture a retrospection that came increasingly to dominate his art, so much so that by the early 1820s when his art became publicly autobiographical, the oil sketch provided the stylistic means whereby painting became "but another word for feeling." The nature that these later works describe is not the nature of the landscape subject but of the perceiving subject, that is to say, Constable's own consciousness in the act of perceiving nature. Unlike Gainsborough's landscapes, Constable's were never escapist; they offered him no refuge from the world of the self. That they gave no such refuge becomes particularly evident and inexpressibly poignant in the late works. What Constable said of Gainsborough's late landscapes is more true of his own: "On looking at them, we find tears in our eyes, and know not what brings them."[118]

It is precisely this not knowing that confirms the power of Constable's art to move us, because it places the power beyond reason and discourse. The translation of the language of the oil sketch into the style of the later works accounts for this power, I would argue, for what the sketch embodies (or rather appears to embody) is feeling itself. Its formal language naturalizes not the social codes inscribed in the representation of nature but rather the perception Constable infused into the landscape, his own feelings and autobiographical meanings. Such feelings and meanings insist on both their uniqueness and their universality. They are unique because they have been formulated out of a particular set of personal circumstances and universal because these circumstances have been rendered in a system of strokes and notations that read as emotion itself. Remarking to Fisher in 1824 on the criticism his increasingly sketchlike execution aroused, he justified his procedure: "The language of the heart is the only one that is universal—and Stern says that he disregards all rules—but makes his way to the heart as he can."[119] This belief in the universality of feelings both motivated Constable's art and makes it nearly impossible to discuss in any terms other than the ones he himself has defined. Hence the difficulty in analyzing his naturalism, so sensually palpable and so intellectually elusive, as a reflection of historical consciousness, social milieu, or class ideology. That such an analysis, which seems both a violation of the works' "humanity" and a necessity, has only recently been undertaken testifies both to the success of Constable's stylistic insistence that his art be read through his autobiography and to his formal ability to universalize his intimate history.

What the language of the heart displaces is the language of society. Constable's naturalization of his autobiographical perception of landscape was a logical end point of the naturalization of the sign that formed the social discourse of the eighteenth century. Through naturalization, Constable's landscapes bypass the explicitly social referent and make claims to something more universal. Whereas nature in the early works was still defined according to the actual appearance of the landscape, by the early 1820s nature had come to mean human nature, the nature of the individual perceiving subject. Such a transition was anticipated by the very need that originally drove Constable to paint the landscape of his youth, the need to retreat from the psychosocial implications of his place in the *patria* and to recover that place by personalizing the landscape. Thus

the oil sketch can be seen as a paradigm for the origin, dilemma, and achievement of Constable's naturalism. And it is finally in the formal language of the
sketch that one hears the social discourse that the sketch itself is so anxious to
silence.

THE SIX-FOOTERS

Writing to Constable in 1821, John Fisher offered this observation on a small
landscape the artist had sent him: "It is most pleasing when you are directed to
look at it—but you must be *taken* to it. It does not *solicit attention*—And this I
think true of all your pictures & the real cause of your want of popularity."[120]
Despite his often-voiced resolution never to pander to public taste and opinion,
Constable was becoming increasingly aware of the need to exhibit attention-
getting works at the Royal Academy if he were going to be noticed in the midst
of the spectacular landscapes by Turner and John Martin. He made good his
intention, as he said, "to pay court to the world" in 1819 when he exhibited his
first six-foot landscape (or "six-footer"), *The White Horse* (Figure 61).[121] The work
succeeded in attracting favorable notice from the critics and earned Constable an
associateship in the Academy. The series of six-foot landscapes initiated by *The
White Horse* established Constable's reputation as a landscape painter. They are
critical to the history of the rustic landscape—a history they culminate and conclude. Most simply, their monumentality, breaking with the traditional scale of
the genre, gestures dramatically to call attention to themselves and their subject.
The gesture belongs both to a turning point in Constable's career and to the
more general crisis of a genre whose subject had been eclipsed in importance.
The ambivalent alienation that had characterized Constable's practice of the
genre (his need to reject and recover his father's land) is intensified in the monumental landscapes by his new commercial and professional ambitions. And if
Constable successfully transmitted this alienation to an urban audience, he did
so because distance from rural experience and an accompanying nostalgia for it
had already predisposed that audience to alienation. In short, the personal dramas
of Constable's relationship to the countryside could now be infused into a more
broadly based structure of feeling, whose origins were entirely different.

The scenes depicted in these landscapes cover at the most a four-mile stretch
on the canalized Stour River, from Stratford Mill to Flatford Mill and Lock. The
river had been turned into a canal in the 1740s and, unlike the canals of the late
eighteenth and nineteenth centuries, it boasted no elaborate feats of engineering
such as aqueducts, embankments, tunnels, lifts, or inclined planes. Instead it

FIG. 61. John Constable, *The White Horse*, exhibited at the Royal Academy 1819 (50 × 72½ in.). The Frick Collection, New York.

was a homely affair, and even in places where the river had been artificially re-directed, the improvements had by 1820 the look of nature.[122] The canal locks had been built and were maintained by the Stour River Navigation Company. Constable's father and later his brother were responsible for inspecting the con-dition of Dedham and Flatford locks, which were adjacent to their mills. Con-stable's paintings of the area around Flatford thus form, as Graham Reynolds has said, "a map of his father's possessions."[123] At the time Constable embarked on his large canal scenes, his brother, feeling the effects of the postwar depression, was fretting over the financial well-being of the family business. "I have found more sleepless nights within a twelve month than in all the former years of my life, not that this year has proved worse, nor so bad as the former, but one gets more loaded as one proceeds, & anxiety will arise, & Trade has been very flat & has ever since I began; let's hope it will mend but I see no prospect, our Trade is overdone, & cannot be a good one, competition is so great."[124] Abram's economic troubles led him to sell the family house on the main street of East Bergholt and to move to a smaller dwelling at Flatford. His letters to John during this period continually exhort him to "exert [himself] and earn some money now."[125]

The six-footers are thus linked to the economic crisis in the countryside that put economic pressure on Constable himself, now the father of a growing family. The artistic ambition behind the paintings—to become better known at the Academy and to win public support for his style of landscape—coincided with an economic one, since such support would enlarge his income and free it from dependence on Abram's management of the family business. In an extension of the pattern discussed earlier, Constable, in choosing scenes directly connected to his family's business, was attempting (if only as an artist) to "manage" it profitably. The canal, a sign of his family's involvement in the industrial transformation of the countryside, became a sign as well of Constable's own commercial exploitation of the countryside in the six-footers. The fact that the canal looked like part of the *natural* configuration of the area both occulted the dramatic transformation of the countryside by capital and justified Constable's own representation of it as "rustic landscape." The paradigm is an old one, familiar from the eighteenth century.

In all the six-footers except *Stratford Mill* work is being done, and in every case it is related to the commercial life of the canal. In *The White Horse* (see Figure 61), the men ferry a horse from one towpath to another; in *The Hay Wain* (Plate 5), the haymakers in the distant field show that a harvest is underway, while two men return from the direction of Flatford Mill in an empty cart, having presumably delivered their hay; in *A View on the Stour* (Figure 62), men pole a gang of barges below Flatford Lock; in the 1824 and again in the 1829 version of *A Boat Passing a Lock* (Figure 63), the Flatford lockkeeper opens the pound lock for a passing barge; and in *The Leaping Horse* (Figure 64), a horse towing a barge is made to jump over a cattle guard on the towpath below Dedham. The men in these works appear absorbed in the tasks they are performing. (This is also true of the figures in *Stratford Mill* [R.A. 1820], who seem wholly given over to the tranquillity of a familiar routine.)[126] Absorbed in their work,

FIG. 62. John Constable, *View on the Stour, near Dedham*, exhibited at the Royal Academy 1822 (51 × 74 in.). Henry E. Huntington Library and Art Gallery, San Marino, California.

they are also absorbed (as Barrell has noted) into the landscape. Oftentimes, like the fisherman in *The Hay Wain*, they are barely distinguishable from it. This blending has two effects: it naturalizes the laborers' presence in the landscape, and, by extension, it naturalizes the work they are shown performing there. Not only men and nature are shown in harmony but also industry and nature. The land is formed for cultivation and the river for navigation: work is the natural attitude in such a place where man's commercialization of nature comes to signify his oneness with nature.

The figures' absorption in the landscape makes them oblivious to the spectacle of nature around them. Nature for them is no more than the site and the substance on which they labor. Consequently, our own delight in this nature, its lush textures and richly shadowed colors, differentiates our consciousness as viewers from that of the figures. No small figures in the foreground (as in Claude or even Gainsborough) either direct our gaze toward the landscape or participate in our viewing of it. The natives of this place, whatever their thoughts, do not share our response to nature. Our awareness of an intrinsic difference reenacts

FIG. 63. John Constable, *A Boat Passing a Lock*, dated 1826, exhibited at the British Institution 1829 (40 × 50 in.). Royal Academy of Arts, London.

Constable's own aesthetic alienation from his homeland. Estranged from its life, we are nonetheless attracted to its beauty. Our consciousness becomes a consciousness of loss, nostalgically oriented toward what it has left behind in order to constitute itself. Our inclusive response to the landscape is thus a sadly limited one, for we can only experience it as a spectacle and not as the "lived." In the very act of spectatorship, therefore, we are installed in Constable's personal double bind, which has now been generalized into a public exercise of aesthetic perception.

FIG. 64. John Constable, *The Leaping Horse*, exhibited at the Royal Academy 1825 (56 × 73¾ in.). Royal Academy of Arts, London.

Along these lines, John Barrell has argued that the paintings embody a paternalistic fantasy of rural social harmony. The fantasy depends, he claims, precisely on turning the laborers into "automata," who, devoid of the strong physical presence of, say, Jean-François Millet's peasants, do not troublesomely intrude on our consciousness and upset the myth of the happy rural laborer at peace with nature and with society at large.[127] I contend that Constable's naturalization of the workers, with their corresponding depersonalization, is not this one-sided. While conforming in part to the project of naturalization, the six-footers undercut it in a significant way. For what can be seen as Constable's nostalgic harkening back to a world that, if it ever existed, was disappearing also

has a more strictly contemporary pertinence. For instance, the paintings fragment their portrayal of rural work into isolated, isolating moments and gestures
involving only single figures or very small groups. Labor is represented at the
fractional level of segments: a lock is opened, a horse is ferried or jumped, a
barge is hauled, a cart driven back from the mill. The actions have the discrete
integrity of snapshots, but, like workers' actions on an assembly line, they lack
completeness. It is hard to see in these marginal and piecemeal activities a whole
process of production. To the extent that labor in these paintings alludes to an
organizing center, that center is outside the landscape represented, in Flatford
Mill from which the hay wain returns or in the towns and markets for which the
barges are destined. Constable shows men laboring in a system of production
that they neither control nor see to its end. The laborers are as blindly caught
up in this system of production as they are visually absorbed into the landscape.
Nor, in a sense, is there much difference between the landscape and the system
of production, since the efficiently hedged and neatly ploughed fields of the
landscape and the mills, locks, and quays of its river constitute little more than
the setting and apparatuses of production. Constable has effectively turned the
landscape into a kind of open-air factory. Thus the figures' "calm, endless, and
anonymous industry," which Barrell puts at the basis of Constable's reactionary
ideal,[128] is ambiguous. Quite as much as it points to a preindustrial fantasy of
organic production, it points to a contemporary model of alienated labor—endless anonymous industry indeed.

To underscore the ambiguity of Constable's representation of labor, one
might contrast his six-footers with the contemporaneous landscapes Samuel Palmer painted at Shoreham. In an 1825 sketch by Palmer entitled *A Rustic Scene*,
a man finished plowing for the day is shown unhitching his ox, preparing to
return home (Figure 65). The rural banality of the action, however, is undercut
by the fantastic landscape in which it takes place. The landscape is pregnant with
meaning, swelling and undulating with growing things: pears dangle from trees
and wheat crowds the fields as far as the eye can see. In the idealizing style of
the landscape, the regularized, repetitious pattern of forms emphasizes the
beauty of their contours as well as their interlocking compositional harmonies.
Such nature for Palmer mirrors the bounty of its divine creator. Man's role in it
is that of steward, and the landscape is as much his reward as his work. Even
though its style is extraordinary, something about the work recalls Constable's
peaceful and sun-filled landscapes of the teens; yet there is a difference. In Constable's paintings the laborer's work is never so completely overwhelmed by the
presence of its reward as it is in Palmer's. In Palmer's Shoreham there is never a
gray day, a chill wind, a fallow field, or a difficult row to hoe. His figures do not

PLATE 1. Thomas Gainsborough, *Mr. and Mrs. Robert Andrews*, ca. 1748–1749 (27½ × 47 in.). National Gallery, London.

PLATE 2. Thomas Gainsborough, *Wooded Landscape with a Seated Figure*, ca. 1747 (24⅝ × 30¾ in.). Tate Gallery, London.

PLATE 3. John Constable, *Dedham Vale*, 1802 (17⅛ × 13½ in.). Victoria and Albert Museum, London.

PLATE 4. John Constable, *A Water-Mill: Flatford Mill, Suffolk*, exhibited at the Royal Academy 1812 (26 × 36½ in.). Anonymous loan, Corcoran Gallery of Art, Washington, D.C.

PLATE 5. John Constable, *The Hay Wain*, exhibited at the Royal Academy 1821 (51¼ × 73 in.). National Gallery, London.

PLATE 6. John Constable, *Dedham Vale*, exhibited at the Royal Academy 1828 (57⅛ × 48 in.). National Gallery of Scotland, Edinburgh.

PLATE 7. Ford Madox Brown, *An English Autumn Afternoon*, 1852–1855 (28¼ × 53 in.). City Museum and Art Gallery, Birmingham.

PLATE 8. John William Inchbold, *In Early Spring*, ca. 1855, exhibited 1871 (20 × 13¾ in.). Ashmolean Museum, Oxford.

FIG. 65. Samuel Palmer, *A Rustic Scene*, dated 1825 (7¹/₁₆ × 9⁵/₁₆ in.). Pen and brush drawing in sepia mixed with gum and varnish. Ashmolean Museum, Oxford.

work by the sweat of their brows because they have never left Eden. Whereas Constable's landscapes, particularly the six-footers, register the impact of industrialism and struggle with its implications, Palmer's seek to naturalize divine presence and earthly salvation. They embody the view of the outsider, the son of a London Baptist bookseller whose desire for spiritual oneness with God assumed such hallucinatory proportions as to temporarily blind him to reality. Deeply moved by what he took to be the spiritual simplicity and directness of rural life, he could not risk shattering his illusions with a closer look.

How, one might ask, did Constable, unlike Palmer, come to register within the ideology of naturalism a negative, or at least ambivalent, perspective? A suggestive analogy may be drawn between the content of the six-footers, their themes of labor and production, and Constable's own experience of producing them for the Academy exhibition to sell to an anonymous market. Never before had Constable committed himself so completely to producing for the market.

He had prided himself on his obscurity and contented himself with the patronage of a happy few, usually friends. But he became caught up in an elaborate, graduated process of production that both required several stages (drawings, sketches, studies) and nullified them in the emergence of the finished, final product. That he found this state of affairs unsatisfactory can be inferred from the way he valued his sketches.[129] His mixed feelings about creating "*grandes machines*" for the art market are inscribed in the six-footers, where the context of rural labor gives these feelings additional social significance. Hence while Constable would have been incapable of criticizing the plight of the laborer in an industrial, capitalist economy (or even of sympathizing with it), he could, as an unwilling participant in this economy, register it accurately, if only in his own personal ambivalence toward it. The six-footers allow one to grasp, then, how nostalgia for an older order masks an ambivalent submission to the new. Far from merely repeating the traditionalism he espoused, Constable came to betray (reveal, undermine, desert) it.

In the opposition between the laborer's activity in nature and the spectator's consciousness of nature, neither the term *laborer* nor the term *spectator* is entirely sufficient. If the first endorses a desirable intimacy, it also represents a limited existence, and as the second transcends these limits, it also thereby condemns itself to alienation. As an artist, however, Constable played the role of both laborer and spectator. The artist-laborer shares the figures' oneness with nature but, thanks to the artist-spectator, not their mindless commercialization of nature. Conversely, the artist-spectator rises to a consciousness of nature, and the artist-laborer keeps this consciousness from succumbing to the detachment of a purely picturesque sensibility. On the old ambivalence toward the commercial life of the *patria* (embodied in the activities of its canal), Constable superimposed a new ambivalence toward the conditions of producing Academy pieces for the art market, and both ambivalences have been superseded in a dialectic of aesthetic perception.

Constable's portrayal of the laborers' naive relation to nature continued the sentimentalization of the "simple life" in the rustic landscapes of Gainsborough and the picturesque painters. Yet a break is evident in the way these celebrations of naïveté conceived man's separateness from nature. Whereas for Gainsborough and the picturesque painters the category of the social (codified in, among other things, artistic style) was responsible for separating man from nature, for Constable this separation came about through consciousness itself (whose activities include the act of painting). These different ideas about man's separation from nature correspond to suitably different modes of painting: for Gainsborough, the pastoral; for Constable, the naturalistic. Playing off their elegantly urbane style against the "little dirty subjects" they depict, Gainsborough's landscapes make visible the discrepancy between the civilized refinement both proffered and consumed as the artist's style and the "naturalness" that this style took for its subject. Style did not come between Constable and his subject because, as noted in the discussion of his natural painture, style had in principle become a transparency. As naturalism it claimed both to free nature from the artificial human codes that represent it and to restore to nature its transcendent difference. Yet this difference is precisely what throws the artist back on himself, making him aware of his own isolated consciousness. The exile from Eden that Gainsborough would have attributed to the imposition of civilization was for Constable an existential condition. The observer, because he is capable of observing nature, can never become one with it. The transparent clarity with which nature is recognized as an object reinforces the separation between nature and the seeing subject. It is no accident that naturalistic styles of art typically give way to various forms of expressionism. For by focusing so exclusively on the object, naturalism not only dialectically constitutes a subject, but in keeping this subject from expression it generates the reflexive energy that will be its own undoing. Inasmuch as it seems to efface itself as a rhetorical mediation between the artist and his subject, naturalism in effect licenses the artist to seize the object directly in an act of projection. As Constable, from *The Hay Wain* on, increasingly projected himself onto the landscape, the naturalism of the six-footers eroded and a new expressionism emerged in his work.

Constable's naturalism always contained the expressionistic dimension that the six-footers bring to the fore. It surfaces in the traditional distinction he maintained in the very early works between the sketch, in which the subject's feeling could be indulged, and the finished work, which restrains such feeling. It surfaces again in the radical ambiguity of the views framed by the windows of his father's house, in which the subject has either abjectly surrendered the task of perception to the object (the windows) or has triumphantly absorbed the object as its metonymy. Even in the alternation of views from the house with views of it (or, in other words, of the view with the site of viewing), one senses something of the subject's attempt to use "objectivity" to grasp himself as much as the object. But if Constable's naturalism was always captive to a dialectic between subject and object, the dialectic typically took the form of a polarization: sketch versus work, window-as-frame versus window-as-eye, view from the house versus view of the house. In works like *The Leaping Horse* (see Figure 64) or the two versions of *A Boat Passing a Lock* (see Figure 63), however, Constable painted neither his emotions nor the empirically observed landscape but their fusion. The uncanny emotionalism of these works highlights rather than obscures their naturalistic observations. Misunderstood by the critics who found it sketch-like and "unfinished," Constable's execution, with its raw surfaces and eccentric tonal structures, is precisely what resolves the opposition between subject and object in an act of projection and possession. The six-footers thus embody and complete the entire pattern of retreat and recovery that governs Constable's re-sponse to the landscape of the Stour Valley. The activities of the laborers that are their subject matter evoke an original oneness with nature; the implied activity of the artist-spectator, however, simultaneously evokes alienation. Constable's execution, uniting the immediate activity of a laborer with the analytic distance of a spectator, is the concrete formal means whereby feeling and consciousness are fused in the landscape.

Constable's execution enabled him not only to fuse himself with the land-scape but also, in doing so, to affirm himself in the face of a hostile and anony-mous public. His execution became the assertion of the self, of its shaping con-sciousness and emotion, in the presence of the market no less than nature. The art market was only the latest version of the authority (embodied earlier in his father and in artistic tradition) whose prescriptions Constable characteristically displaced. For although he desired to "pay court to the world" and paint for the art market, Constable felt that to give in to the popular taste represented by this market was to debase himself and his art. "I now fear (for my family's sake)," he wrote to Fisher in 1821, "I shall never be a popular artist—a Gentleman and Ladies painter—but I am spared making a fool of myself."[130] Although he at-tempted with the six-footers to gain public recognition, they were for this reason the place where Constable felt most impelled to hold the line. He marked his alienated distance from the market by cultivating an execution that he knew would be unpopular. "My execution annoys most of them," he wrote Fisher, "and all the scholastic ones."[131] And though he claimed to "have cut [his] throat" with his pallet knife,[132] he continued to paint his Academy pieces in a fervent impasto until his death.

Constable's ambivalence toward the art market (that is, his desire to succeed in it on his own terms) is reflected in the formal development of the six-footers and in his metaphorical use of scenes of rural labor and commerce to address the problem of his own alienated production. If Constable's six-footers are the cul-mination of the rustic landscape, it is not because they definitively embody the myth of an established harmony between nature and economic practices that has stood behind the genre since its emergence with Gainsborough. One can cer-tainly detect a sociopolitical program in the paintings, but I have tried to show how they register the various checks and impasses of this program as well. The vision of man in harmony with nature is enjoyed at the price of acknowledging a split between those who have the vision and those who mediate it. And not only are spectators divorced from the community whose ideal they are presumably meant to consume, but this community also seems fragmented and decentered from within. Most important, in Constable's six-footers the conditions of rural labor are depicted as *plein air* variants of urban-industrial conditions, so that in important respects the two can no longer be distinguished. Subtending the entire tradition of the rustic landscape is a clear sense of the country as, in relation to the city, an autonomous place with its own distinct ways of ordering things. When the country starts to be colonized by the new urban-industrial modes of organization and when the country comes to be seen as an extension or outpost of urban values, then a genre such as the rustic landscape not only (in almost a literal sense) loses ground but also loses its grounding. This is the profound significance of the six-footers. Though Constable continued to paint rustic landscapes till the end of his life, with the six-footers such landscapes fundamentally ceased to be rustic. Instead of bringing the rustic landscape to perfection, the six-footers took it to the point of impossibility.

A "CHANGE OF WEATHER AND EFFECT"

The increasing melancholy of Constable's work from the mid-1820s onward stems largely from his despondency over Maria's failing health and his despair after her death in 1828, but it is also linked to his unhappiness with the state of English politics during the agitation for reform. Constable feared that the Reform Bill, if passed, would endanger Maria's inheritance, which he had hoped to pass on intact to his children. Leslie reports that Constable "talked much of all that was to be feared from the measure" and made himself ill with worry over it.[133] Constable faced drastic changes in this period, and they all seemed changes for the worse. The equation of change with loss is central to his late painting, in which his underlying ambition is not merely to transcend change but to arrest it altogether.

The repetition of subjects that characterizes Constable's later work is in itself nothing new. Just as Constable both posits and resists a single focus in his compositions, so he always tended both to establish and to refuse a single version of his subjects, which, like Willy Lott's cottage, he painted repeatedly. Yet the tendency to repeat subjects became much more pronounced in his later works, and from 1820 on his repertory of subjects and views remained virtually constant: such Stour Valley subjects as Lott's cottage, Dedham Mill and Lock, Dedham Church, and the Glebe Farm along with other subjects like Salisbury Cathedral, Old Sarum, and Hampstead Heath. Some of Constable's contemporaries complained about the repetition. Even John Fisher, his closest friend, warned him about the danger of monotony in his paintings. In the fall of 1824, when Constable was preparing *A Boat Passing a Lock* for the Academy exhibition, Fisher counseled in a letter: "I hope that you will a little diversify your subject this year as to *time of day*. Thompson [*sic*] you know wrote, not four Summers but *four Seasons*. People are tired of mutton on top of mutton at bottom mutton at the side dishes, though of the best flavour & smallest size."[134] Constable's reply is unrepentant: "I regard all you say but I do not enter into that notion of varying ones plans to keep the Public in good humour—subject and change of weather & effect will afford variety in landscape."[135] His response points to another important feature of his art in the 1820s, the shift of emphasis from specific views and objects to the varying conditions in which they may be seen.

Rosenthal has remarked how Constable's increasingly abstract style coincided with what had become an abstracted nature, "seen in terms of essences, wind and light."[136] Constable's interest in representing different states of weather and various effects of light began with the 1819 cloud studies he did at Hampstead (where he moved to preserve the delicate health of his wife and children from the pollution of London) and continued to mark his work to the end of his life. During this period, the "change of weather & effect" became no less important to the work than its subject; and storms, clouds, rainbows, and other transitory aerial effects came to carry as much meaning as the familiar sites over which they played, transforming Constable's sun-filled naturalism into a meteorological expressionism.

In short, Constable's art in this period is organized by the contrast between a principle of repetition and a principle of difference, between the sameness of the subjects and the infinite diversity of the conditions under which they are seen. Repetition confers on subjects an aura of permanence and stability that seems to outlast the various transitory states of nature in which they appear. Caught in the midst of an indifferent-to-hostile nature, ever changing and ever effecting changes, they endure, like Hadleigh Castle, as noble monuments to their own survival. Constable's preoccupation with changing meteorological conditions was not simply the naturalist's pure surrender to the phenomenal world for which many art historians have taken it. Rather it served to render an ideal of transcendent survival, all the more tenacious for its bleakness. The point of representing, say, the Valley Farm now in sunshine, now in storm or twilight was not to erode its identity under the pressure of changing appearances but to consolidate its identity as a place that, despite and by means of such appearances, emerges recognizably intact. Repetition in Constable served his ongoing struggle to assimilate change, to control and triumph over it.

Interesting adjuncts to this need to assimilate change are the pastiches that Constable made in the last few years of his life, which seem to be composite

FIG. 66. John Constable, *Hampstead Heath with a Rainbow*, ca. 1836 (20 × 30 in.). Tate Gallery, London.

pieces drawn from memory or perhaps earlier pencil sketches. One such obvious pastiche from about 1836 is *Hampstead Heath with a Rainbow*, painted originally for George Jennings and now in the Tate (Figure 66). The view is the familiar one over Branch Hill Pond; however, in the center Constable has placed a windmill that in reality was never there.[137] The central portion of the painting, comprising the windmill, the cottage, and the rainbow, is transposed wholesale from an oil sketch done about 1824 of a Brighton windmill that Constable painted many times (Figure 67).[138] It has been suggested that this Hampstead windmill is "a nostalgic allusion to his Suffolk childhood."[139] But in fact this pastiche, like the others, is an example of decorative picture making. When a Hampstead scene is combined with a Brighton one, both places lose their specificity and the painted scene becomes a collage of motifs and effects. Taking bits and pieces from this place and that and recombining them is a profoundly ahistorical process and is directly at odds with the localism thus far associated with Constable. Nevertheless, the development is logical given the preoccupations of his late paintings. For in cutting these scenes and objects loose (literally) from their historical and geographical ground, Constable replaced their specific meanings and associations with more general, universal ones. Constable, it seems, traded

FIG. 67. John Constable, *A Windmill among Houses with a Rainbow*, ca. 1824 (8¼ × 12 in.). Victoria and Albert Museum, London.

his realism for a metaphysical surrealism, for what is at stake in these bits and pieces is not identity but essence, their ineffable and ineffaceable objecthood. Like Constable himself, they survive out of context in a time that is out of joint.

If the repetition of subjects establishes their universal essence, the tonality of Constable's late works—what he called the chiaroscuro of nature—reduces this essence to a ruin.[140] Constable's chiaroscuro consists of tonally contrasting zones of the landscape that create strong compositional patterns of light and dark as well as effects of evanescent natural light. Certain objects are highlighted with a glittering intensity that makes them stand out from the strong overall light pattern. Though such individuation of objects was a fundamental principle of Constable's early naturalism, in the late works the principle is applied so selectively that it becomes expressionistic. Comparing the 1802 *Dedham Vale* (Plate 3) with the version painted twenty-six years later (Plate 6), one sees immediately how strongly emphasized the trees in the foreground have become.[141] Lighted from behind and monumentalized against a threatening sky, they now seem to overshadow the landscape, dwarfing rather than framing the spire of Dedham Church and transforming the composition from a picturesque "view" into a drama of the elements. Aged and disfigured by time (the tree to the left is now blasted), they assume an almost human pathos.

Constable intentionally sought out subjects and scenes that would evoke such associations and on occasion made direct (if ironic) allusion to their allegorical significance.[142] He wrote to David Lucas, the collaborator on his book of mezzotints entitled *English Landscape Scenery*, "I have added a 'Ruin' to the little Glebe Farm—for, *not* to have a symbol in the book for myself, and of the 'Work' which I have projected, would be missing the opportunity."[143] The statement glosses the prominence of ruins in the imagery of late Constable, where one finds not only the Hadleigh Castle ruin referred to in this letter but also the ruins at Cowdray, Arundel, Old Sarum, and Stonehenge.[144] In almost every case it is as though the weather were implicitly responsible for the state of ruination—as though the tempests off the coast of Essex had battered down the walls of Hadleigh Castle or the storms sweeping Salisbury Plain had worn away the city of Old Sarum and toppled the monoliths at Stonehenge.

In these late works, the landscape has been reduced to a play of light. In *Dedham Vale* or *Salisbury Cathedral from the Meadows* (Figure 68), light patterns delimit the space and highlight objects. This chiaroscuro of nature is highly ephemeral. While the weather in earlier paintings is common, recurring weather one might readily observe, in the late work it is extraordinary, even unique. It is likely that one could look at clouds like those in *Scene on a Navigable River* (see Figure 41) at least as long as one would normally look at the painting itself. But even an ordinary look at *Salisbury Cathedral from the Meadows* with its rainbow and flash of lightning must be longer than our vision of such effects could be in actuality.[145] In his late landscapes, through weather and effect, Constable renders time in order to freeze it. This is the declared intention behind his *English Landscape Scenery* project: "To give 'to one brief moment caught from fleeting time', a lasting and sober existence, and to render permanent many of those splendid but evanescent Exhibitions, which are ever occurring in the changes of external Nature."[146] Although this capturing of fleeting effects may be Constable's intention, the actual effect of the mezzotints is quite different and close to that of the late works. Precisely because the transitory light effects that are so important to the compositional order of the landscapes are at the same time so obviously fugitive, the sensation one has in looking at the scenes is not of permanency but of change (Figure 69). The mastery and control of nature Constable sought in freezing "weather and effect" were undermined in the end by the virtuosity of the rendering. Considering that nature for Constable had a double significance in that it was both landscape and self, one understands why at this melancholy time the issue of nature's control became paramount. The bitter resignation of

FIG. 68.   John Constable, *Salisbury Cathedral from the Meadows*, exhibited at the Royal Academy (59¾ × 74¾ in.). Lord Ashton of Hyde. On loan to National Gallery, London.

his late correspondence with Fisher barely masked a deep despair. Excusing his neglect of their correspondence, he wrote in 1830, "Time and events—and moral duties—and all the sad vicissitudes and concerns of life—have greiviously {*sic*} usurped its place—and I feel bereaved of much which used to urge & cheer my anxieties & progress in the difficult mode of life which is my lot."[147] His lot was to control his own moods as much as those of nature, and it was the enormousness of this task that became the drama of the late works.

The eighteenth-century view of nature as existing independently of social and cultural forms prepared the way for the empirical, scientific investigation of

FIG. 69. John Constable, *Old Sarum*, dated 1832. Mezzotint (second plate) from the second edition of his *Various Subjects of Landscape Characteristic of English Scenery*, 1832.

nature in the nineteenth century. Founded on the absolute autonomy of the category of nature, this investigation provided the context in which Constable's naturalism developed. Implicitly, his naturalism presupposed a division between nature and culture that obliges an artist to choose between two modes: "In the one, the Artist, intent only on the study of departed excellence, or on what others have accomplished, becomes an imitator of their works, or he selects and combines their various beauties; in the other he seeks perfection at its PRIMITIVE SOURCE, NATURE."[148] Constable did not so much disregard the landscape tradition as subsume it under the new rubric of naturalism. His achievement stands at the end of a gradual shift in artistic standards first voiced by Gilpin in his advice on drawing from nature. By making art subservient to the standard of nature, he not only subsumed the landscape tradition but also animated it by introducing into it an element of uncontrol. Whereas the traditional landscape made order out of nature's chaos, the natural landscape embraced this chaos in the blind hope of finding an order that was not art's. The naturalist painter who opts for nature, then, chooses it over culture, against it. The fiction of nature's separateness enabled Constable to free himself from authority in the form of burdensome cultural legacies both personal and professional. At the same time, the realm of this freedom was determined and inscribed by the cultural and paternal values against which it came into being.

The chaos and uncontrol nature both promises and threatens provide the key to Constable's late works, in which for the first time he fully faced the formal consequences of naturalism. In the familiar pattern of subversion and sublation of authority that governed his naturalism, Constable introduced nature's chaos into these works in order, it seems, to subdue it. He did this not only by freezing nature's "evanescent Exhibitions" but also by cataloguing them, as he did in *English Landscape Scenery*. Intended as a manifesto for his own style of landscape, *English Landscape Scenery* inventories various subjects characteristic of English scenery from pictures painted by Constable. Accompanying several of the plates are texts that explain the natural phenomena exhibited there, like the rainbow in his mezzotint of Stoke-Nayland Church: "When the Rainbow appears at Noon, the height of the sun at that hour of day causes but a small segment of the circle to be seen, and this gives the Bow its low or flat appearance: the Noonday-bow is therefore best seen 'Smiling in a Winter's day,' as in the Summer, after the sun has passed a certain altitude, a Rainbow cannot appear."[149] It is ironic, yet true to form, that at the moment Constable publicly defended his introduction of nature's uncontrol into the tradition of landscape painting, he should also set about systematizing it. Because the oeuvre on its own could not be trusted to do this, Constable reorganized and summarized it by selective examples. In *English Landscape Scenery* early works are grouped with late ones, the plates being arranged in sequences of four that are intended to show a range of landscape types; the project's ahistoricism is mitigated by its scientism and formalism.[150] Impatient, as it were, with the very thing that had caused him to paint these landscapes in the first place—their personal historical significance—Constable sought to universalize their message. In doing so he shifted terms; as in the late paintings he displaced an original ambivalence toward authority onto an ambivalence toward chaos and change. He subsumed the motivation for his naturalism in a critical appraisal of the consequences of that naturalism. In *English Landscape Scenery*, then, Constable could defend his naturalism only by at the same time repudiating it.

The scientism that characterizes Constable's late thinking about art is an extension of this pattern, respectfully preserving nature's otherness in the same gesture that ideally masters it. "Painting is a science," Constable told a lecture audience in 1836, "and should be pursued as an inquiry into the laws of nature. Why, then, may not landscape be considered as a branch of natural philosophy, of which pictures are but experiments?"[151] Science provided Constable with a model for comprehending nature in terms of laws. As a systematic inquiry into such laws, painting could impose stability and predictability on nature. The model of science allowed Constable to conceive his naturalism as fidelity to nature, even as—rather like nineteenth-century science—it aspired to appropriate and control it. The coincidence of Constable's scientism with the most explicitly allegorical phase of his work is therefore not contradictory since in both cases he attempted to retrieve the otherness that is also nature's supreme value.

Such a pattern is not unique to Constable. The eighteenth century's preoccupation with the natural masked a profound acculturation of nature, and the picturesque concern with an unspoiled nature was consonant with its industrial despoliation. In the tradition of the rustic landscape from the eighteenth century on, the ostensible isolation of nature as a category and a value facilitated its being regularly appropriated by cultural subjects and social groups in a strategy of self-justification and self-preservation. Always desired for itself but always made to say something other than itself, nature never appeared except as part of a personal and social allegory. Nature provided Constable with both a means to free himself from traditional authority and, finally, a reason to embrace it. In this sense nature, like the family, the school, the factory, and culture, teaches the necessity of discipline, one of the first lessons of an industrial society.[152]

The highest laws of biological science are expressed in their simplest terms in the lives of the lowest orders of creation.

William B. Carpenter,
Nature and Man:
Essays Scientific and Philosophical

MIDDLE GROUNDS AND MIDDLE WAYS: THE VICTORIAN SUBURBAN EXPERIENCE OF LANDSCAPE

In 1865 a contributor to the *Cornhill Magazine* regretfully observed the falling off of interest in landscape at the Royal Academy's annual exhibition: "While figure pictures have still the chance of being hung according to their merits, landscapes are being gradually excluded or placed in positions so unfavorable as to render them invisible."[1] To clinch his point, he noted that in twenty-five years only two landscape artists had been elected to the Academy ranks. It would be a mistake, however, to conclude from such remarks that the Victorians had little love for landscape, although their preoccupation with it took different forms from that of the preceding period. For instance, while the ranks of landscape painters in the Royal Academy shrank, the number of new watercolor societies with their largely amateur membership increased markedly.[2] Rather than decline, landscape painting by 1860 simply changed course as a new interest in scientific phenomena and naturalistic representation replaced an older taste for picturesque topography and rustic scenery. What waned was not an interest in landscape but a particular tradition of landscape representation—specifically, the genre of the rustic landscape developed from Gainsborough to Constable and grounded on the rural experience of agricultural industrialization.

By 1860 the great period of enclosure was over, and the rural economy it had created, having diversified its investments, was no longer strictly dependent on agrarian production. Demographically England had become an urban society, and since Waterloo the countryside had gradually lost the political and economic power it had previously commanded. In the urbanized world of Victorian England, the countryside was a somewhat distant realm, the object of eager inquiry to be enjoyed as a distraction and a relief. This shift in the perception of the countryside, extending from Constable's Hampstead landscapes to the landscapes of the Pre-Raphaelites and their followers in the 1850s and 1860s, marks the development of the naturalization of the sign from an imperative cultural confusion to a confused cultural imperative. For the rural countryside that had been intended to justify capital's transformation of nature had been (with increasing obviousness) diminished by this very process, and its status as metaphor had necessarily become more ambiguous. By the time of Victoria, rustic landscapes like those of Ford Madox Brown took for granted the diminished stature of the countryside and its ambiguous signification. Painting the countryside, like going to the countryside, became a matter of urban ritual, whose performance was felt to be important, though its meaning was no longer clear.

TERRA COGNITA

Surveying the conditions that prevailed in the economically depressed countryside of his *Rural Rides*, William Cobbett concluded that "there is nobody, no not a single man, out of the regions of Whitehall, who can pretend, that the country can, without the risk of some great and terrible convulsion, go on, even for twelve months longer, unless there be a *great change of some sort* in the mode of managing the public affairs."[3] Beginning at the end of the 1820s a great change did occur, though it was not the saving reform of the old country hegemony Cobbett desired. The repeal of the Test and Corporation Acts in 1828 allowed non-Anglican Protestants to participate in government, and the Reform Bill of 1832 extended the franchise to the non-landowning middle class. The Poor Law (1834) and the Municipal Reform Act (1835) established nationally centralized administrations with authority over local systems of poor relief and government. The paradoxical pattern of increasing democratization with increasing governmental control and intervention has continued to this day: liberalization invariably interlocks with the government regulation that it seems both to demand and to justify. For my purposes this pattern of centralization is important because it signaled the decline of country hegemony and the shift of power to the commercial and urban middle classes. The contestation of the Corn Laws, resulting in the formation of the Anti-Corn Law League in 1839 and in the ultimate repeal of the Corn Laws in 1847, was the most visible manifestation of the shift. Inheriting the countryside's former power, the urban, industrial interests now defined the dominant social problems and perceptions as well. The most significant social agitation in the 1830s and 1840s came from trade unions and the Chartists, whose complaints and demands were directed to and oriented by the industrial conditions in the towns.

The new reforms did not represent simply a victory of urban interests over rural ones: they in fact resulted from a growing cooperation between the agricultural and manufacturing classes and revealed the rural economy adapting itself to the commercialized industrial world. Because of the agrarian depression, landowners began to diversify their income, which no longer depended exclusively on agriculture but relied on a variety of ventures such as canal and bank stocks, municipal bonds, railway shares, urban real estate, quarries, mines, brickworks, and so on.[4] This economic diversification changed the physical appearance of the countryside as more canals and railroads were built along with potteries, ironworks, and brickworks and as new towns sprang up around these industries. Diversification, moreover, called forth a reformed government to regulate, direct, and control from a center this complex of overlapping interests. Parliamentary commissions and trade and borough councils took over the functions of local magistrates and justices of the peace in managing local affairs. As a result, the countryside became increasingly urbanized as a bureaucratic administration centralized in London replaced local provincial control.

The bureaucratic view of rural life is best seen in the eleven-volume *Report from His Majesty's Commissioners on the Administration and Practical Operation of the Poor Laws* (1834) that was the basis for the Poor Law of 1834.[5] The law classified the poor into various categories (the able-bodied, the aged, the sick, the orphaned, lunatics) and prescribed uniform standards of treatment for each group. Newly elected boards of guardians, working under the authority of the Poor Law Commission, took over from the parish vestries the task of supervising and caring for the poor. The rural society described by the commissioners' report consisted of diverse but stable classes; on these groups' diversity the report based its encyclopedic range, and on their stability it based its accuracy. The interviews, letters, and personal testimonies in the report came from "many thousand witnesses, of every rank and of every profession and employment, members of the two Houses of Parliament, clergymen, country gentlemen, magistrates, farmers, manufacturers, shopkeepers, artisans and peasants, different in every conceivable degree in education, habits and interests, and agreeing only in their practical experience as to the matters in question."[6] The report's sociological investigation of what was seen largely as a rural problem indicates the degree to which rural life and social experience had become exotic phenomena to be understood only through the systematic and quasi-scientific collection of data. Analogously, the growth of naturalist societies in nineteenth-century England reveals that nature itself was falling increasingly outside quotidian experience and becoming the subject of specialized investigation.[7] As rural life became less accessible in the nineteenth century, the province of the specialist or administrator who undertook to describe it grew. Furthermore, precisely because it was set at a remove, like a terra incognita that needed to be mapped out, the country could seem knowable in ways that the city, more complex and overwhelming, could not.[8]

The project of knowing the countryside extended to knowing its poorest inhabitants. The report of the Poor Law Commission, however, nearly always rephrased the testimony of the poor from a standpoint "above" them or juxtaposed their direct narratives of experience with the more distanced and condensed overviews of their social superiors:

> The laborer feels that the existing system, though it generally gives him low wages, always gives him work. It gives him also, strange as it may appear, what he values more, a sort of independence. He need not bestir himself to seek work; he need not study to please his master; he need not put any restraint upon his temper; he need not ask relief as a favour. He has all a slave's security for subsistence, without his liability to punishment. . . . All the other classes of society are exposed to the vicissitudes of hope and fear; he alone has nothing to lose or to gain.[9]

The report allows the laborer to speak only by speaking for him, and the paternalistic assurance with which it presumes to know what he "feels" and "values" rivals that of any omniscient Victorian novelist. The proper management of the poor required such implicitly objective psychological profiles to make this troublesome and historically mute class knowable, its movements predictable, and its control more efficient.

Government centralization and urbanization tended to bring about a corresponding valorization of urban experience. Increasingly, rural isolation seemed to be causally connected to poverty and ignorance. Contrasting the lot of the town mechanic with that of the farm laborer, William Howitt argued: "The mechanic has his library,—and he reads, and finds that he has a mind, and a hundred tastes and pleasures that he never dreamed of before—the clod-hopper has no library, and if he had, books in his present state would be to him only so many things set on end upon shelves. He is as much of an animal as air and exercise, strong living and sound sleeping can make him, and he is nothing more."[10] Howitt went on to illustrate his observation with this paraphrase of lines from Wordsworth's *Excursion*:

> What kindly warmth from touch of fostering hand,
> What penetrating power of sun or breeze
> Shall e'er dissolve the crust wherein his soul
> Sleeps, like a caterpillar sheathed in ice?

This torpor is no pitiable work
Of modern ingenuity: no town
Or crowded city may be taxed with aught
Of sottish vice, or desperate breach of law,
To which in after years he may be roused,
This boy the fields produce: —his spade and hoe—
The carter's whip that on his shoulder rests,
In air high-towering with a boorish pomp,
The scepter of his sway; his country's name,
Her equal rights, her churches and her schools—
What have they done for him? And, let me ask,
For tens of thousands, uninformed as he?[11]

Rural life, without the direct experience of the larger world or the indirect experience of this world as manifested in politics, religion, or education, was felt not only to brutalize the individual but also to threaten the social order. Society had arrived at that *"queer* state," according to Cobbett, "when the rich think, that they must *educate* the poor in order to ensure their *own safety."*[12] Because of government centralization, provincialism had become a national concern; urban values and their intrusion into the countryside came to be seen as necessary and benign civilizing influences. Howitt's observation that the gentry's annual visit to the metropolis improved the character of rural life suggests that a formerly pleasant amusement had acquired the status of a moral duty.[13] The imposition of an urban sensibility on rural experience became the Victorian ideal of naturalness and rusticity; its purest expression was the development of the suburb.

The urbanization of the countryside and the suburbanized ethic of rusticity led to the demise of rustic landscape painting. One effect of urbanization was to transform rural life from a common experience to a popular pastime. Accessibility by railway and omnibus made the countryside a kind of city park, a place to escape to, and the removal of the country from daily life made rural nature an object of specialized, even scientific, study. Occasionally the combination of such specialized study of nature and improved means of transportation into the countryside gave rise to new amusements, as in the early 1830s when plant spotting from train windows became the pastime of professional and amateur naturalists alike.[14] On the whole, however, the study of natural history in the nineteenth century, as the extraordinary number of naturalist societies and publications indicates, was a serious business, if also a popular one. Even its trivialization, as in a deck of children's playing cards from about 1843 (Figure 70), reveals the social value of mastering tongue twisters like *ichthyology* and knowing about fish, birds, and shells. Whether the countryside was used as a city park or appropri-

FIG. 70. Children's playing cards, ca. 1843. The Museum of London, London.

ated as the province of the naturalist or specialist, actual or substantial rural experience was eroded: the countryside was either trivialized by the suburban excursion or formalized by a quest for knowledge. In neither case was the experience of the countryside the central social experience that arbitrated all others.

THE "TOWN PILGRIM OF NATURE"

Constable's Hampstead landscapes anticipated the Victorian ideal of urbanized rusticity that made nature the site of spectacle and scientific investigation. At the same time that Constable's six-footers were revealing the obsolescence of the rustic landscape, his art took a new point of departure in the suburban landscapes of Hampstead. If the rural scenes of the six-footers convey the effects of the demographic shift from country to city, the Hampstead landscapes painted at the same time suggest the concomitant demographic shift from city to suburb. One displacement caused the loss of actual rural experience, and the other brought about a factitious recovery of such experience. The spaces depicted in the Hampstead landscapes are thoroughly suburban ones—their rusticity is tenuous, and they are fundamentally oriented toward somewhere else. London's smoky skyline dominates the horizon (Figures 71, 72), and from the high ground of the heath figures gaze toward other suburban towns in the distance (Figure 73). The most obvious evidence of this other-directedness is the network of roads linking Hampstead to the metropolis and knitting it up in a web of suburbs. On these roads city dwellers frequently stroll, taking the air out on the heath (Figure 74). Little in this nature escapes the imprint of urbanism; even the early cloud studies painted at Hampstead show chimney pots and rooftops through the trees (Figure 75). Such nature or rusticity as the heath represents appears as the exception rather than the rule of human existence. Nature has become the object of an excursion, a change of scene. And this change of scene is quite different from the scenery sought out by the picturesque traveler of the previous century. Constable makes the difference clear in a letter to John Fisher that dia-

FIG. 71. John Constable, *View at Hampstead, Looking towards London*, dated December 7, 1833 (4½ × 7½ in.). Watercolor. Victoria and Albert Museum, London.

grams a panorama not of mountains, forests, and sea but of the towns surrounding the heath.[15] Like the suburb itself, Constable's Hampstead landscapes situate the experience of nature well within an urban context.

When Maria's health demanded clean air and Constable's profession easy access to London, they moved to Hampstead, which occupied an acceptable middle ground between urban congestion and rural isolation. The Constables were not alone in finding the suburban compromise attractive.[16] During this period

FIG. 72. John Constable, *View of London with Sir Richard Steel's House*, exhibited at the Royal Academy 1832 (8¼ × 11¼ in.). Paul Mellon Collection, Upperville, Virginia.

dissatisfaction with both urban and rural life increased. In 1826 William Hazlitt, weighing the disadvantages of each, concluded that ideally a person should
pass his youth in the city and retire to the country in later life. "We may find in
such a one," Hazlitt claimed, "a social polish, a pastoral simplicity. He rusticates
agreeably, and vegetates with a degree of sentiment."[17] Only those fortified by
urban civility, Hazlitt seems to say, can withstand rural boorishness. And even
the positive aspects of country life—its calm and its beauties—are best appreciated from the standpoint of urban, urbane values. The enormous popularity of
books like Mary Russell Mitford's five-volume *Our Village* (1824–1832) and Elizabeth Gaskell's *Cranford* (1853) indicates the urban reader's enlightened senti-
mentalism about rural life. (One is also reminded here of Howitt's and Wordsworth's descriptions of field hands and of Constable's depictions of canal workers,
in which to its natives the countryside remains forever unintelligible or the mere
material for their labor.) Practically, Hazlitt's whimsical call for an enlightened
rusticity, admitting urban manners, amusements, and values and located, if any-
where, in the shuttle between city and country, was answered in the development
of the mixed mode of the suburb.

FIG. 73. John Constable, *Branch Hill Pond, Hampstead Heath, with a Boy Sitting on a Bank*, ca.
1825 (13 × 19½ in.). Tate Gallery, London.

FIG. 74.   John Constable, *Hampstead Heath*, ca. 1821 (21¼ × 30¼ in.). Fitzwilliam Museum, Cambridge.

The English suburb, emerging from a new mode of exploiting the country-side, implied a new perception of land. Previously a view of the land as mere capital had stood behind such exploitation. The improvements of enclosure, for instance, had been attempts to manage this capital wisely and efficiently by bringing all available land into production. Similarly, industry had found no more in the countryside than the economic advantages of abundant raw materials (coal, iron), convenient sources of power (waterfalls, rivers), and cheap labor (the dispossessed agricultural worker). This practical view of the land as capital to be exploited had been complemented and compensated for by an aesthetic view of the land as scenery to be appreciated. The conspicuous consumption of the land-scape garden had lain in its taking vast areas out of production and putting them in the service of an ideal of natural beauty. Valuing precisely what had been neglected by the modern forces of industrialization, the picturesque sensibility had preserved the landscape in an archaic state of quaintness. Suburban land, however, was both capital *and* scenery—scenic capital and capital scenery. Sub-urban development joined the exploitation of the land with an appreciation of

FIG. 75. John Constable, *Study of Sky and Trees with a Red House, at Hampstead*, dated September 12, 1821 (9½ × 11¾ in.). Victoria and Albert Museum, London.

its natural rustic beauties, for it was precisely these beauties that enhanced the economic opportunities of exploitation.[18] The more rustic-looking a suburb, in fact, the more prestigious it was to live there.[19] The suburbs most coveted in the 1820s, such as Hampstead, Denmark Hill, Camberwell, and Dulwich, all made a fetish of rusticity in their detached and semidetached "villas," each screened from both its identical neighbors and the main thoroughfares by a tiny decorative garden or "jungle."

The fetish of rusticity in the early Victorian suburb represented the survival of the popular picturesque sensibility and the incorporation of its aesthetic precepts into a program of social planning. Both the sharp divergence of suburban architectural forms and landscape plans from urban ones and their derivation mainly from picturesque models of rustic villas, ornamented cottages, and cozy villages expressed the suburb's ambivalent relationship to the city.[20] A central figure in the transition from the late eighteenth-century picturesque mode of architectural and landscape design to the suburban dream of *rus in urbe* was the Regency architect John Nash, whose plans for Regents Park (1810) included placing terraced houses and crescents in a landscape setting instead of the urban grid and whose designs for Park Villages East and West (1824) prefigured the better class of suburban tracts of the 1840s and 1850s.[21] For the creatively aware developer or the reformist landowner, the suburb presented the opportunity to fulfill the old eighteenth-century dream of the picturesque village. Indeed the two basic models for the early Victorian garden suburb came from designs for the estate village, such as Milton Abbas (1773–1787), designed by Sir William Chambers and Capability Brown to replace the original market town demolished by Lord Milton to make room for his landscape garden, and from designs for the industrial village, such as Cromford (1787–1797), built by Joseph Arkwright for his mill laborers.[22] Given its formal roots in these eighteenth-century models of planned picturesqueness, the early Victorian suburb came freighted with a set of ideological meanings and assumptions that were to be played out in an urban context. Designs meant to have a restorative effect on the lives of the dispossessed agricultural and industrial laborers were now intended to mitigate the anomie of the middle-class and upper middle-class commuter. In this sense the picturesque sensibility remained throughout the Victorian period an ever-present promise of community. Significantly, population figures for the suburbs south of London and around Liverpool show that at least two-thirds of their inhabitants in the mid-nineteenth century were rural born and had moved to the suburbs not from the city but from the surrounding countryside.[23] Such statistics suggest that the picturesque nostalgia clinging so tenaciously to the suburb in its houses, gardens, and planning transmuted a dream of rusticity even the countryside itself could not embody. In its purest form the suburb was an abstraction of the rustic tradition, a utopian ideological construction that provided a refuge from the disappointing realities of both urban and rural life.

Its promise of a model community was based on an idealization of individualism and privacy. The suburb was a flight from both the old suffocating hierarchy of the country village and the new bureaucratic impersonality of the city. This rather paradoxical conception of community appeared precisely at the time when England was emerging as a centralized industrial nation. The suburb reflected the increasing tendency for Englishmen to separate their social lives into work and leisure and their social geography into workplace and home. With its detached and semidetached houses and private gardens, the suburb provided its inhabitants with tenuous and thus tightly maintained privacy. The importance attached to domestic privacy resulted in a kind of domestic narcissism. The

suburban house and garden became the repository of the owner's personal iconography, whether expressed by whimsical gnomes in the garden or, more extrav-
agantly, by eccentricities like those Constable illustrated in his painting of the
Grove, a house in Hampstead owned by a retired admiral who ringed his roof
with ship's railings to provide himself with a landlocked lookout (Figure 76).[24]

FIG. 76. John Constable, *The Admiral's House, Hampstead*, ca. 1820–1825 (14 × 11⅞ in.). Tate
Gallery, London.

As the suburban house provided a haven from the world, the suburban garden provided an escape into nature. Like the suburb itself, it derived from popularized notions of picturesqueness. The garden, as disseminated by John Claudius Loudon in his *Suburban Gardener and Villa Companion* (1838), was based on the late work of Humphry Repton.[25] Repton's work in the early 1800s marked an important shift in gardening away from the large-scale plans of Brown and the picturesque impossibilities of Uvedale Price and Richard Payne Knight to a more flexible and pragmatic approach that considered the pocketbook and taste of the client as much as the "capabilities" of his grounds. Repton came to disapprove of Brown's principle of setting the house in a sea of smooth-shaven lawn, and his modification consisted of placing formally arranged flower beds and shrubs close to the house as a transition between it and the park beyond. These balustraded terraces and parterres were often planted with annuals and with exotic plants introduced into England from the colonies. Repton also urged that older garden elements such as avenues of trees, trellised walkways, and hedged borders be incorporated into the new garden.[26] The eclectic result of these compromises seemed a logical extension of picturesque variety. This variety of garden styles, however, differed significantly from the variety of natural forms urged by Price and Knight. "Repton's School," as Loudon noted, "may be considered as combining all that was excellent in the former schools, and, in fact, as consisting of the union of artistical knowledge of the subject with good taste and good sense."[27] Repton's work thus opened the door to a historicism in gardening that could be indulged with antiquarian eagerness while being rationalized as thoroughly pragmatic.

The "good sense" planted by Repton was faithfully tended by Loudon, whose writings always stressed the practical over the theoretical. His own plans represented a change from the picturesque school to what he called the gardenesque, "the chief characteristic of which," he wrote, "is the display of the beauty of trees, and other plants, individually."[28] Such display was intended to please "botanical amateurs," and accordingly flowers were contained in formal beds unmixed with trees and shrubs, which were kept in "arboretums" planted to look like small-scale versions of the older landscape garden. An important feature of the gardenesque garden was the glass greenhouse that in large gardens took on fanciful shapes and in smaller ones was often attached to the house. For Loudon the gardenesque had a great advantage over the picturesque in being "particularly adapted for laying out the grounds of small villas,"[29] and thus "the suburban residence, with a very small portion of the land attached, will contain all that is essential to happiness, in the garden, park and demesne of the most extensive country residence."[30]

Two striking characteristics of Loudon's gardenesque philosophy are its emphasis on practicality—its adaptability to the small suburban tract and to the pocket of the middle class—and (related to the first) its botanical interest. Lacking the huge tracts of land and extensive vistas that gave the landscape garden its intrinsic value as a display of wealth and power, the suburban gardenesque gardener had to impress not with land but with plants. Rare varieties of trees, flowers, fruits, and shrubs became the pride of these gardens, a pride mixed with scientific interest. The garden in which choice extracts from nature invited study, cross-pollination, grafting, and experimentation as well as just looking was consistent with the tendency of the period to view nature scientifically. Aided by such books as Loudon's *Encyclopaedia of Gardening* (1822), *Encyclopaedia of Plants* (1829), and *Encyclopaedia of Trees and Shrubs* (1841) as well as by the eternal summer of his greenhouse, the amateur horticulturalist could amaze his neighbors with melons in January and with new varieties of old favorites like roses and asters. Less landscape than laboratory, the early Victorian garden reflected

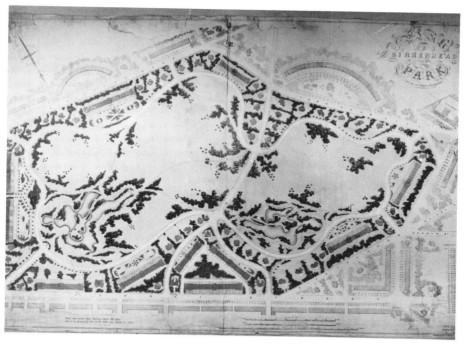

FIG. 77. Joseph Paxton, a plan for the suburb of Birkenhead Park, 1843. Liverpool City Libraries, Liverpool.

the increasing emphasis of horticultural books on the growth and maintenance of particular species of plants instead of on their place in garden design.

Large-scale landscape design survived in the laying out of the suburban tract.[31] For instance, the plan of Birkenhead Park (Figure 77), a suburb outside Liverpool designed by Joseph Paxton in 1843, includes what at first glance appears to be an eighteenth-century landscape garden with its belts and clumps of trees, circuit walks, and irregular plantings. Closer inspection, however, reveals the houses arranged along its boundaries, each set back from the street, separated from its neighbors by "green walls" of trees and shrubs, and sharing with them large greenhouses fronted with formal parterres. The park ringed by villas was at once a private, a communal, and a public space. Garden suburbs like Birkenhead, popular with the upper middle classes in the nineteenth century, formed a model even for urban design. During the Victorian period the shaded, grassy city square, fenced in wrought iron and surrounded by row houses, became a commonplace of urban planning, metamorphosing spectacularly in America into Frederick Law Olmsted's extensive "people's garden" for New York City.[32] Like the interior park at Birkenhead, these city squares were intended to bring nature into the city and to afford its inhabitants a privatized place to congregate and commune with nature. In short, the earliest attempts at comprehensive city planning embodied the suburban promise of nature and civilization in symbiotic harmony.[33] Originally a flight from urbanism, suburbanism returned to the city in the later Victorian period to reform it.

Much of this harmonious vision was anticipated in Constable's Hampstead landscapes, which eliminate the dilemmas of alienation and ambivalence that characterized the countryside proper in the six-footers. By explicitly including the spectator, the Hampstead landscapes relax the problematic tensions of position and perception in the six-footers. The 1821 *Hampstead Heath* (see Figure 74) is a good example of how this process works. In this landscape, laborers work in a gravel pit while strollers from the city walk the heath, taking in its views. Equally absorbed in their activities, the laborers and the strollers are both accommodated in a landscape whose mixed character makes it appropriately a place where some work and others merely watch. The spectator, whose unrepresentability in the six-footers debarred his being at home in the landscape, is now portrayed so that his presence is casually taken for granted. In suburban Hampstead, the role of the spectator has become thoroughly unexceptional, disembarrassed of the burden of singularity and withdrawal. This landscape authorizes seeing as much as working. Consequently, rather than signaling our alienation from the landscape, our own role as spectators is what allows us to enter into it, much like the Hampstead strollers. Economic and aesthetic forms of exploitation

FIG. 78. John Ritchie, *Hampstead Heath*, 1859 (32½ × 53½ in.). Present whereabouts unknown.

FIG. 79. John Constable, *Study of Cirrus Clouds*, ca. 1822 (4½ × 7 in.). Victoria and Albert Museum, London.

no longer war with one another but coexist happily in the same space. Later, during the high Victorian period, Constable's scattered strollers become in John Ritchie's *Hampstead Heath* (Figure 78) a cheery and unabashed swarm of touring parties or "town pilgrim[s] of nature," to whom the reduction of landscape to spectacle represents no loss.[34]

If Constable's Hampstead landscapes anticipated the Victorian taste for nature as spectacle, they also announced the more serious Victorian interest in the naturalist's study of nature. The two preoccupations might seem entirely disjunct: one appears to celebrate the seeing subject, the other to investigate the objects seen. Yet one effect of viewing nature as spectacle is to naturalize the spectator's role, which is thereby tranquilized to a point where it can effectively be bracketed. The sheer obviousness of the spectator's presence thus facilitates viewers' "objective" attention to what is seen. This pattern is at work in the Hampstead landscapes. Precisely because Constable reduces nature in them to the uncomplicated status of scenery, he can explore the incidents of weather and effect with more minute and attentive naturalism than he had ever before achieved. At Hampstead Constable painted his quasi-scientific studies of cloud formations and types, often inscribed with the proper meteorological names (Figure 79; see also Figure 75).[35] Charles Leslie remarked of Constable's art during the early Hampstead period that it was "never more perfect, perhaps never so perfect."[36] In the new landscape of the suburb—as devoid of private associations and past traditions for Constable as it was for the developer—his landscape painting took on a new purity: of spectacle or science.

THE SPECTACLE AND THE SPECIMEN

Spectacle and science name the dominant orientations toward landscape during the Victorian period, when discussions of landscape urged the claims of either one or the other. An exchange between two eminent Victorian authorities on landscape, John Ruskin and Ford Madox Brown, is characteristic. Catching sight of a painting of Hampstead on a visit to Brown's studio in 1855, Ruskin asked Brown why he had chosen "such a very ugly subject." "Because," Brown replied, "it lay out my back window."[37] The painting in question was *An English Autumn Afternoon* (Plate 7), in which Brown depicted a pair of young lovers enjoying the view from the back of his lodgings looking out toward Highgate. Brown described the scene as "a literal transcript of the scenery around London," adding,

> The smoke of London is seen rising half-way above the fantastic shaped, small distant cumuli, which accompany particularly fine weather. The upper portion of the sky would be blue as seen reflected in the youth's hat; the grey mist of autumn only

rising a certain height. The time is 3 p.m., when late in October the shadows already lie long, and the sun's rays (coming from behind in this work) are preternaturally glowing, as in rivalry of the foliage.[38]

As this description suggests, one finds in Brown's landscape a conjunction both of the minutely observed with the general impression and of the mundane with the extraordinary; a rather ordinary suburban landscape is transformed by the rays of the setting sun into a glowing, vibrant vision. In a Hampstead view by Constable (see Figure 74), a different formal vocabulary conveys a different set of associations. Constable's Hampstead scene consists of an orchestration of tones from dark to light that organizes the space of the landscape into receding planes and selects objects in the space for special emphasis. Brown's landscape, by contrast, is neither tonally nor coloristically "composed"; it does not appear to recede into depth atmospherically, and nothing in it is picked out for special attention. Its spatial flatness and compositional nonselectivity make all its parts seem equally important in a way that superficially recalls Constable's landscapes of the teens. Nevertheless, Brown's landscape goes beyond these early landscapes of Constable's in making a radical departure from traditional landscape composition. The difference has to do with the amount of detail in Brown's work that accumulates extraordinarily as the eye travels back into the landscape. In the middle ground and in the distance, Brown's paint handling, instead of becoming broader, becomes increasingly minute. Coupled with the oval format, which echoes the eye's own field of vision, this disorderly profusion of detail makes us feel that we (like the lovers in the foreground) stare wide-eyed and unfocused at the scene before us. With its random collection of detail—including such homely objects as a dovecote, a backyard poultry pen, property-line fences, and the overall erratic plantings of trees and shrubs that come from each man cultivating his garden—the landscape seems composed bit by bit, in a way that counters the grand designs of both Ruskin's "Nature" and the previous century's agricultural improvers. The Victorian developer's practice of carving up large-scale, regularly planned agricultural spaces into small suburban lots, thus moving from large-scale composition to small-scale composition, was perfectly embodied in the Pre-Raphaelites' minutely detailed landscape style, which consciously opposed the sweeping naturalism of the previous generation.

Ruskin's distaste for Brown's work is curious when one considers that his own first formative experience of landscape was similarly suburban. The suburb in Ruskin's case was Herne Hill, Camberwell, where he lived with his parents in a semidetached villa after their removal from London when he was four. Ruskin's autobiography, *Praeterita*, warmly evokes childhood memories of this landscape: "The view from the ridge from both sides was, before railroads came, entirely lovely: westward at evening, almost sublime, over softly wreathing distances of domestic wood;—Thames herself not visible, nor any fields except immediately beneath; but the tops of twenty square miles of politely inhabited groves."[39] One would think from this passage that Ruskin was describing the scene painted by Brown. But it is clear from Ruskin's theory of landscape as evolved in *Modern Painters* that this childish delight in suburban scenery was only preliminary to a deeper understanding of landscape. In *Modern Painters* landscape painting is treated as much more than a matter of representing scenery. It is, or ought to be, a means by which one discovers the "truth of nature," immanent with divine presence.[40] To include in his works "the greatest number of the greatest ideas,"[41] the landscape painter must first represent scenes that are lofty enough to embody them. A landscape like that of Hampstead was simply unequal to sustaining the conceptual demands that Ruskin put upon landscape.

Given his discountenance of the suburban landscape as a subject for landscape painting, it is not surprising that Ruskin gave the rustic landscape proper a minor and even negative role in *Modern Painters*. This five-volume treatise, the period's most important critical discussion of landscape, evolved from an aesthetic defense of Turner's art to a theory about the role of art and nature in society. Naturalization plays an important part in Ruskin's formulation of his thesis. For him landscape or nature is always an "environment" with a determining effect on culture and society. He contrasts two Alpine communities, showing how their physical situations contributed to their opposite characters and ways of life.[42] His criticism of past and present landscape painting styles leads to criticism of the national characters and cultures that produced the styles and then to the real landscape, whose physical properties become the base for society and its representations. He scientifically inventories the elements of the real landscape.[43] Rocks, mountains, trees, clouds, sunsets, and water are analyzed according to their specific appearances and their geological and meteorological properties. The more forcefully a real or painted landscape displays these appearances and properties, the more aesthetic value it has in that it reveals clearly the creative power and wisdom of the Deity. Such a definition of landscape by necessity excludes humble rural scenes and suburban ones like Brown's *English Autumn Afternoon*. Ruskin's greatest frustration with his friends the Pre-Raphaelites was that they "wasted" their talents and summers on just such inferior subjects.[44] The most powerful effect his criticism had was to encourage artists like William Holman Hunt, John William Inchbold, John Brett, and Thomas Seddon to leave England in search of timelessly "noble" scenes like the Alps, the Holy Land, and the Roman Campagna.

Nature and landscape for Ruskin were meant to be spiritually lofty and grandiose; hence they could never be industrial. In attacking Constable's naturalism and the Pre-Raphaelites' subject matter, he attacked his own culture's economic transformation of the landscape and the process of naturalization that had facilitated it. In *Modern Painters* Ruskin attempted to turn around this naturalization so that it would criticize instead of justifying the industrial landscape, holding up to it another standard of nature Ruskin felt to be truer.[45] But the social ideal embodied in this superior landscape was similarly flawed. The utopia Ruskin envisioned and described in works like *Time and Tide* is familiarly paternalistic, a society in which the cultured "upper classes . . . keep order among their inferiors, and raise them always to the nearest level with themselves of which those inferiors are capable."[46] His vision constituted an attack on the materialistic values of industrial society while leaving the boundaries of power in place. Naturalization, as the example of Ruskin makes clear, is always involved in maintaining the status quo, in continuing to represent the given relationship of men to the means of production as "natural." Having traveled full circle politically, nature and art arrived in Ruskin's socialist utopia at the place where they had stood before the revolution.

In spite of what Ruskin saw as its conceptual impoverishment, the suburban landscape, as even *Praeterita* suggests, was not without its charms. Its beauty lay not in its naturalness (or even lack of it) but in the token bits of nature that still clung to it: the tops of its groves, the individually cultivated beauties of its flowers, trees, and shrubs. Similarly, one's pleasure in Brown's Hampstead scene consists in selecting this tree or that hedge for special study in much the way one would enjoy the gardenesque designs of Loudon. Such a process of selection eases the initial anxiety of looking at this landscape in which the numerous details threaten to neutralize or cancel out one another. The painting's *horror vacui* resists the attempt on our part to make compositional sense of the landscape. By focusing on this or that detail of the landscape, however, we both minimize the self-canceling effect of the details and more nearly meet, if we do not fulfill, our own desire for order. Our selective perception therefore is a necessary compensation for the landscape's apparent randomness. Just as the painting presents the scene as a profusion of seemingly meaningless and unconnected details taken out of their natural context and juxtaposed in a random, man-made order, we in perceiving the landscape also fragment it by decontextualizing its details in focusing on them (as we must) one by one. Thus the isolation of specific details for attention repeats at the level of perception the process of decontextualization performed by Brown when he painted in the Pre-Raphaelite technique each tree and shrub leaf by leaf. More important, this perceptual isolation echoes the effect of the suburb itself as it divides nature into small-scale yards and parks. Hence the aesthetic experience of Brown's Hampstead scene cultivates and is cultivated by a thoroughly suburban experience of nature.

In the urbanized Victorian world the notion of the landscape as spectacle implied a related notion of the landscape as diversion. For Brown this sense of spectacle was contained in the landscape's compositional disorder and its correspondingly ephemeral optical sensuousness.

> Looked out for landscapes this evening; but although all around one is lovely, how little of it will work up into a picture! . . . How despairing it is to view the loveliness of nature towards sunset, and know the impossibility of imitating it! . . . What wonderful effects I have seen this evening in the Hayfields! the warmth of the uncut grass, the greeny greyness of the unmade hay in furrows or tufts with lovely violet shadows, and long shades of the trees thrown athwart all, and melting away one tint into another imperceptibly; and one moment more a cloud passes and all the magic is gone. Begin tomorrow morning, all is changed; the hay and the reapers are gone most likely, the sun too, or if not it is in quite the opposite quarter, and all that was loveliest is all that is tamest now, alas! It is better to be a poet! still better a mere lover of nature, one who never dreams of possession.[47]

Significantly, Brown was mystified that so little of nature's loveliness could be worked up into a picture. He failed to see the connection between the character of his response to the scene and his difficulty in representing it as landscape. Like the responses of the Pre-Raphaelites, Brown's response to landscape worked at a more atomistic level than, say, Constable's. He responded not to the overall sweep of a panorama or a meteorological event but to the almost unrepresentable aspects of the scene, the warmth of the uncut grass and the imperceptible tints of sunset. His response was purely sensual, unmediated by any past or personal associations or "dreams of possession." The habit of association as formulated in the writings of Alison and Knight at the end of the eighteenth century (and practiced by Constable) no longer functioned in such an experience of landscape. It was not that landscape had lost all meaning and become a merely figurative mode of painting but rather that the meaning one brought to it was less personal. Whereas for Constable emotion and representation in the face of nature were complementary processes, for Brown they frustrated one another. The shift in sensibility is significant. The landscape would not work up into a picture not because it had been made "ugly" by suburbanism but because at some fundamental level it was no longer an inevitable part of experience and therefore became difficult to represent. It was no longer a place where one sought oneself (à la Wordsworth or Constable); instead it had become a place where one sought to lose oneself. For Brown the "truth of nature" lay not, as it did for Constable, in its manifestation of the self nor, as it still did for Ruskin, in its manifestation of divine presence but rather in the riot of spectacle itself.

Landscape was, in fact, a diversion for Brown in more ways than usual. He thought of his landscapes as potboilers, peripheral to his main artistic projects such as the contemporary history paintings *Work* and *The Last of England*. He relegated his landscapes to secondary status and abandoned them when they began to "take up too much time to be profitable."[48] More positively, however, they also provided a therapy, a salutary holiday from his exhausting preoccupation with history painting. Indeed, Brown's best landscape work was done during the 1850s when he was suffering physically and psychologically from lack of critical recognition and its attendant woes, poverty and despair. During this period,

FIG. 80. Ford Madox Brown, *Walton-on-the-Naze*, dated 1860 (12½ × 16½ in.). City Museum and Art Gallery, Birmingham.

which Brown described as an "intensely miserable" time when he was "very hard up, and a little mad . . . broken in spirit and but a melancholy copy of what [he] once was,"[49] the countryside offered a restorative change of scene, and Brown and his wife Emma made excursions there either on foot or by omnibus.

Walton-on-the-Naze, a landscape from 1860, commemorates one of these outings (Figure 80). In it the artist, his wife Emma, and their little girl, their backs to the viewer, gaze out at the harbor, which is spanned by a breathtaking rainbow. The couple holds hands secretly while the child in her excitement pokes her mother with a sand shovel to get her attention. Brown described the action as follows: "The lady and little girl, by their let-down hair, have been bathing— the gentleman descants learnedly on the beauty of the scene."[50] As in *An English Autumn Afternoon*, an implied narrative informs the work, and as in the earlier painting, it is a narrative of diversion. If landscape in these works provokes a liberation of desire—in the young couple's wooing or in the older couple's furtive hand-holding, its brilliant evanescence also reaffirms the transitory, diversionary nature of this desire. "The beauty of the scene" is that it arouses but never fulfills "dreams of possession." Like the evanescent colors of twilight or the pangs of sexual desire, it fades. The end of a narrative of diversion is always that one is diverted back: the spell is broken and one stirs, perhaps consults the time, and hastens back to "real life." Here again Brown struggled to represent the unrepresentable. With its exaggerated color and narrative devices, *Walton-on-the-Naze* commemorates, by approximating, the things it can never possess. The result is a style of landscape in which realism and unreality are interfused. Brown's urban view of the countryside as a temporary departure from everyday routine is common to many other mid-Victorian painters. For instance, William Powell Frith's *Ramsgate Sands* of 1854 spawned a whole subgenre of seaside holiday paintings, some of which, like William Gale's *The Convalescent* of about 1862 (Figure 81), make explicit the period's trust in the salubrity of a change of scene. One might also recall the beaming strollers in John Ritchie's *Hampstead Heath* (see Figure 78).

In a formal sense Brown's landscapes perform the distraction that they are also about. Much as the scenery that is *in* the painting offers the figures a break from their ordinary preoccupations, so too the landscape that *is* the painting aspires to provide its spectators with a sensual experience to refresh eyes dulled by urban routine. Allen Staley has called these landscapes "hallucinatory,"[51] a word that congenially evokes their vivid color and extreme two-dimensionality. The minute Pre-Raphaelite detail, the intensity of the color, and the narrowness of its tonal range are such that one senses rather than sees the landscape beneath the optical glare emanating from it.

FIG. 81. William Gale, *The Convalescent*, ca. 1862 (12 × 18½ in.). Private collection, Great Britain.

A reverse yet complementary strategy stands behind the work of a painter like John William Inchbold, in whose works like *In Early Spring*, painted in 1855 (Plate 8), the quasi-scientific exactness of detail ministers perfectly to a clear, detached vision. Inchbold's low vantage point, as opposed to Brown's traditional high one, enables the viewer to focus on the details of the foreground. Inchbold's lack of deep space results from composition and not from indifference to tonal structure. Moreover, his details are nowhere so profuse as Brown's, and the scale of his composition, more suggestive of the close-up than the panorama, allows a more selective approach to them. Instead of canceling each other out, they add up. They seem purposefully selected to describe or exemplify. Such use of naturalistic detail, rendered with a hyperrealistic attention to light and surface texture, is profoundly interconnected with naturalism in its scientific sense. One could easily imagine Inchbold's landscape behind glass in a museum of natural history. Its various species of flowers, plants, grasses, trees, and animals all but make up a habitat study, in the manner of those popularizations of Victorian natural science, the terrarium and the vivarium.[52] Like such three-dimensional representations of nature, Inchbold's landscape (which could stand for many others) copies the style of pre-Darwinian Victorian science as it isolates trees, rocks, and clouds and bestows on them minute, even microscopic, attention.

Biologists and chemists of the pre-Darwinian period assumed that the seeming diversity of nature rested in fact on a simple foundation.[53] The work of Sir Humphry Davy and Michael Faraday, for instance, stressed the wonderful "economy" of nature that could unite both organic and inorganic matter under the same chemical elements and laws. Such unity in nature led many scientists to postulate an eventual convergence of all the sciences under a few simple laws governing elemental phenomena such as heat and electricity. Nature's diversity seemed a mask, worn to confound the ignorant, that needed to be stripped away through a study of biological and chemical laws, experimentation, and observation of the natural specimen *in vivo* and *in vitro*. As the great biologist William B. Carpenter explained, "the highest laws of biological science are expressed in their simplest terms in the lives of the lowest orders of creation."[54] Under this system, the humblest parts of creation could be analyzed for their universal significance; hence nothing was too small or insignificant to be afforded the minutest attention, and the results of the analysis could be broadly applied. Such a vision of nature's harmonious unity and economy not only stimulated scientific inquiry but also informed the definition of naturalism Ruskin urged on the Pre-Raphaelites and on artists like Inchbold.[55]

Inchbold's quasi-scientific attention to detail, like Brown's sensuous profusion of detail, forces us to perceive the landscape bit by bit rather than to take it all in as a single entity. The experience of nature, whether as spectacle or as science, is decontextualized; the nature of this experience in turn suggests an important connection between the suburban attitude toward nature and the scientific one. In both the suburb and the laboratory, we experience the natural specimen, not nature; we observe the example of the larger phenomenon. In the laboratory, through the close study of nature decontextualized, we believe we come to understand nature's context. Such an assumption generated phenomena as diverse as the Victorian rock garden that attempted to recreate the Alps in miniature and the preservation of specimens through improved methods of taxidermy. Both these experiences of nature were synecdochic. The part had come to stand for the whole, with the result that the whole seemed less accessible to the imagination; less real, in a sense, than the part; less comprehensible; yet all the while increasingly subject to laws and formulas. The long process of objectifying nature that began with enclosure culminated in the Victorian natural object, the specimen housed in a well-dusted bell jar.

One is tempted to speculate that the Victorian fascination in general with the little, the miniature, was symptomatic of this same process. From Tom Thumb's sensational London visit to the delight in dolls and mechanical toys, one sees a similar desire to experience the world through the small-scale example. The world at large, it seems, was too unmanageable. Moreover, in light of England's imperialistic expansion at this time, decontextualized, empirically observed example had administrative uses. The report of the Poor Law Commission, for instance, with its method of selecting examples and formulating models from them, was itself a model of such decontextualized empiricism and resembled the reports sent back to England from foreign offices across the continent of Asia.

Though the Victorian tendency to reduce experience to the characteristic "example" was not wholly the result of the chaos of mass urbanization, nevertheless close connections between the two can be seen throughout the period. One thinks, for instance, of the scene from Charles Dickens's *Dombey and Son* in which Florence Dombey flees into the heart of London:

> With this last adherent, Florence hurried away in the advancing morning, and the strengthening sunshine, to the City. The roar soon grew more loud, the passengers more numerous, the shops more busy, until she was carried onward in a stream of life setting that way, and flowing, indifferently, past marts and mansions, prisons, churches, market-places, wealth, poverty, good and evil, like the broad river side by side with it, awakened from its dreams of rushes, willows, and green moss, and rolling on, turbid and troubled, among the works and cares of men, to the deep sea.[56]

Significant here is not just the overwhelming urban diversity and congestion evoked by Dickens's description of London but also the implication that nature takes on the character of human life and vice versa. The stream of life and the river "side by side with it" seem one and the same. More important, the "example" of Florence's individual experience is threatened by the metaphor that almost swamps the description of that experience. Nature and society are fused in a way that jeopardizes the very principle of novelistic representation, namely, the rendering of the world through the example of individual experience. The global proportions of Dickens's novels, an important feature of their realism, can in the end be seen as a way to combat this threatening alliance of indifferent nature and society. Their realistic scope naturalizes the implausibility of the coincidences that continually shrink the world down to size. Narrative unfolding in Dickens always sets the primacy of the individual experience against, as much as in, the world, and in doing so reaffirms the status of the novel as an example.

That in *Dombey* Dickens seeks a metaphor for urban life in nature makes one wonder if the reverse process (seeking a metaphor for nature in urban life) might not also have operated at this time. Perhaps it can be found to some degree in popular post-Darwinian views of nature, in which the experience of the specimen (as opposed to the species) in its habitat resembles the experience of urbanism, with the result that the naturalist who leaves the specimen behind in the bell jar and goes into the field finds nature at best an indifferent "stream of life," and at worst "red in tooth and claw."[57] Similarly, social Darwinism and its theoretical offspring seem more the extensions of a particular urban-industrial experience than of an actual Darwinian analysis of nature. Under the motto "survival of the fittest," the long process of conflating nature and society produced some of its grimmest sociological effects.

THE RUSTIC STAGE

As the countryside offered an occasion for amusement, of both the sightseeing and the popular-scientific kind, its ways could be viewed with interest, detachment, or suspicion by an audience that did not feel implicated in them. Neither the social and economic eclipse of the countryside nor the proliferation of suburbs that trivialized it therefore can be taken to indicate that it had ceased to play a significant role in the cultural preoccupations of Victorian England. Even without its former importance and its attendant ability to affirm the "natural" position and status of the landowning classes, the countryside nevertheless became increasingly significant as a universal stage on which the dramas of poverty and financial ruin, sexual desire and transgression, illness and death could be played out to their fullest. Victorian rustic genre paintings mark a transition from the late eighteenth-century forms that implicitly dealt with the social consequences of enclosure and rural industrialization to a new tendency to universalize such issues as occasions for *general* identification.

For instance, the Victorian fascination with romantic sexual love found its characteristic representation in rural landscapes. It is hard to feel in William Mulready's *Open Your Mouth and Close Your Eyes* of 1839 (Figure 82) that the artist makes a specific comment on rural life.[58] Rather, he proffers an image of sexual play whose force is safely tempered by a geographical and social remoteness. In another Mulready painting, *The Sonnet* of 1839 (Figure 83), in which a young countryman presents his beloved with a poem, the sexual dimension of the scene is defused by its abundant charm. The young woman's naive pleasure and the young man's equally naive self-consciousness allude to country manners only by evoking a universally applicable picture of courtship. With the Pre-Raphaelites and their followers, this universalized rural landscape often became blatantly allegorical. In *The Long Engagement* by Arthur Hughes, for instance, the ivy that obscures the initials carved into a tree chronicles the no-longer-young couple's years of waiting. Likewise, the details of the landscape in *The Hireling Shepherd* by Holman Hunt must be read symbolically if the moral tale is to unfold.[59]

Not only erotic content but a whole range of social "problems" as well were dressed in rural clothes. A good example is the pair of paintings of stonebreakers

FIG. 82. William Mulready, *Open Your Mouth and Close Your Eyes*, exhibited at the Royal Academy 1839 (12½ × 12 in.). Victoria and Albert Museum, London.

exhibited at the Royal Academy in 1858 by Pre-Raphaelite followers John Brett and Henry Wallis (Figures 84, 85). In Brett's work, a small boy sits breaking stones in the noonday sun while his dog plays with his cap and a bird twitters in the tree. As in most Pre-Raphaelite works, nature—here, a view of Box-Hill, Surrey—contributes to the narrative poignancy of the painting: the child laborer

FIG. 83. William Mulready, *The Sonnet*, exhibited at the Royal Academy 1839 (14 × 12 in.). Victoria and Albert Museum, London.

must work even as all nature plays.[60] In Wallis's painting the stonebreaker, this time a grown man, has mortally succumbed to his arduous task. His body is collapsed against a hillock, his legs splayed, and his hands held as though they still gripped a mallet. The sun has just set, and the landscape is permeated with its fading glow; a weasel, herald of the night, emerges from its den. The landscape precisely echoes and aggrandizes the anecdote. The stonebreaker expires with the day; his body, growing cold in the fading light, is reduced to mere

FIG. 84. John Brett, *The Stonebreaker*, exhibited at the Royal Academy 1858 (19½ × 26½ in.). Walker Art Gallery, Liverpool.

matter. Like the landscape, he will soon be swallowed up in darkness. Tragically, cynically, the painting exemplifies with a vengeance the romantic dream of man's oneness with nature.

Like such Pre-Raphaelite prostitute paintings as Hunt's *Awakening Conscience*

FIG. 85.   Henry Wallis, *The Stonebreaker*, exhibited at the Royal Academy 1858 (25⅜ × 31 in.). City Museum and Art Gallery, Birmingham.

or such social genre paintings as Richard Redgrave's *The Seamstress*, Brett's and Wallis's treatment of their subject seems to be an implicit call for reform.[61] For the most part stonebreaking was not an occupation but a form of relief that rural counties and industrial districts used as a device for keeping the highways in good repair while providing for the destitute.[62] Broken stones were used to surface roads according to the Macadam method, and during the 1840s and 1850s, as a result of the growth of suburbs, a great deal of road work was being done, especially in the counties like Surrey that bordered London.[63] Because highway work was so closely intertwined with rural poor relief, a reform of one necessarily involved a reform of the other. As early as 1819, John Loudon McAdam himself blamed the poor condition of the king's highways on the use of "inefficient" pauper labor, and in 1833 this use of pauper labor became a special subject of the Poor Law Commission, which concluded not only that it was generally "unprofitable" as a form of relief and highway maintenance but also that it tended to demoralize the workers by encouraging a "dissolute idleness."[64] The recommendations made by the committee and written into the Poor Law of 1834 did little to remedy the situation.[65] What these earlier inquiries into the profitability of pauper labor overlooked was the issue raised by Brett and Wallis—the inhumanity of the task of stonebreaking itself.

To characterize the moral sensibility informing Brett's and Wallis's works one need only compare the two Victorian representations of stonebreaking with what is perhaps the earliest English version of the subject, George Walker's illustration (Figure 86) of "road workers" from his book *The Costumes of Yorkshire* (1814).[66] Neither too young for their labors nor destroyed by them, Walker's figures work in organized teams, unlike the solitary confinement of Brett's or Wallis's stonebreakers. Rather than the forgotten castoffs of an indifferent industrial society, Walker's men appear a small, but nonetheless significant, unit of its overall organization. That the image was one of forty aquatints etched after Walker's sketches, showing a whole range of occupations from peat cutting to cloth dressing performed by the working classes in the north of England, reinforces this impression. Significantly, the issue of labor could not be addressed directly for, as the title of the book indicates, such depictions were still accommodated under the rubric of picturesqueness: the laborers and their labors were presented as incidents of native costume and local color. Moreover, Walker depicted stonebreaking as he depicted other occupations, as part of an industrial process that had no trouble organizing and regulating itself. For Walker this form of outdoor relief was merely an unexceptional contribution to local economy, whereas for Brett and Wallis it was an inhuman punishment for having been born poor. The liberal consciousness that informs their representations was alien to Walker who, in typical post-Speenhamland fashion, saw no difference

FIG. 86.   George Walker, *Road Workers*, ca. 1814. Colored lithograph by Ernst Kaufmann, published in the second edition (1855) of George Walker's *Costumes of Yorkshire*, 1814.

between relief and wages in the overall scheme of economy. Whereas in 1814 stonebreaking appeared as a small segment of a well-integrated industrial system, by 1858 it had become a quintessential example of what was perceived as being wrong with that system.

It is possible that Brett and Wallis were influenced in their choice of subject by Gustave Courbet's notorious *Stonebreakers*, exhibited in the Paris Salon of 1850, or by some other French version of the subject.[67] It is also worth recalling that as early as 1852 Madox Brown had started his masterpiece *Work*, which shows the repair of a road in Hampstead by a team of navvies.[68] (One might even think of Ruskin's road-building project at Oxford.) What seems clear is that during this time the industry of road building figured large in the Pre-Raphaelite circle of friends and associates as a subject worthy of address. The equivocal status of stonebreaking, as both labor and relief, allowed Brett and Wallis to mask an obvious criticism of industrial society with a less controversial and more specific criticism of rural poor relief. The setting of their works, as the milestone in Brett's painting makes clear, was not the city but the country, and the "problem" the works treated could be seen as peculiarly rural, that is to say, both geographically and sociologically remote. Skirting the industrial issues of wages and hours by focusing on a form of rural poor relief, the paintings could make a universal appeal to contemporary humanitarian and philanthropic concern for the poor. The quotation from *Sartor Resartus* that accompanied Wallis's work—Carlyle's blanket condemnation of the evils of hard labor—assumes something of this generality.[69] As the quotation suggests, Wallis was using the example of the rural stonebreaker to criticize industrialism, yet the indirectness of both the allusion and the example disembroils his message from specific controversies and gives it a quasi-universal ethos. The clear moral force with which the paintings argue that children should not have to do hard labor or that men should not be killed by their work draws its power, as well as, finally, its inconsequence, from the fact that it exacts from its audience little actual or precise commitment.

It is often remarked that the Victorian fondness for genre paintings of this type was merely a taste for narrative art; and, depending on the critic, this taste is seen as either a vulgar debasement or another charming instance of Victorian camp. These views obscure both the social and cultural frustrations and concerns these paintings express and the role of art in addressing them. In short, Victorian genre painting accords perfectly with Ruskin's and Arnold's belief in the moral and pedagogical responsibility of art and their faith that it could effect social changes for the better. That this notion of art was so widely accepted and practiced indicates its art-historical importance. But what was the significance of the paintings' depiction of the countryside and rural life? Besides serving in genre paintings as a stage on which current urban industrial problems and concerns could be safely enacted, the countryside was also depicted more positively as an allegorical model of the organic society, in which all classes worked in harmony according to a plan that tended naturally toward the greatest good for the greatest number. The recurring theme of labor and work in the paintings of the period was the primary means of alluding to this organic ideal. One thinks of Brown's *Work* (1852–1865) and of William Bell Scott's *Coal and Iron* (1855–1860), but also of landscapes like Brown's *Hayfield* of 1855 (Figure 87) and John Frederick Herring's *Harvest* of 1857 (Figure 88).

The Hayfield represents Brown himself at the end of a long day of painting, leaning against his camp stool and umbrella and watching the last of the laborers depart from the field. Brown's painting differs from the usual representations of the artist in the landscape in that he is not alone with nature but shares the field with the reapers and like them is exhausted by his work. Instead of being alienated from the life of the landscape, Brown has become a part of that life. Like the work of the field hands, the activity of painting is presented as demanding,

FIG. 87. Ford Madox Brown, *The Hayfield*, 1855 (9⁹⁄₁₀ × 13½ in.). Tate Gallery, London.

time-consuming, and physical. What differences remain between painting and reaping, and between the artist's class status and that of the field hands, are made to seem unimportant and secondary to the fact of work itself.[70]

In Herring's *Harvest*, work in all its socioeconomic diversity stands even more explicitly for social unity. The numerous rural classes represented in the painting—the laborers, the farmer lounging at the edge of the field, and the landowner on horseback in the distance—are seen against a landscape that with its fields, church, village, park, and manor house echoes and hence endorses this diversity. Much as the eighteenth-century conversation piece painters "naturalized" their well-to-do sitters by placing them in a landscape setting that reaffirmed the values of their class, Herring valorized the class system as a whole by representing it in a landscape that is itself ordered by this same social hierarchy. Distinctions of class—the laborer's activity and the landowner's leisure—are accommodated in a landscape that makes such differences seem natural and even unimportant in the context of the collective interdependence of worker and landowner and their mutual dependence on the land. Collectivism is acceptable only along vertical class lines ("the rich man in his castle, the poor man at his gate"),

FIG. 88. John Frederick Herring, Sr., *Harvest*, 1857 (41¹³/₁₆ × 73³/₁₆ in.). Yale Center for British Art: Paul Mellon Collection, New Haven.

where it does not threaten the established social fabric. Such "organicism" acquires its full ideological importance in the context of the counterambitions of the trade unions and working men's societies.

As these examples of Victorian landscape make clear, the countryside, or rather the urban vision of it, came to provide the setting for problems that were not specifically rural at all. Instead of focusing on rural experience, the representation of the countryside modeled urban culture. No longer played off against the city as its traditional opposite, the countryside seemed instead to distill and clarify urban experience. It was as though the country formed a repository of ideals through which urban experience both was perceived and found its ultimate truth. Objectified as spectacle or science, the countryside took on an ideal form and performed the ideological function of providing urban industrial culture with the myths to sustain it. The actual encroachment on the countryside by industry, city, and suburb, together with the absorption of rural symbolism into urban values and experience, in no way, then, diminished the importance of the countryside as a cultural ideal. Believed in more as it exists less, it has become one of our modern superstitions.

NOTES

1. There are already a number of fine surveys of English landscape painting, the most recent being Louis Hawes's *Presences of Nature: British Landscape, 1780–1830* (New Haven, Conn., 1982) and Michael Rosenthal's *British Landscape Painting* (Ithaca, N.Y., 1982). See also Martin Hardie, *Watercolour Painting in Britain*, 3 vols. (London, 1966–1968); Luke Herrmann, *British Landscape Painting of the Eighteenth Century* (London, 1973); Leslie Parris and Conal Shields, *Landscape in Britain, c. 1750–1850*, Tate Gallery catalogue (London, 1973); and Christopher White, *English Landscape, 1630–1850*, Yale Center for British Art catalogue (New Haven, Conn., 1977).

2. Michel Foucault, *The Order of Things: An Archaeology of the Human Sciences*, trans. anonymously (London, 1970), and his *Discipline and Punish: The Birth of the Prison*, trans. Alan Sheridan (London, 1977). See also Hans-Georg Gadamer, "The Problem of Historical Consciousness," trans. Jeff L. Close, *Graduate Faculty Philosophy Journal* 5, no. 1 (Fall 1975): 8–56.

3. A thorough critique of the limitations of the traditional approaches to the social history of art is offered by T. J. Clark in his introduction to *Image of the People: Gustave Courbet and the Second French Republic, 1848–1851* (Greenwich, Conn., 1973). This book and a second by Clark, *The Absolute Bourgeois: Art and Politics in France, 1848–1851* (Greenwich, Conn., 1973), are good examples of the scholarly richness provided by an interpretive and methodologically self-conscious approach to the social history of art.

4. For Marx, the structure of society consisted of two main levels: the infrastructure, or economic base, which is articulated by the means and relations of the productive forces, and the superstructure, which is composed of two parts, the political and legal

mechanisms of the state and the ideological mechanisms such as religion, philosophy, and education. The ideological portion of the superstructure houses art. See Louis Althusser, *For Marx*, trans. Ben Brewster (New York, 1969), pp. 51–85, and his *Lenin and Philosophy and Other Essays*, trans. Ben Brewster (New York and London, 1971), pp. 134–48; see also Louis Althusser and Etienne Balibar, *Reading Capital*, trans. Ben Brewster (London, 1977).

5. Althusser, *Lenin and Philosophy*, pp. 127–86.

6. For analyses of the relationship between ideology and form, see Terry Eagleton, *Criticism and Ideology* (London, 1976), and Pierre Macherey, *A Theory of Literary Production*, trans. Geoffrey Wall (London, 1978).

7. See Althusser, "A Letter on Art," in *Lenin and Philosophy*, pp. 221–27. D. A. Miller provides an important critique of Althusser's concept of the function of "internal distanciation" in literary texts. Instead of seeing ideological contradiction within the text as a simple ideological "bind" revealed by the text's distanciation from its own program, he argues, "we need rather to be prepared to find in the source of 'incoherence,' the very resource on which the text draws for its consistency; in the ideological 'conflict,' a precise means of addressing and solving it; in the 'failure' of intention on the part of the text, a positive advantageous *strategy*" ("Discipline in Different Voices: Bureaucracy, Police, Family, and *Bleak House*," *Representations* 1 [February 1983]: 63). My own readings of ideology are indebted to this observation of Miller's.

8. Roland Barthes, *Mythologies*, trans. Annette Lavers (New York, 1972), *S/Z: An Essay*, trans. Richard Miller (New York, 1974), and *Writing Degree Zero*, trans. Annette Lavers and Colin Smith (New York, 1977).

9. Barthes, *S/Z*, pp. 22–26.

10. E. P. Thompson, *The Making of the English Working Class* (Harmondsworth, Middlesex, 1977).

11. Raymond Williams, *The Country and the City* (New York, 1973).

12. John Barrell, *The Idea of Landscape and a Sense of Place, 1730–1840: An Approach to the Poetry of John Clare* (Cambridge, Eng., 1972), and James Turner, *The Politics of Landscape: Rural Scenery and Society in English Poetry, 1630–1660* (Oxford, 1979). Along these lines, Carole Fabricant's valuable reevaluation of Jonathan Swift's work maps the intersections between Swift's "mental landscape" and that of his native Ireland. See her *Swift's Landscape* (Baltimore, 1982).

13. David H. Solkin, *Richard Wilson: The Landscape of Reaction*, Tate Gallery catalogue (London, 1982), and Michael Rosenthal, *Constable: The Painter and His Landscape* (New Haven, Conn., 1983).

14. John Barrell, *The Dark Side of the Landscape: The Rural Poor in English Painting, 1730–1840* (Cambridge, Eng., 1980).

15. John Hayes, *The Drawings of Thomas Gainsborough*, 2 vols. (New Haven, Conn., and London, 1970), and his *Landscape Paintings of Thomas Gainsborough*, 2 vols. (London, 1982); Graham Reynolds, *Catalogue of the Constable Collection in the Victoria and Albert Museum* (London, 1973), and his *Later Paintings and Drawings of John Constable*, 2

vols. (New Haven, Conn., 1984); Leslie Parris, Conal Shields, and Ian Fleming-Williams, *Constable: Painting, Watercolours, and Drawings*, Tate Gallery catalogue (London, 1976); and Leslie Parris, *The Tate Gallery Constable Collection* (London, 1981).

16. Kenneth Clark, *Landscape into Art*, 2d ed. (New York, 1976), and Ernst H. Gombrich, *Art and Illusion: A Study in the Psychology of Pictorial Representation*, 2d ed. (Princeton, N.J., 1972).

17. See, in particular, Ronald Paulson, *Emblem and Expression: Meaning in English Art of the Eighteenth Century* (Cambridge, Mass., 1975).

CHAPTER ONE

1. The phrase is William Gaunt's (*The Great Century of British Painting* [London, 1972], p. 25). The most important art-historical treatment of the enclosure period is John Barrell's *Dark Side of the Landscape: The Rural Poor in English Painting, 1730–1840* (Cambridge, Eng., 1980). For analysis of native scene painting, see Kenneth Clark, "On the Painting of the English Landscape," *Proceedings of the British Academy* 21 (1935): 27–39; and Geoffrey Grigson, *Britain Observed: The Landscape through Artists' Eyes* (London, 1975). A comparison between Dutch and English rustic landscape styles is found in the Arts Council of Great Britain's catalogue *The Shock of Recognition: The Landscape of English Romanticism and the Dutch Seventeenth Century* (London, 1971).

2. The most important primary sources on enclosure in Suffolk are Arthur Young, ed., *The Annals of Agriculture*, vols. 19 and 20 (London, 1784–1785), and his *Farmer's Tour through the East of England* (London, 1771). Equally important is his son's (also Arthur Young) *Agriculture in Suffolk* (London, 1798). Modern historical treatments of enclosure are W. H. R. Curtler, *The Enclosure and Redistribution of Our Land* (Oxford, 1920); J. L. Hammond and Barbara Hammond, *The Village Labourer, 1760–1832* (London, 1920); G. E. Mingay, *English Landed Society in the Eighteenth Century* (London, 1963); Gilbert Slater, *The English Peasantry and the Enclosure of the Common Fields* (London, 1907); and W. E. Tate, *The English Village Community and the Enclosure Movements* (London, 1967). The topographical impact of the enclosure movements is discussed in Thomas Sharp, *The English Panorama* (London, 1955). Enclosure could mean either the fencing off of a parish's common grazing land for cultivation or efficient stocking or the division and redistribution of arable land lying in open fields for more efficient maintenance.

3. J. H. Plumb, *England in the Eighteenth Century* (Harmondsworth, Middlesex, 1974), p. 153.

4. Tate, *English Village Community*, p. 365.

5. The genre of rustic landscape includes the work of artists like John Crome, John Sell Cotman, and the other Norwich painters as well as the work of David Cox, William Delamotte, Peter De Wint, George Lambert, George Robert Lewis, John Linnell, and Cornelius and John Varley, artists who, while not directly influenced by Gainsborough and Constable, nevertheless did paint native, rural scenes. I concentrate on the

work of Gainsborough and Constable because they are the most innovative artists of the rustic landscape. The achievement of Constable, an admirer of Gainsborough, is clearer in light of the formal qualities and ideological values Gainsborough first attached to the rustic landscape.

6. Mavis Batey, "Oliver Goldsmith: An Indictment of Landscape Gardening," in *Furor Hortensis: Essays on the History of the English Landscape Garden in Memory of P. H. Clark*, ed. Peter Willis (Edinburgh, 1974), p. 57. David Streatfield, in a perceptive account of the English landscape garden presented at the Clark Library in 1978, points out that villages destroyed by gardens were often replaced by such model villages as Milton Abbas, designed by Capability Brown in 1774 ("Art and Nature in the English Landscape Garden: Design, Theory, and Practice, 1700–1818," in *Landscape in the Gardens and the Literature of Eighteenth-Century England* [Los Angeles, 1981], p. 59). In the case of Nuneham Courtenay, Lord Harcourt moved the villagers from their old cottages to two rows of brick cottages along the Oxford-Henley road (Dorothy Stroud, *Capability Brown* [London, 1965], p. 82).

7. Batey, "Goldsmith," p. 57.

8. Miles Hadfield, *Gardening in Britain* (London, 1960), p. 183.

9. Ibid., p. 207.

10. Stroud, *Capability Brown*, p. 129.

11. Hadfield, *Gardening in Britain*, p. 183.

12. See Peter Willis, *Charles Bridgeman and the English Landscape Garden* (London, 1977), p. 19; and S. A. Mansbach, "An Earthwork of Surprise: The Eighteenth-Century Ha-Ha," *Art Journal* 42 (Fall 1982): 217–21.

13. Hadfield, *Gardening in Britain*, p. 210.

14. Quoted by S. Lang, "The Genesis of the Landscape Garden," in *The Picturesque Garden and Its Influence outside the British Isles*, ed. Nikolaus Pevsner (Washington, D.C., 1974), p. 4.

15. Uvedale Price and Richard Payne Knight's feud with Brown and his successor, Humphry Repton, is surveyed in Christopher Hussey, *The Picturesque: Studies in a Point of View* (London, 1927), and in Walter John Hipple, Jr., *The Beautiful, the Sublime, and the Picturesque in Eighteenth-Century British Aesthetic Theory* (Carbondale, Ill., 1957).

16. With the exception of Batey, garden historians have tended to minimize the impact of enclosure in their accounts of English landscape gardening. Christopher Hussey (*English Gardens and Landscapes, 1700–1750* [London, 1967], pp. 15–16) mentions enclosure but goes no further than to admit that it enabled landowners to take out of production the large number of acres needed for a landscape garden. Similarly, David Streatfield has noted that the great scale of the Brownian garden could not have been achieved without the enclosure acts. He also goes on, however, to contrast the design of the garden with the redesigning of the enclosed countryside. He insightfully points out that "inside the park the imagination could roam freely, seeking inspiration from an idealized re-created nature unfettered by the sight of workers laboring" (p. 59). Literary critics assessing its impact on landscape poetry have offered the most pioneering analyses

of the effects of enclosure. John Barrell's two volumes, *The Idea of Landscape and a Sense of Place, 1730–1840: An Approach to the Poetry of John Clare* (Cambridge, Eng., 1972), and *The Dark Side of the Landscape*; James Turner, *The Politics of Landscape: Rural Scenery and Society in English Poetry, 1630–1660* (Oxford, 1979); and Raymond Williams, *The Country and the City* (New York, 1973), make important contributions to the study of enclosure. And although she does not discuss English landscape and enclosure, Carole Fabricant, in her account of Swift's responses to the changing landscape of his native Ireland, provides a model for a sustained analysis of the interactions between the poet's mental landscape and the social, political, and economic reality of the natural landscape (*Swift's Landscape* [Baltimore, 1982]).

17. Sharp, *English Panorama*, p. 54.

18. Humphry Repton lists "Four Rules of Gardening" in his *Enquiry into the Changes of Taste in Landscape Gardening* (London, 1806), p. 23:

> *First*, it must display the natural beauties, and hide the natural defects of every situation. *Secondly*, it should give the appearance of extent and freedom, by carefully disguising or hiding the boundary. *Thirdly*, it must studiously conceal every interference of art, however expensive, by which the natural scenery is improved; making the whole appear the production of nature only; and *fourthly*, all objects of mere convenience or comfort, if incapable of being ornamental, or of becoming proper parts of the garden scenery, must be removed or concealed.

19. A number of plans that show the way Capability Brown screened the estate's farmland from the garden are reproduced in Stroud's *Capability Brown*. In them one can see how naturalized the garden was in comparison with the more regularized farmland around it.

20. As John Barrell has noted,

> All nature was a garden, but only when seen from one particular "station" or point of view. The method also encouraged the careful disposition of contrasted tones in the landscape, by the use of differently colored vegetation, which created also the illusion of depth in a restricted area; and this practice shows how able the 18th-century connoisseur was to separate the impressions he received of a landscape from the reality he knew to exist. Perhaps in no other of the 18th-century landscape arts was the landscape kept so carefully remote from the observer, or did it depend so much on his willingness, his anxiety even, to see ideal structures in what he saw. (*Idea of Landscape*, p. 48)

Dorothy Stroud discusses Repton's use of screening and framing devices in *Humphry Repton* (London, 1962), p. 35. See also Willis, *Charles Bridgeman*, pp. 19–23.

21. Quoted by Hadfield, *Gardening in Britain*, p. 216. Young was describing Duncomb, a garden in Yorkshire on an escarpment above the River Rye Valley. First designed (possibly by Bridgeman) in the second decade of the eighteenth century, Duncomb was an early example of a landscape garden. Subsequent owners continued to alter the garden to suit the increasing taste for the natural in gardening. Young saw the garden in 1768.

22. Pope's recommendations to the gardener are best summed up by lines from his *Epistle to Lord Burlington* (1731):

> In all let Nature never be forgot
> But treat the Goddess like a modest fair,
> Nor over-dress, nor leave her wholly bare.

23. Marx was the first to discuss this phenomenon and to analyze it in the context of bourgeois economic values. See *Grundrisse: Introduction to the Critique of Political Economy*, trans. Martin Nicolaus (New York, 1973), pp. 83–84. The concept is also important for literary critics analyzing realism in narrative prose. See especially Roland Barthes, *S/Z: An Essay*, trans. Richard Miller (New York, 1974), *Mythologies*, trans. Annette Lavers (New York, 1972), and *Writing Degree Zero*, trans. Annette Lavers and Colin Smith (New York, 1977); and Gerard Genette, *Figures II* (Paris, 1969). Barthes's model of naturalization is also used by Turner (*Politics of Landscape*, pp. 186–95).

24. This pattern of naturalization is outlined by Williams in his chapter "The Morality of Improvement," in *Country and City*, pp. 60–68. The image of the mother hen with her chicks was also used by Jean-Baptiste Greuze in his *L'Accordée de village* (1761).

25. Worn in the service, this cuff was popular with civilians from 1750 on and was often adopted by the fop. See Barbara Phillipson and Phillis Cunnington, *Handbook of English Costume in the Eighteenth Century* (London, 1936), p. 188.

26. Ronald Paulson, *Emblem and Expression: Meaning in English Art of the Eighteenth Century* (Cambridge, Mass., 1975), p. 123.

27. Lang, "Genesis of the Landscape Garden," pp. 3–23.

28. For a perceptive discussion of meaning in Watteau, see Norman Bryson, *Word and Image: French Painting of the Ancien Régime* (Cambridge, Eng., 1981), specifically chapter 3, "Watteau and Reverie," pp. 58–88.

29. Joseph Addison, *Selections from Addison's Papers Contributed to the Spectator*, ed. Thomas Arnold (Oxford, 1886), p. 263.

30. Philip Dormer Stanhope, *Letters Written by Lord Chesterfield to His Son*, ed. Ernest Rhys (London, 1889), p. 9.

31. Quoted by John E. Mason, *Gentlefolk in the Making: Studies in the History of English Courtesy Literature and Related Topics, 1531–1774* (Philadelphia, 1935), p. 97. I am indebted to the work of Ellen D'Oench of Yale University both for this reference and for other references to eighteenth-century courtesy literature I use in this chapter. It was she, in her dissertation on Arthur Devis, who first proposed comparing gestures in conversation pieces with those in etiquette books (see n. 40).

32. Mathew Towle, *The Young Gentleman and Lady's Private Tutor* (London, 1770), p. 186.

33. Ibid., p. 143.

34. Francis Nivelon, *Rudiments of Genteel Behavior* (London, 1737), n.p.

35. Henry Home (Lord Kames), *Elements of Criticism* (New York, 1866), p. 230.

36. Thomas Sheridan, *Courses of Lectures on Elocution* (Providence, R.I., 1796), p. 166.

37. Jean-Baptiste Du Bos, *Réflexions critiques sur la poésie et sur la peinture*, 3 vols. (Paris, 1755), 3:217.

38. Towle, *Private Tutor*, p. 40.

39. Although manners during the period were usually described as "natural" or "reasonable" (Jonathan Swift, *Works*, 9 vols. [Dublin, 1747], 9:263), Norbert Elias (*The Civilizing Process: The History of Manners* [New York, 1978]) has shown that the historical trend in manners has been toward greater elaboration.

40. See Ellen Gates D'Oench, *The Conversation Piece: Arthur Devis and His Contemporaries*, exhibition catalogue of the Yale Center for British Art (New Haven, Conn., 1980), pp. 15–18, and "Arthur Devis (1712–1787): Master of the Georgian Conversation Piece" (Ph.D. diss., Yale University, 1979), pp. 90–100. See also Stephen V. Sartin, *Polite Society: Portraits of the English Country Gentleman and His Family by Arthur Devis, 1712–1787*, exhibition catalogue of the Harris Museum and Art Gallery (Preston, Lancashire, 1983).

41. Quoted in Ellis Waterhouse, *Painting in Britain, 1530–1790* (Harmondsworth, Middlesex, 1969), p. 134.

42. Phillipson and Cunnington, *English Costume*, p. 164.

43. Ibid., p. 85.

44. The law in effect was the Act of 1671 that prohibited the killing of game by all except owners of land worth £100 a year, lessees of land worth £150 a year, the eldest sons of esquires or of persons of higher degree, and the owners of franchises. See E. W. Boville, *English Country Life* (London, 1962), p. 174; Hammond and Hammond, *Village Labourer*, pp. 163–67; and G. M. Trevelyan, *English Social History* (Harmondsworth, Middlesex, 1967), p. 294. John Berger also mentions the way the Andrewses are naturalized as landowners in his discussion of the painting in *Ways of Seeing* (Harmondsworth, Middlesex, 1972), pp. 106–7.

45. The scene is identified by John Hayes as the Andrews estate, Auberies, near Sudbury (*Gainsborough* [New York, 1975], p. 203). Waterhouse (*Painting in Britain*, p. 174) has called the portrait "an eccentric masterpiece," whose naturalness found no favor among Gainsborough's clients, who instead preferred the artificial backdrops of portraits like *Heneage Lloyd and His Sister*. Adrienne Corri ("Gainsborough's Early Career: New Documents and Two Portraits," *Burlington Magazine* 125 [April 1983]: 210–16) provides important new material about this portrait. Robert Andrews's father, Robert senior, was a wealthy man who lent sizable amounts to landowners; one of those most in his debt was Frederick, prince of Wales. Andrews had guaranteed a loan of £30,000 to the prince. When the prince died, Andrews and his friends in the Scottish faction lost a powerful ally. Many of Gainsborough's early sitters, like the son and daughter-in-law of Robert Andrews, were from Frederick's circle, and many of his Bath patrons were also friends of the prince. Corri dates Gainsborough's final return to Sudbury as 1751, the date of the prince's death. Before that, she believes, Gainsborough was in London, where he lived for a time in Andrews's household.

46. Marx, *Grundrisse*, p. 83. Marx sees this image of individual production as a typical eighteenth-century conceit, "which in no way expresses merely a reaction against

over-sophistication and a return to a . . . natural life." In a society of free competition, the individual appears detached from the bonds that in earlier historical periods made him part of a communal ideal; thus he appears as an individual type that does not arise historically but is posited by nature. In other words, he becomes the naturalized sign of capitalism.

47. Hayes, *Gainsborough*, p. 203. Since birds often carried erotic connotations, the dead pheasant might have seemed inappropriate and thus been left unfinished.

48. Basil Taylor, *Painting in England, 1700–1850: From the Collection of Mr. and Mrs. Paul Mellon* (Richmond, Va., 1963), p. 118; and Hayes, *Gainsborough*, p. 203.

49. In England the *ferme ornée* followed Addison's suggestion that "a man might make a pretty landscape of his own possession" (*The Spectator* no. 414 [June 25, 1712], quoted in John Dixon Hunt and Peter Willis, eds., *The Genius of the Place: The English Landscape Garden, 1620–1820* [London, 1975], p. 142). Stephen Switzer's *Ichnographia rustica* (1718) listed a *ferme ornée*, "Manor of Paston Divided and Planted with Rural Gardens," in which a circuit walk enclosed groves, paddocks, and cornfields. That the 1742 edition of the *Ichnographia* refers to only three *fermes ornées*, Streatfield takes to indicate their unpopularity (p. 19). Switzer stressed as its chief attraction the *ferme ornée's* inexpensive construction, but given the economic signification of the landscape garden, this low cost could have been the very reason the *ferme ornée* was unpopular.

The circuit walk used by Southcote seems to derive from the work of William Kent at Stowe and Rousham. Henry Hoare also used this device at Stourhead. Thomas Whately (*Observations on Modern Gardening* [London, 1770], p. 63) described Southcote's *ferme ornée*: "The decorations are communicated to every part, for they are disposed along the sides of a walk which, with its appendages, forms a broad belt round the grazing grounds and, on a more contracted path, through the arable. The walk is properly a garden; all is within the farm; the whole lies on two sides of a hill." See also Hadfield, p. 200. Young's *Annals*, 6:176, contains suggestions by Thomas Ruggles of the improvements a "picturesque farmer" might make, which on the whole follow the general pattern of the *ferme ornée*.

50. Shenstone's Leasowes is better documented than Southcote's Woburn Farm. A description of the garden by editor Robert Dodsley is contained in *The Works in Verse and Prose of William Shenstone, Esq.*, 3 vols. (London, 1765), 2:291. In that same volume, see also Shenstone's own essay "Unconnected Thoughts on Gardening," p. 133. Another source of information on the Leasowes is *The Letters of William Shenstone*, ed. Marjorie Williams (Oxford, 1939). To date the most complete discussion of the Leasowes is John Riely, "Shenstone's Walks: The Genesis of the Leasowes," *Apollo* 110 (September 1979): 202–9. In his essay Riely reproduces for the first time six drawings by Shenstone of the garden, as well as an engraving of Virgil's Grove after a painting of 1748 by Thomas Smith. Both the drawings and the engraving are remarkable in that they focus on the urns, ruins, streams, plantings, and framed prospects of the circuit walk and neglect views of the interior farmland. In addition to Riely, see Derek Clifford, *A History of Garden Design* (New York, 1963), pp. 141–43; Paulson, *Emblem and Expression*, pp. 19–

34; and Kimerly Rorschach, *The Early Georgian Landscape Garden* (New Haven, Conn., 1983), pp. 39–45. For the development of the *ferme ornée* in France, see Dora Wiebenson, *The Picturesque Garden in France* (Princeton, N.J., 1978), pp. 98–99.

51. Both Hayes (*Gainsborough*, p. 205) and Paulson (*Emblem and Expression*, p. 216) have pointed out the correspondence between the branches of the tree and the disposition of Plampin's legs. Both see it as an attempt to integrate figure and ground. Whereas Hayes sees it, for the most part, as a formal device to involve the figure with the landscape, Paulson sees it as part of Gainsborough's thematic statement: man is a part of nature. My own observations, indebted to Hayes and Paulson, nonetheless go further in suggesting a possible sociocultural origin for Gainsborough's use of visual parallels between man and nature.

52. The portrait of Richard Savage Lloyd is in the Yale Center for British Art, New Haven, Connecticut; the Heneage Lloyd conversation piece is in the Fitzwilliam Museum, Cambridge, England; and the Brown family portrait is in the collection of the Marchioness of Cholmondeley, Houghton, England.

53. *The Morning Herald* (London), August 4, 1799, n.p.

54. Letter to Henry Bate dated March 11, 1788, from Paul Mall. For the full text of this important letter, see Mary Woodall's edition of *The Letters of Thomas Gainsborough* (London, 1961), p. 35.

55. Ellis Waterhouse, *Gainsborough* (London, 1958), p. 12.

56. Hayes, *Gainsborough*, p. 201.

57. *The Morning Herald*, August 4, 1788, n.p.; and John Hayes, *The Drawings of Thomas Gainsborough*, 2 vols. (New Haven, Conn., and London, 1970), 1:54–63. Both give an account of the formative influences on Gainsborough's art. Hayes believes that Gainsborough's teacher, the French engraver Hubert Gravlot, influenced his techniques and figure style and that the seventeenth-century Dutch painters influenced his landscape style.

58. *The Morning Chronicle* (London), August 8, 1788, n.p.

59. Walter Thornbury, *The Life of J. M. W. Turner* (London, 1862), quoted by Hayes, *Drawings*, p. 57.

60. Woodall, *Letters*, p. 91 (a letter to Thomas Harvey dated May 22, 1779, from Paul Mall).

61. This device appears in Ruisdael's *La Forêt* in the Louvre, which Gainsborough carefully copied around 1747. This drawing is now in the Whitworth Art Gallery, Manchester. Mary Woodall ("A Note on Gainsborough and Ruisdael," *Burlington Magazine* 66 [January 1935]: 40–45) was the first to remark that the drawing was a copy of the Ruisdael.

62. The *Woodcutter Courting a Milkmaid* is in the collection of the duke of Bedford. Paulson (*Emblem and Expression*, p. 226) sees Gainsborough's space as convoluted and ultimately deriving from rococo pattern books. Hayes (*Drawings*, 1:12) does not discuss Gainsborough's space in any great detail, emphasizing instead the perfectly balanced tensions of the compositions themselves. Neither writer takes into account the screening

devices, the compacted spaces of the landscapes, or the focus on incidental, naturalistic detail in the foreground. But the space associated with the rustic landscapes of Gainsborough can be found in the majority of illustrations in John Hayes, *The Landscape Paintings of Thomas Gainsborough*, 2 vols. (London, 1982), vol. 2, in particular figures 8, 15, 30, 31, 35, and 56 from the Suffolk period; 76, 80, 82, and 87 from the Bath period; and 117, 118, 120, 136, 143, 158, and 160 from the London period.

63. Woodall, *Letters*, p. 99 (a letter to William Jackson dated only August 23 from Bath).

64. Ibid., p. 35 (a letter to Henry Bate dated March 11, 1788).

65. One could apply Jay Appleton's behaviorist habitat theory to Gainsborough's confined and sheltered spaces. Appleton sees such spaces as providing the viewer with an aesthetic pleasure derived from observing an environment favorable to the satisfaction of sexual, oral, nurturing, eliminative, and shelter-seeking needs. (*The Experience of Landscape* [London and New York, 1975], pp. 73–74.) Transhistorical in scope, Appleton's habitat theory and prospect-refuge theory are too insensitive to the social and economic realities of a particular period and culture to be of use here.

66. G. W. Hoskins, *The Making of the English Landscape* (London, 1955), p. 113.

67. Sharp, *English Panorama*, p. 300. In the eighteenth century the total acreage enclosed amounted to 6,400 acres; in Essex, 6,510 acres; and in Sussex, 1,500 acres. There are no figures for Kent. These eastern counties were relatively untouched in comparison with the counties to the west and north. According to Sharp, in the west 35,000 acres of Cambridge and 96,596 acres of Oxford were enclosed; in the north the totals were much higher: 112,880 for Nottingham; 60,143 for Derbyshire; 70,504 for Norfolk; and 175,280 for Leicester (pp. 268–71).

68. Hoskins, *English Landscape*, p. 142.

69. Williams, *Country and City*, chapters 7, 9, and 13. More directly relevant is John Barrell's discussion of this poetry and the social attitudes it describes. Barrell sees it as forming, like Gainsborough's landscapes, a bridge between the older pastoral mode of the sixteenth and seventeenth centuries and the eighteenth-century georgic mode of depicting landscape. See his chapter on Gainsborough in *The Dark Side of the Landscape*, pp. 35–88.

70. *Woody Landscape with Milkmaid and Drover* is in a private collection, England. See Hayes, *Landscape Paintings of Gainsborough*, 2:426–27.

71. There are a number of copies of this work. The Gainsborough original is in a private collection in England and has been catalogued by John Hayes (see his *Landscape Paintings of Gainsborough*, 2:367–68).

72. Oliver Goldsmith, "The Deserted Village," *Poems and Plays of Oliver Goldsmith*, ed. Austin Dobson, 27 vols. (London, 1891), 11:59–62. Barrell points out that Gainsborough's figures, often mixing labor with leisure, create an ideal of rural life that balances productivity with pleasure (*Dark Side of the Landscape*, pp. 35–37).

73. Woodall, *Letters*, p. 115 (a letter to William Jackson dated only June 4 from Bath).

74. Ibid.

75. Ibid., p. 101 (a letter to William Jackson dated September 2, 1767, from Bath).

76. Ibid., pp. 101–3 (a letter to William Jackson dated only September 14 from Bath).

77. Ibid., p. 35 (a letter to Henry Bate dated March 11, 1788, from Paul Mall).

78. Ibid., p. 117 (an undated letter to William Jackson).

79. Ibid., p. 53 (a letter to the earl of Dartmouth with no date but probably— according to Woodall—April 1, 1771).

80. Ibid., p. 43 (a letter to Sir William Chambers dated April 27, 1783).

81. Ibid., p. 99 (a letter to William Jackson dated only August 23 from Bath).

82. Hayes, *Gainsborough*, p. 217.

83. This painting was bought by the fourth duke of Rutland before 1787 and is still today at Belvoir Castle. The date of the work is problematic: Hayes believes it to be from 1773 (*Gainsborough*, p. 217), and Waterhouse (*Gainsborough*, p. 119) believes it to be the cottage-door scene exhibited at the Royal Academy in 1782 as "The Woodcutter's Return." I agree with Hayes's dating and think it probable that another cottage-door scene (perhaps the Cincinnati *Cottage Door with Children Playing*) was exhibited at the Academy in 1782. An ironic sidelight to the history of this painting is that the duke of Rutland was rapidly enclosing the land around Belvoir Castle in Leicestershire around the time he purchased the Gainsborough. It is believed that Crabbe wrote his poem *The Village* partly in response to the dire effects the duke's enclosures had on the countryside (Williams, pp. 91–92). Obviously the duke's fondness for humble cottage scenery was purely aesthetic and was satisfied more amply by art than by nature. Barrell (*Dark Side of the Landscape*, p. 67) points out the political relevance of this image by relating it to contemporary tracts addressed to the laboring class that evoke, like the painting, happy images of rest and contentment after a hard day's work.

84. Williams, *Country and City*, p. 78. Although Williams uses the term in relation to Goldsmith, what he says applies equally well to Gainsborough: "We need not doubt the warmth of Goldsmith's feelings about the men driven from their village: that connection is definite. The structure becomes ambiguous only when this shared feeling is extended to memory and imagination, for what takes over then, in language and idea, is a different pressure; the social history of the writer."

85. This view is similar to that of John Hayes ("Gainsborough's Later Landscapes," *Apollo* 95 [August 1964]: 21):

> The persistence of the cottage-door theme in these later years reflects the significance which Gainsborough attached to it as an expression of his sentimental attitude towards life, an attitude which was close in spirit to the nostalgia of Goldsmith's *Deserted Village*, to the image of a contented peasantry evoked in certain works by Greuze or to the self-deception of Marie Antoinette on her specially built farm at the Petit Trianon, Versailles.

More recently, Marcia Pointon has declared Hayes's interpretation a "serious misunderstanding of the philosophical associations of the cottage in English 18th-century thought," and has linked Gainsborough's "Cottage Doors" to the literature of rural retirement exemplified by the work of William Shenstone. According to Pointon, the landscapes are purely vehicles for contemplation ("Gainsborough and the Landscape of Retirement," *Art History* [December 1979]: 441–55). What Pointon overlooks is that Shenstone's literature is itself simply another manifestation of the broader cultural tendency Hayes has described. Unlike Hayes and Pointon, Carole Fabricant illuminates the meanings and deeper social implications of this ideology of retirement as it applies to gardening and literature ("Binding and Dressing Nature's Loose Tresses: The Ideology of Augustan Landscape Design," *Studies in Eighteenth-Century Culture* 8 [1979]: 109–35). Earlier explorations of the Augustan literature of retirement include Maren-Sofie Røstvig, *The Happy Man: Studies in the Metamorphoses of a Classical Ideal*, 2 vols. (New York, 1954); and Maynard Mack, *The Garden and the City: Retirement and Politics in the Later Poetry of Pope, 1731–1743* (Toronto, 1969).

86. This landscape is in the collection of the Honorable Michael Astor.

87. The unfinished *Diana and Actaeon* is in the collection of Her Majesty the Queen, Buckingham Palace. One might tentatively include in this list of paintings with a voyeuristic theme a late, unfinished figure study in the Tate that has traditionally been called "Musidora" after the heroine of an episode in James Thomson's poem *The Seasons*, whose lover secretly sketched her while she was bathing. It is sometimes thought that this work was intended for Macklin's Poet's Gallery, but there is no evidence for this claim. The title given the work in the sale catalogue of Gainsborough's studio is simply "A Nymph at the Bath." It is possible that the Thomson association was made only after Gainsborough's death. The figure, as Graham Sawyer has pointed out, is derived from a statuette by Adriaen De Vries ("A Note on Thomas Gainsborough and Adriaen De Vries," *Journal of the Warburg and Courtauld Institutes* 14 [1951]: 134). Whether a Musidora or not, in the context of Gainsborough's other late works the figure does take on voyeuristic overtones.

88. This interpretation tallies with the one given by Ronald Paulson, *Hogarth: His Life, Art, and Times*, abridged by Ann Wilde (New Haven, Conn., and London, 1974), pp. 115–16; and with Sean Shesgreen's in his *Engravings by Hogarth* (New York, 1973), plate 17.

89. One can draw a parallel between the classical system of codification and what Roland Barthes has described as "classical language": "There is no genre, no written work of classicism which does not suppose a collective consumption, akin to speech; classical literary art is an object which circulates among several persons brought together on a class basis; it is a product conceived for oral transmission; for a consumption regulated by the contingencies of society: it is essentially a spoken language, in spite of its strict codification" (*Writing Degree Zero*, p. 49). An alternative to this classical language, says Barthes, is the romantic use of language by a writer like Victor Hugo, who developed a "particular and thematic use of language, which could no longer be understood with reference to a tradition, but only in the light of the formidable reality lying behind his own existence" (ibid., p. 59).

90. It might be more accurate to say that the classically composed landscapes date from the late 1760s (reaching a peak in the early 1770s) and that the seascapes date from 1781 and the mountain scenes from 1783 when Gainsborough visited the Lake District. The classicizing compositions in the landscapes neither outnumber nor are opposed to the more eccentrically composed rustic landscapes. For the most part the classically composed landscapes are loosely joined together snatches of incident. Rather than keep the brightest lights for his horizon, Gainsborough scattered them throughout or used them in the foreground. As a result, the compositions lack the order and deep space of a Claudian landscape and seem closer in spirit to the rustic landscapes, with their fragmented and compacted spaces.

91. Both Waterhouse (*Gainsborough*, p. 37) and Hayes (*Gainsborough*, p. 32) see the late Gainsborough as something of a subject painter and believe that works like the *Diana and Actaeon*, *Woodman*, and *Two Shepherd Boys with Dogs Fighting* exemplify what Gainsborough had in mind when he talked of becoming a "serious fellow." John Barrell (*Dark Side of the Landscape*, pp. 82–83) discusses Gainsborough's late pictures of ragged country children as images of the "industrious poor," which by the end of the century were very popular with the upper classes. Jean Starobinski, cited by Barrell, sees Gainsborough naturalizing the extreme poverty of the poor in these works (*L'Invention de la liberté, 1700–1789* [Geneva, 1964], p. 163).

92. Most of these works are in the *exemplum virtutis* mode of painting discussed by Robert Rosenblum (*Transformations in Late Eighteenth-Century Art* [Princeton, N.J., 1967]). Scenes of rustic charity, however, are more problematic than their urban or historical counterparts. Significantly, these scenes abounded in England during the period of enclosure. One thinks of Francis Wheatley's *Rustic Benevolence* (1797) in the British Museum, Edward Penny's *Generosity of John Pearmain* (1782) in the Paul Mellon Collection, and Gainsborough's own *Charity Relieving Distress* (1784) in the collection of Sir Francis Cassel, which depicts a housemaid at the back door of a country house handing out food to a peasant family. More so than Morland's works, all three paintings are, at some level, indictments of enclosure. Wheatley depicts a well-worn observation that the poor take care of their own. Penny's picture refers to a real-life incident: when the few possessions of a poor widow were seized in payment for taxes owed, John Pearmain was moved to pity by the scene and paid the taxes. The political implications of Gainsborough's painting are less radical than those of Wheatley's, yet Gainsborough's painting hardly makes the case for bourgeois heroism and generosity that the Penny and Morland paintings make. The benevolence that Gainsborough depicts was typical of the servant class. One reads with interest in William Cobbett's *Advice to Young Men* about the economic disasters that can befall a household whose too-generous servant girls virtually rob their masters to give to the poor, many of them old neighbors, friends, and relations. Whereas Morland and Penny see generosity as the virtue of the upper classes, Wheatley and Gainsborough see it as the habit of the lower classes. Nevertheless, while depicting what was becoming a sad necessity because of enclosure, all the paintings of rustic charity deny, in an important sense, that enclosure was destroying the foundations of rural so-

ciety. All the paintings show traditional rural modes of support for the poor, not either the new bureaucratic systems and institutions like the "Speenhamland system" and the workhouse or the alternative more popular among the poor, emigration to the city. These paintings are, in short, attempts to reaffirm the integrity of rural society precisely at the moment when it was most in danger of disintegrating.

93. For a rather different reading of Morland, see Barrell, *Dark Side of the Landscape*, pp. 89–129.

CHAPTER TWO

1. Joshua Reynolds, *Discourses on Art*, ed. Robert Wark (London, 1969), p. 223.

2. Ibid.

3. Ibid., p. 219.

4. Ibid., p. 218.

5. Ibid., p. 222.

6. Philip Thicknesse, *A Sketch of the Life and Paintings of Thomas Gainsborough, Esq.* (London, 1788), pp. 5–6.

7. Ibid., p. 11.

8. Ibid., p. 14.

9. John Pinkerton, ed., *A General Collection of Voyages and Travels* (London, 1808), p. 644. I am indebted to John Hayes for this reference.

10. Ibid., p. 68.

11. Uvedale Price, *An Essay on the Picturesque As Compared with the Sublime and the Beautiful* (London, 1842), p. 408.

12. Ibid., p. 512.

13. John Walter Hipple, Jr., *The Beautiful, the Sublime, and the Picturesque in Eighteenth-Century British Aesthetic Theory* (Carbondale, Ill., 1957), p. 249.

14. For a discussion of this development in art criticism see Adel M. Holcomb, "More Matter with Less Art: Romantic Attitudes toward Landscape Painting," *Art Journal* 36 (Summer 1977): 303–6.

15. *John Constable's Correspondence*, ed. R. B. Beckett and (for vol. 7) Leslie Parris, Conal Shields, and Ian Fleming-Williams, 7 vols. (Ipswich, Suffolk, 1962–1975), 6:77–78 (hereafter cited as *Correspondence*). Constable possessed a copy of Thicknesse's account, which Allan Cunningham tried to borrow in 1829. For the contents of Constable's library, see *Correspondence*, 8:25–52. Both John Hayes (*The Landscape Paintings of Thomas Gainsborough*, 2 vols. [London, 1982], 2:41) and Michael Rosenthal (*Constable: The Painter and His Landscape* [New Haven, Conn., 1983], p. 137) have also noted the correspondence between Thicknesse's account and Constable's letter.

16. Hayes, *Landscape Paintings of Gainsborough*, 1:183.

17. William Whitley, *Art in England, 1800–1820*, 2 vols. (New York, 1968), 1:228.

18. Ibid., 1:288.

19. W. H. Pyne, *Etchings of Rustic Figures for the Embellishment of Landscape* (London, 1814–1815), p. 6.

20. Allan Cunningham, *Lives of the Most Eminent British Painters* (London, 1893), p. 255.

21. Ibid., p. 273.

22. George William Fulcher, *Life of Thomas Gainsborough, R.A.* (London, 1856), p. 32.

23. Ibid., p. 171.

24. For an account of Gainsborough's influence on later artists, see Hayes, *Landscape Paintings of Gainsborough*, 1:237–93.

25. William Gilpin, *Three Essays: On Picturesque Beauty; On Picturesque Travel; and On Sketching Landscape* (London, 1803), p. 3.

26. Ibid., p. 59.

27. Ibid., pp. 66–67.

28. Ibid., p. 57.

29. Ibid., p. 67.

30. See especially his chapters "Of the Use of Pictures," "Of the Pathetic Fallacy," and "The Moral Landscape" in volume 3; "Of the Turnerian Picturesque," "The Mountain Gloom," and "The Mountain Glory" in volume 4; and part 9 in volume 5 of *Modern Painters* (New York, 1910).

31. Price, *Essay on the Picturesque*, p. 68.

32. Ibid., p. 70.

33. Ibid., p. 132.

34. Ibid., p. 232.

35. Ibid., p. 233.

36. Ibid.

37. Ibid., p. 61.

38. Ibid., p. 69.

39. John Dixon Hunt and Peter Willis, eds., *The Genius of the Place: The English Landscape Garden, 1620–1820* (New York, 1975), pp. 32–33.

40. Price, *Essay on the Picturesque*, p. 84.

41. Ibid., p. 87.

42. This is Ruskin's point in *Modern Painters*, "Of the Turnerian Picturesque," 4:1–14.

43. Price, *Essay on the Picturesque*, p. 91.

44. Ibid., p. 151.

45. Gilpin, p. 7.

46. Archibald Alison, *Essay on the Nature and Principles of Taste* (Edinburgh, 1825), p. 172.

47. See Christopher Hussey, *The Picturesque: Studies in a Point of View* (London, 1927), and Hipple, *Beautiful, Sublime, and Picturesque.*

48. Richard Payne Knight, *An Analytical Inquiry into the Principles of Taste* (London, 1805), p. 196. Knight had previously endorsed Price's theories in his poem *The*

Landscape (1794). In the preface to the second edition of the poem (1795), however, Knight argued that Price's distinction between the beautiful and the picturesque was "an imaginary one" and that the picturesque was "merely that kind of beauty which belongs exclusively to the sense of vision—or to the imagination, guided by that sense." This preface is included in the 1842 edition of Price, *Essay on the Picturesque*.

49. Knight, p. 462.

50. Ibid., p. 460.

51. Ibid., p. 464.

52. J. H. Plumb, *England in the Eighteenth Century* (Harmondsworth, Middlesex, 1974), p. 152.

53. David Thomson, *England in the Nineteenth Century* (Harmondsworth, Middlesex, 1950), p. 11. Hereafter cited as D. Thomson.

54. Thomas Bewick, *Memoir of Thomas Bewick* (1862) (London, 1961), p. 154.

55. William Cobbett, *Rural Rides* (1830) (Harmondsworth, Middlesex, 1977), p. 227.

56. G. W. Hoskins, *The Making of the English Landscape* (London, 1955), p. 218.

57. Quoted in D. Thomson, pp. 14–15.

58. William Howitt, *Rural Life in England*, 2 vols. (London, 1838), 1:158.

59. E. W. Boville, *English Country Life* (London, 1962), p. 118.

60. E. P. Thompson, *The Making of the English Working Class* (Harmondsworth, Middlesex, 1977), pp. 62–64.

61. A fine account of agriculture in Suffolk (both Gainsborough's and Constable's home county) can be found in Joan Thrisk, ed., *Suffolk Farming in the Nineteenth Century* (Ipswich, Suffolk, 1958). In Constable's town of East Bergholt, the high, dry land of the commons was enclosed immediately after the French Napoleonic wars (ca. 1816) as more and more land was given over to growing wheat.

62. Other period sources on the rising poor rates besides Arthur Young, ed., *The Annals of Agriculture*, 46 vols. (London, 1770–1813), are David Davies, *The Case of Labourers in Husbandry* (London, 1795); Thomas Ruggles, *The History of the Poor*, 2 vols. (London, 1795); and Fredrick Morton Eden, *The State of the Poor* (London, 1797). The finest modern survey of the problem is still J. L. Hammond and Barbara Hammond, *The Village Labourer, 1760–1832* (London, 1920). E. P. Thompson deals with the phenomenon in the larger context of industrialism in *The Making of the English Working Class*. Other solid, but less profound, analyses are J. D. Chambers and G. E. Mingay, *The Agricultural Revolution, 1750–1880* (London, 1966); and W. E. Tate, *The English Village Community and the Enclosure Movements* (London, 1967). For a specific analysis of conditions in Suffolk see Thrisk, *Suffolk Farming*.

63. "By nineteen out of twenty enclosure Bills the poor are injured, and some grossly injured," Young declared in the *Annals*, 30:52.

64. Quoted in E. P. Thompson, *English Working Class*, p. 243.

65. The average price of wheat from 1776 to 1794 was 44s, 7d a quarter bushel. In 1795, the price of wheat jumped to 108s. See W. Smart, "Antecedents of the Corn Law of 1815," *English Historical Review* 24 (1909): 470–87.

66. E. P. Thompson, *English Working Class*, pp. 71, 158.

67. Eden, p. 100.

68. Arthur Young, *General View of the Agriculture of the County of Lincoln* (London, 1799), p. 439.

69. Quoted in Hammond and Hammond, p. 14.

70. The Speenhamland solution was preferred to Samuel Whitebread's proposal for a minimum wage. Strong opposition in Parliament to Whitebread's bill was formulated by Pitt, who argued that the price of labor must find its own "natural" level in the market. See Hammond and Hammond, pp. 115–20, and Gertrude Himmelfarb, *The Idea of Poverty: England in the Early Industrial Age* (New York, 1984).

71. D. Thomson, pp. 15–16.

72. See especially the 1794 survey of poor houses conducted by Ruggles, in his *History of the Poor*.

73. Thrisk, p. 35.

74. Ruggles, 1:55, 102; 2:17, 86, 99.

75. Davies, p. 55.

76. Young, *Annals*, 14:166–67.

77. Price, *Essay on the Picturesque*, p. 152.

78. Gilpin, p. 45.

79. See also F. D. Klingender's analyses of industrial scenes in his *Art and the Industrial Revolution* (New York, 1968).

80. This painting is in the John Paul Getty Museum in Malibu, California. It was engraved by Charles Knight and published by Bull and Jeffrye in 1787.

81. The four paintings, sometimes called *The Four Times of Day*, are in the Yale Center for British Art, New Haven, Connecticut. They were engraved by H. Gillbank and published in 1800 by J. Daniell.

82. Both paintings are in the National Gallery of Scotland in Edinburgh. They were engraved by H. Hudson for J. R. Smith in 1790.

83. This engraving was done by G. Keating in 1797 and published by John Jeffrye.

84. Cited in Elizabeth Wheeler Manwaring, *Italian Landscape in Eighteenth-Century England* (New York, 1925), p. 200.

85. Jane Austen, *Northanger Abbey*, ed. R. W. Chapman (London, 1971), p. 111.

86. Manwaring, p. 134.

87. Wordsworth turned Price's own arguments against him, complaining to Sir George Beaumont that Foxley impoverished and monotonized the landscape (*Letters of William and Dorothy Wordsworth: The Middle Years*, ed. E. De Selincourt [Oxford, 1937], 2:466. This letter is quoted in Martin Price's interesting essay "The Picturesque Moment," in *From Sensibility to Romanticism: Essays Presented to Frederick A. Pottle*, ed. Fredrick W. Hilles and Harold Bloom [Oxford, 1965] , pp. 259–89).

88. George Kubler, *The Shape of Time: Remarks on the History of Things* (New Haven, Conn., 1973), p. 39.

89. Jean Baudrillard, *Le Système des objets* (Paris, 1968).

90. The opposition between the reproducible and the unique that can be seen in a given object may also operate between objects as well—the art of the avant-garde does not make a radical break with academic art so much as it combines with it to produce another version of the opposition between the reproducible and the unique that governs aesthetics in the modern world.

91. Price, "Picturesque Moment," p. 227.

92. Gilpin, p. 51.

93. Quoted in Price, "Picturesque Moment," p. 280.

CHAPTER THREE

1. *John Constable's Correspondence*, ed. R. B. Beckett and (for vol. 7) Leslie Parris, Conal Shields, and Ian Fleming-Williams, 7 vols. (Ipswich, Suffolk, 1962–1975), 6:78. Hereafter cited as *Correspondence*.

2. Ibid.

3. Writing to his future wife Maria Bicknell in the spring of 1814, he said, "You once talked to me about a journal. I have a little one that I made last summer that might amuse you could you see it—you will then see how I amused my leisure walks, picking up little scraps of trees, plants, ferns, distances &c &c" (ibid., 2:120).

4. Graham Reynolds, *Catalogue of the Constable Collection in the Victoria and Albert Museum* (London, 1973), p. 84.

5. Though a good deal of this correspondence was collected by his friend Charles R. Leslie and quoted by him in his biography of Constable, only recently do we have a complete and fully annotated edition in R. B. Beckett's six-volume collection, with the seventh and last volume edited by Leslie Parris, Conal Shields, and Ian Fleming-Williams. The volumes are organized by correspondents as follows: (1) The Family at East Bergholt, 1807–1837; (2) Early Friends and Maria Bicknell (Mrs. Constable); (3) C. R. Leslie, R.A.; (4) Patrons, Dealers, and Fellow Artists; (5) Various Friends, with Charles Boner and Artist's Children; (6) The Fishers; (7) Further Documents and Correspondence.

6. David Thomson, *England in the Nineteenth Century* (Harmondsworth, Middlesex, 1950), p. 4.

7. Joan Thrisk, ed., *Suffolk Farming in the Nineteenth Century* (Ipswich, Suffolk, 1958), pp. 18, 20–21, 22–23.

8. William Cobbett, *Political Register* (March 17, 1821), 38:750. Quoted in J. L. Hammond and Barbara Hammond, *The Village Labourer, 1760–1832* (London, 1920), p. 188.

9. E. P. Thompson, *The Making of the English Working Class* (Harmondsworth, Middlesex, 1977), pp. 442–49.

10. D. Thomson, pp. 35–36.

11. E. P. Thompson, *English Working Class*, p. 245. See also Hammond and Hammond, pp. 162–70, 216–300; Alfred James Peacock, *Bread or Blood: A Study of the*

Agrarian Riots in East Anglia in 1816 (London, 1965); and Eric J. Hobsbawm and George Rudé, *Captain Swing* (New York, 1968).

12. Charles R. Leslie's biography, *Memoirs of the Life of John Constable,* was first published in 1843 and was popular enough to merit a second edition in 1845. The second edition has been the basis for subsequent editions by Andrew Shirley (London, 1937) and Jonathan Mayne (London, 1951). The *Memoirs* cited here are Mayne's edition. Studies of Constable since Leslie that are mainly biographical are Robert G. Plymouth (Lord Windsor), *John Constable, R.A.* (London, 1905); E. V. Lucas, *John Constable the Painter* (London, 1924); Sydney Key, *Constable* (London, 1948); Lawrence Gowing, *Constable, 1776–1837* (London, 1960); Graham Reynolds, *Constable: The Natural Painter* (London, 1965); Basil Taylor, *Constable: Paintings, Drawings, and Watercolours* (London, 1973); Reg Gadney, *Constable and His World* (London, 1976); and John Walker, *John Constable* (New York, 1978).

13. As these remarks suggest, I shall not offer a strictly chronological account of Constable's development, of which several excellent studies already exist in any case. See Taylor, *Constable*; Reynolds, *Catalogue* and *Natural Painter*; Leslie Parris, Ian Fleming-Williams, and Conal Shields, *Constable: Paintings, Watercolours, and Drawings*, catalogue of the Constable bicentenary at the Tate Gallery, 1976; John Baskett, *Constable Oil Sketches* (London, 1966); and Ian Fleming-Williams, *Constable: Landscape Watercolours and Drawings* (London, 1976). My discussion will place the art in a number of chronological series, depending on the particular issue under consideration. Without surrendering all sense of historical development, the procedure will, I hope, register how complex, devious, and multileveled this development is.

14. John Barrell, *The Dark Side of the Landscape: The Rural Poor in English Painting, 1730–1840* (Cambridge, Eng., 1980), and Michael Rosenthal, *Constable: The Painter and His Landscape* (New Haven, Conn., 1983).

15. Barrell, *Dark Side of the Landscape*, p. 135.

16. Ibid., p. 134.

17. Rosenthal, *Constable*, pp. 207–13.

18. *Correspondence*, 6:88.

19. Ibid., 3:49.

20. Studies of the family's intermediary role tend to focus on its internalization of social structures of power and authority. Such internalization makes the family an extension of society. See Jacques Donzelot, *The Policing of Families*, trans. Robert Hurley (New York, 1979); Erich Fromm, "The Theory of Mother Right and Its Relevance for Social Psychology," in *Crisis of Psychoanalysis* (New York, 1934); Max Horkheimer, "Authority and the Family," in *Critical Theory: Selected Essays,* trans. Matthew J. O'Connell and others (New York, 1972); Herbert Marcuse, *Eros and Civilization* (New York, 1962). For social histories of the family see Philippe Ariès, *Centuries of Childhood: A Social History of Family Life*, trans. Robert Baldick (New York, 1962); Christopher Lasch, *Haven in a Heartless World: The Family Besieged* (New York, 1979); and Lawrence Stone, *The Family, Sex, and Marriage in England, 1500–1800* (New York, 1977).

21. In his psychological reading of Turner's and Constable's landscapes, Ronald Paulson demonstrates how Constable suppressed traditional literary meaning in his landscapes by infusing them with personal associations, specifically his love for Maria Bicknell. In this context Paulson analyzes the compositions of the early Stour Valley landscapes, such as *Golding Constable's Kitchen Garden*, and discusses the meaning of Constable's late works like *The Cenotaph* (*Literary Landscape: Turner and Constable* [New Haven, Conn., 1982]).

22. Louis Althusser discusses the relevance of psychoanalytic theory to the study of ideology in "Freud and Lacan," in *Lenin and Philosophy and Other Essays*, trans. Ben Brewster (New York and London, 1977).

23. Raymond Williams, *The Country and the City* (New York, 1973), p. 166.

24. *Correspondence*, 1:35.

25. Ibid., 1:52.

26. Ibid., 1:107.

27. Ibid., 2:102.

28. Ibid., 2:128.

29. Ibid., 2:90.

30. Ibid., 2:78.

31. Ibid., 2:125.

32. Ibid., 2:220.

33. For a detailed account of Golding Constable's business and holdings, see Beckett's discussion in the *Correspondence*, 1:5–6. See also Parris, Fleming-Williams, and Shields, *Constable*, pp. 31–32.

34. Leslie, in his *Memoirs* (p. 3) reports that at sixteen or seventeen Constable had become "devotedly fond of painting" and had made friends with an amateur artist of the village, John Dunthorne. This is also the time when Constable is thought to have worked in his father's mill on the commons. An outline carving of a windmill found on one of its timbers is signed by Constable and dated 1792. See Parris, Fleming-Williams, and Shields, *Constable*, p. 36.

35. *Correspondence*, 2:13–14.

36. Ibid., 2:10.

37. Ibid., 2:17–18.

38. Ibid., 1:63, 85, 86, 94.

39. Beckett infers this from two letters by Constable's mother that obliquely refer to a past falling-out between Golding and Dr. Rhudde (see *Correspondence*, 1:46–47, 76).

40. His mother's efforts culminated in the winter of 1811 when she asked John to copy a drawing of East Bergholt Church to present to Dr. Rhudde. The drawing was made, presented, and graciously received, but it did not soften Rhudde toward Constable (see *Correspondence*, 1:56).

41. *Correspondence*, 2:170, 171.

42. One of these was the local physician Dr. Travis, who supplied the Constables with gossip from the rectory (see *Correspondence*, 1:141–43, 147–49).

43. Ibid., 1:74.

44. The relevance of late eighteenth-century theories of associationism for Constable's work is discussed in Rosenthal, *Constable*, pp. 71–76, and Paulson, *Literary Landscape*, pp. 128–29, 147–48, 151–57. Constable mentioned in a letter to Maria dated 1814 that he preferred Alison's theories to Burke's (*Correspondence*, 2:131). The first thorough exploration of Constable's habit of associating certain scenes with Maria was given by Charles Rhyne in a lecture at the College Art Association meeting of January 1970, entitled "Constable's Views of East Bergholt Common: Observation and Emotion."

45. Through such metaphoric and metonymic structures of meaning Paulson sees Constable breaking with the more traditional literary landscape tradition of Claude and Turner (*Literary Landscape*, p. 108).

46. Three of the drawings were made from Gun Hill, Dedham, on the Essex side of the Stour; a fourth was done from a spot further east. All are in pen and ink and watercolor.

47. Constable's topographical accuracy has been verified by Colonel Attfield Brooks, who has identified numerous Suffolk and Essex scenes Constable painted, including the view depicted in the Whitworth drawing (Alastair Smart and Attfield Brooks, *Constable and His Country* [London, 1976], p. 26).

48. This painting was first identified (in print) as a view from the upstairs windows of Golding Constable's house in the Tate exhibition catalogue of 1976, where it is attributed to the period around 1800 (see Parris, Fleming-Williams, and Shields, *Constable*, p. 46). Professor Charles Rhyne, who with Graham Reynolds will produce a catalogue raisonné of Constable's work, believes the work to be later, perhaps closer to 1804. My reasons for placing it nearer 1800 have to do with the flatness of Constable's modeling of the trees and shrubs, which corresponds to his work of 1800–1802.

49. Parris, Fleming-Williams, and Shields, *Constable*, p. 46. Charles Rhyne, however, believes Constable represented the view exactly as it was then since there is no evidence that Constable altered views in any drawings or paintings at this time. Rhyne proposes that the gardens were later additions to the house grounds. Yet this proposal does not explain why Constable shows a cow track leading up to the back of the house rather than toward the farm buildings, which, as in his 1815 painting *Golding Constable's Flower Garden* (Figure 39), were to the left of the stone wall visible in the Downing view.

50. Cited in Geoffrey Grigson, *Britain Observed: The Landscape through Artists' Eyes* (London, 1975), p. 189.

51. The exceptions are the 1802 oil sketches now in the Victoria and Albert Museum and the Yale Center for British Art; several watercolors and chalk drawings from around 1805, a number of which are in the Victoria and Albert Museum; and finally, a few oil sketches from about 1808–1809, in private collections but reproduced in Parris, Fleming-Williams, and Shields, *Constable*, pp. 62–72.

52. A general outline of Constable's artistic activities during this period gives some idea of his topographical and generic eclecticism. In 1801 he sketched in Derbyshire; in 1803 he sketched around Ipswich; in 1804, while in Suffolk, he painted portraits in the mornings and landscapes in the afternoons, and he also sketched in Hursley, Hampshire; in 1805 he was commissioned to paint an altarpiece for Brantham Church;

in 1806 he toured Epsom and the Lake District, sketching at Ambleside, Windermere, Brathay, Borrowdale, and Langdale (he also painted around Bergholt); in 1807 he copied portraits by Reynolds and Hoppner for the earl of Dysart; in 1808 he worked in the Academy life class and later painted in Suffolk; in 1809 he spent the early part of the summer at Epsom and at Malvern Hall, where he painted a portrait of Henry Greswolde Lewis, and visited Bergholt in late August.

53. Leslie first suggested the importance of Maria Bicknell as an influence on Constable's art. Subsequent biographers have noted the change in his style evident from the time of their meeting and, most particularly, the even more dramatic change after Maria's death in 1828. See Reynolds, *Catalogue*, p. 16, and *Natural Painter*, pp. 38, 42, 109–10; see also Taylor, *Constable*, pp. 13, 16–17.

54. *Correspondence*, 2:78.

55. Ibid.

56. Ibid., 2:67.

57. Ibid., 2:132.

58. Both paintings depict nearly the same panorama as that sketched by Constable in 1814 in a drawing entitled *Golding Constable's Gardens*, which is in the Victoria and Albert Museum (see Reynolds, *Catalogue*, R176). Michael Rosenthal securely dates the two paintings 1815 ("Golding Constable's Gardens," *Connoisseur* 187 [October 1974]: 89–91).

59. A number of these Flatford sketches date from 1810–1811. Three of them exhibited at the Tate in 1976 (catalogue numbers 94, 95, 96) relate to Constable's Royal Academy exhibition piece of 1812, *A Water-Mill: Flatford Mill, Suffolk* (Plate 4). This work was recently rediscovered by Charles Rhyne and is now in the Corcoran Gallery of Art in Washington, D.C.

60. *Correspondence*, 2:80.

61. Ibid., 2:54.

62. Ibid., 2:203.

63. Ibid.

64. Ibid., 1:12.

65. Ibid., 2:5.

66. These sketches are all in the Victoria and Albert Museum.

67. John Thomas Smith, *Remarks on Rural Scenery* (London, 1797), p. 5.

68. Ibid., p. 7.

69. Ibid., p. 8.

70. Ibid., p. 10.

71. Ibid., pp. 7–8.

72. Constable's class prejudices emerge sharply in the 1825 journal he kept for Maria. Responding to an event involving the Brighton mechanics' support of the oppressed wool combers and weavers of Bradford, he wrote: "Almost every mechanick, wether master or man, is a rebel and a blackguard—dissatisfied, in proportion to his abilities. He is only kept respectable by being kept in solitude and worked for himself

. . . but directly he is *congregated* with his brethren his evil dispositions are fanned. . . .
Remember that I know these people well—having seen so many of them at my father's"
(*Correspondence*, 2:403). One traces similar sentiments in his mother's disdain for poachers
(ibid., 1:68–70) and his brother Abram's for beggars (ibid., 1:190). These remarks suggest that the family attitude was orthodox in distinguishing these types from the respectable (i.e., working and submissive) poor (see also ibid., 1:160, 249, 267).

73. Along with Figure 48, this sketch is one of two dozen early drawings by
Constable contained in a portfolio left by his sister Mary to her nephew Daniel Whalley
in 1865. The portfolio is now in a private collection. See Parris, Fleming-Williams, and
Shields, *Constable*, p. 40.

74. *Correspondence*, 2:16.

75. This drawing is dated on the verso "23ᵈ Sept. 1799."

76. J. Grieg, ed., *The Farington Diary*, 8 vols. (London, 1920), 1:229. Hereafter
cited as *Farington Diary*.

77. *Correspondence*, 2:11–13, 36–37.

78. This drawing is also from the Whalley portfolio (see n. 73). It is attributed
by Ian Fleming-Williams to 1799 (*Constable: Landscape Drawings*, p. 17). The Gainsborough drawing is from the late 1740s and is now in the Courtauld Institute of Art (Witt
Collection). It has been catalogued by John Hayes in *The Drawings of Thomas Gainsborough*, 2 vols. (New Haven, Conn., and London, 1970), pp. 132–33. The drawing was
in the collection of George Frost, where it is likely Constable saw it.

79. The confusion stems mainly from Sir Charles Holmes's book *Constable, Gainsborough, and Lucas* (London, 1921), in which a large number of Frost drawings were
attributed to Constable. An exhibition in 1961 at the Huntington Art Gallery, compiled
by Robert R. Wark and entitled "John Constable's Drawings and Sketches," presented a
number of Constable's own drawings in the Frost-Gainsborough style, which in turn led
John Hayes ("The Drawings of George Frost," *Master Drawings* 4, no. 2 [1966]: 163–
68) to reattribute to Frost many of the drawings that Holmes thought were by Constable.
Hayes concluded from the Huntington drawings that Constable was indeed influenced—
via Frost—by Gainsborough's technique (see *Drawings*, pp. 74–76). An exhibition organized by Michael Rosenthal in 1974 at Gainsborough's house, Sudbury, helped further
clarify the attribution problems. The most complete account of the Frost/Constable confusion is given by Ian Fleming-Williams and Leslie Parris in *The Discovery of Constable*
(London, 1984), pp. 159–77, where close stylistic analysis of both artists' work sheds
light on the significant differences between them.

80. This is the date attributed to the work by Fleming-Williams and Parris on
the basis of stylistic analysis (*Discovery*, pp. 174–75).

81. In March 1801 Constable complained to Farington that Ramsey Reinagle and
other students at the Royal Academy "only look to the surface and not to the mind. The
mechanism of painting is their delight. Execution is their chief aim" (*Farington Diary*,
1:303). A similar criticism is contained in a letter to John Dunthorne (*Correspondence*,
2:26). Constable's criticism of his fellow students echoes the condemnation in Joshua

Reynolds's first Discourse of students who "make the mechanical felicity, the chief excellence of the art" (*Discourses on Art*, ed. Robert Wark [London, 1969], p. 22).

82. *Farington Diary*, 1:309.

83. *Correspondence*, 2:31–32.

84. I use the term "natural painture," as I believe Constable meant it, to refer to a style of painting. Relying on Andrew Shirley's transcription of the 1802 letter in which the phrase appears, Graham Reynolds believed it to mean "natural painter." Beckett's subsequent transcription suggests that this reading is erroneous (cf. Reynolds, *Catalogue*, p. 48, and *Correspondence*, 2:31–32). The actual 1802 letter has been lost.

85. *Correspondence*, 2:24.

86. The quotations are from the second Discourse (Reynolds, *Discourses*, p. 30). Constable's letter refers to the twelfth Discourse, in which Reynolds, speaking of François Boucher, condemns short cuts to "the art of seeing nature." Parts of the sixth Discourse also pertain to Constable's program as outlined to Dunthorne.

87. *Farington Diary*, 1:432.

88. *Correspondence*, 2:18; 6:66, 78, 157, 258. See also *John Constable's Discourses*, ed. R. B. Beckett (Ipswich, Suffolk, 1970), pp. 39, 57, 58, 68, 69, 72.

89. This is one of several small oil sketches from that year that are now in the Victoria and Albert Museum. The view is from Gun Hill, Dedham. In his edition of Leslie's life of Constable, Andrew Shirley was the first to point out Constable's use of the *Hagar* for this work.

90. Rosenthal (*Constable*, pp. 34–35, 140–53) suggests that the importance of Claude for Constable is both formal and ideological: formal in that Claude provided the young Constable with pictorial structures to use in representing local scenes and ideological in that such structures were popularly imbued with associations with the Golden Age that Constable attached to the Stour Valley. Hence, Rosenthal argues, when in the 1820s Constable experienced an estrangement from the landscape of his youth, the old Claudian formulas gave way and his compositions changed dramatically. I confess I do not see such a radical shift in the compositions of the 1820s. Rather, I feel that the compositional structures for paintings like *View on the Stour* (R.A. 1822) are already in place as early as 1810–1811 and represent Constable's own variations on Claudian motifs. In particular, the oil sketches of Flatford Mill from the lock seem to echo Claude's *Flight into Egypt* (no. 110 in the *Liber Veritatis*) and show Constable's early tendency to lower the viewer's vantage point and to compress the foreground.

91. The similarity between these two works was noted by Parris, Fleming-Williams, and Shields, *Constable*, p. 50.

92. For an insightful analysis of how such naturalism is a precondition for a romantic approach to landscape, see Karl Kroeber, *Romantic Landscape Vision: Constable and Wordsworth* (Madison, Wis., 1975).

93. For Reynolds, the realistic study of an object was a necessary but insufficient condition of artistic achievement, which must proceed to idealize, or improve upon, its object. For William Gilpin, the realistic study was constitutive of the finished work,

with idealizations confined to inessential features that made the study a scene. In discussing composition, he wrote: "Liberties . . . with truth must be taken with caution: tho at the same time a distinction may be made between an object and a scene. If I give the striking features of the *castle*, or *abby*, which is my *object*, I may be allowed some little liberty in bringing my appendages (which are not essential features) within the rules of art" ("On Sketching Landscape," in *Three Essays: On Picturesque Beauty, On Picturesque Travel, and On Sketching Landscape* (London, 1803), pp. 167–68). Gilpin's combination of the study of the object with the artistry of the scene is close to Constable's practice in the 1802 oil sketches. While Constable quoted Reynolds and no doubt intended to treat the landscapes as mere studies, his actual practice was to combine—à la Gilpin—the study and the scene.

94. This sketch is inscribed "Oct.ʳ 13. 1809. E. B."

95. Leslie, p. 18.

96. *Correspondence*, 6:77.

97. This work is inscribed "John Constable pinxt. 1811" and "DEDHAM VALE." Four oil sketches and a pen and wash drawing in the Philadelphia Museum of Art along with Figure 53 appear to have led to the final painting. See Parris, Fleming-Williams, and Shields, *Constable*, p. 76. Since writing this, I have discovered that my analysis of Constable's compositions has affinities with Karl Kroeber's treatment of them. He has likened these charged spots to Wordsworth's "spots of time" that by their organization suggest a temporal coherence between the momentary and the eternal (*Romantic Landscape Vision*, pp. 3–28). Hugh Honour summarizes Kroeber's analysis in his discussion of Constable in *Romanticism* (New York, 1979), pp. 87–89. Neither links the innumerable parts of Constable's compositions to the mulitiplication of the picturesque vignette, nor does either note the role the horizon plays in imposing a unity suggestive of divine order.

98. As in an oil sketch of 1802, Lott's cottage is seen from the south bank of the Stour. Both these works form the germ of Constable's numerous oil and watercolor sketches of the Valley Farm, which climaxed in his monumental painting of it exhibited at the Royal Academy in 1835.

99. For example, among the works already referred to are the family windmill in the center of the Downing College view (Figure 38) and Dedham Church spire in the middle distance of the 1802 *Dedham Vale* (Plate 3). In the 1809 sketch *Man Resting in a Lane* (Figure 53), the center of the composition is occupied by the figure, and in *Dedham Vale: Morning* (Figure 54), in the Proby collection, it is occupied by a herd of cows and a cowman. Similarly, in the Flatford sketches (Figures 56–60) twin poplar trees close off a central perspective; and in the 1815 depictions of the family gardens, a barn marks the center of one view (Figure 39) and the rectory of Dr. Rhudde the center of the other (Figure 40).

100. John Constable, *Various Subjects of Landscape Characteristic of English Scenery from Pictures Painted by John Constable, R.A.* (London, 1830), plate 1.

101. Leslie, p. 285.

102. In addition to the Downing College view, the 1814 pencil sketch of the same view, and the two oil pendants of 1815 showing Golding's gardens, there are a number of pencil sketches of the house and its grounds in the small 1813 and 1814 sketchbooks, which have been catalogued and illustrated by Graham Reynolds (*Catalogue*, pp. 81–89, 96–103) and which have also been published in a facsimile edition with an introduction by Reynolds (*John Constable's Sketchbooks of 1813 and 1814* [London, 1973]).

103. Unfortunately, Professor Rhyne's important work on Constable has not been published. It was presented by him in a lecture entitled "Constable's Views of the East Bergholt Common," delivered at the College Art Association meeting in Washington, D.C., in January 1970 and, in an expanded version, at the Tate Gallery and at Yale University in March and April of 1976. Similar observations have been made by Parris, Fleming-Williams, and Shields in the Tate bicentenary catalogue and summarized in Ronald Paulson, "Toward the Constable Bicentenary: Thoughts on Landscape Theory," *Eighteenth-Century Studies* 10, no. 2 (Winter 1976–77): 256–57; and in Michael Kitson, "The Inspiration of John Constable," *Royal Society of Arts Journal* 124, no. 5244 (November 1976): 738–53. Rhyne argues that the family house was the nexus of all associations for Constable, the basis on which he developed "an iconography of the place." He claims that Constable's representation in the early teens was so exact that we can accurately judge the respective distances and relative heights of objects in the landscape. He also proposes that Constable used a framed piece of glass to study landscape at this time, the windows of the house being similar apparatuses.

104. Rosenthal, *Constable*, pp. 210–11.

105. Thicknesse, *A Sketch of the Life and Paintings of Thomas Gainsborough, Esq.* (London, 1788), pp. 5–6 (see also nn. 14 and 15, chap. 2).

106. *Correspondence*, 6:80.

107. This has already been noted in relation to *Dedham Vale: Morning* (see n. 99).

108. Leslie, p. 288.

109. I do not wish to oversimplify either the complex role of the oil sketch in art history or its (perhaps) even more complex role in Constable's oeuvre. Constable's oil sketching originated in eighteenth-century traditions of *plein air* painting, but he soon shaped that practice to personal ends. A sense of how his work differs from that of his predecessors and contemporaries can be grasped by comparing his sketches with the oil sketches shown in two exhibitions, the Norwich Castle Museum's Decade of English Naturalism, 1810–1820 (1969–1970) and the Arts Council of Great Britain's Painting from Nature: The Tradition of Open-Air Oil Sketching from the Seventeenth to the Nineteenth Centuries (1980–1981). See also Philip Conisbee, "Pre-Romantic *Plein-Air* Painting," *Art History* 2 (December 1979): 413–28; and Paula Rea Radisich, "Eighteenth-Century Plain-Air Painting and the Sketches of Pierre Henri de Valenciennes," *Art Bulletin* 64 (March 1982): 98–104.

110. A pioneering study of the oil sketch and its relation to the Academic traditions of the seventeenth and eighteenth centuries is Rudolf Wittkower's catalogue *Masters of*

the Loaded Brush: Oil Sketches from Rubens to Tiepolo (New York, 1967). For a thorough analysis of nineteenth-century academic oil sketch practices, see Albert Boime, *Academy and French Painting in the Nineteenth Century* (New York, 1971). A symposium in conjunction with an exhibition of oil sketches in Braunschweig (March 1984), entitled "Malerei aus erster Hand: Ölskizzen von Tintoretto bis Goya," provided a comprehensive overview of the oil sketch. An important paper from that symposium (in press), Linda Bauer, "Some Early Views and Uses of the Painted Sketch," details the earliest uses of oil sketches from life.

111. One might add to this collection of sketches a fragmentary view of Flatford Mill painted on the verso of a figure study that was auctioned at the Phillips Gallery, London, in December 1984. I am grateful to Ian Fleming-Williams for alerting me to the existence of this work. There is also a drawing in a private collection in England that shows this view. See Robert Hoozee, *L'opera completa di Constable* (Milan, 1979), no. 115.

112. Ian Fleming-Williams, "John Constable at Flatford," *Connoisseur* 204 (July 1980): 216–19.

113. Charles Rhyne has pointed out to me that the pentimenti over the roofs of the mill in the exhibition work are similar to those in Figure 59.

114. *Correspondence*, 2:54.

115. Kroeber, p. 18. My own interpretation of these sketches owes much to Kroeber's suggestive analysis.

116. *The Prelude*, book 2, lines 314–17.

117. On this subject, see Louis Althusser, "Contradiction and Overdetermination," in *For Marx*, trans. Ben Brewster (London, 1969), pp. 191–203.

118. *Correspondence*, 3:116.

119. Ibid., 6:157.

120. Ibid., 6:18.

121. Ibid., 6:71.

122. For an accurate topographical view of East Bergholt as it looked in Constable's day, see the map of the East Bergholt Enclosure Award in the Suffolk Record Office, County Hall, Ipswich, reference number B150/1/4 (2a).

123. Reynolds, *Natural Painter*, p. 65.

124. *Correspondence*, 1:184.

125. Ibid., 1:249.

126. *The White Horse,* the first of the six-foot landscapes, was exhibited at the Royal Academy in 1819 under the title "A Scene on the River Stour"; it is now in the Frick Collection in New York City. *The Hay Wain*, exhibited at the Academy in 1821 as "Landscape: Noon," is now in the National Gallery, London. *View on the Stour, near Dedham*, exhibited at the Academy in 1822, is now in the Huntington Art Gallery, San Marino, California. The first version of *A Boat Passing a Lock*, a vertical composition, was exhibited at the Academy in 1824; it is owned by the Trustees of the Walter Morrison Pictures Settlement. The second version, a horizontal composition, exhibited at the

British Institution in 1829, is in the Royal Academy of Arts, as is *The Leaping Horse*, exhibited at the Academy in 1825 as "Landscape." *Stratford Mill*, exhibited at the Academy in 1820 as "Landscape," is privately owned. Because of its subject matter, *Stratford Mill* was known after Constable's death as "The Young Waltonians" after Izaak Walton's *The Compleat Angler.*

127. Barrell, *Dark Side of the Landscape*, pp. 134-35, 137, 157.

128. Ibid., p. 149.

129. In addition to the numerous small oil sketches Constable made throughout his lifetime, one also thinks of the full-size sketches he painted for all his large exhibition pieces. Two of the best known are the sketches for *The Hay Wain* and *The Leaping Horse* in the Victoria and Albert Museum. Constable never exhibited these sketches and their existence was not generally known during his lifetime. They first became public at the sale of Constable's effects on May 16, 1838 (see Parris and Fleming-Williams, *Discovery*, pp. 17-19).

130. *Correspondence*, 6:63.

131. Ibid., 6:157.

132. Ibid., 3:87.

133. Leslie, p. 198. As a staunch Tory, Constable was opposed to Whig policies and in particular to the Reform Bill introduced by Lord John Russell in March 1831. In October of that year Leslie urged Constable to stop harassing himself "with useless apprehensions of the future." Constable replied, "No Whigg government ever did or can do good to *this* peculiar country—they are always the blocks as well as the wiggs—and always when in power, are our worst stumbling blocks" (*Correspondence*, 3:48-49).

134. *Correspondence*, 6:180.

135. Ibid., 6:181.

136. Rosenthal, *Constable*, p. 166.

137. Another pastiche from this period that takes similar liberties with the actual site is *A Cottage at East Bergholt* (1836) in the Lady Leaver Art Gallery, Port Sunlight, England. See Graham Reynolds, *The Later Paintings and Drawings of John Constable*, 2 vols. (New Haven, Conn., 1984), 1, figure 36:20, pp. 292-93.

138. Reynolds has also noted the transplanting of this windmill from Brighton to Hampstead (*Later Paintings*, 1, figure 36:7, pp. 288-89).

139. Parris, Fleming-Williams, and Shields, *Constable*, p. 188.

140. For Constable's various explanations of the term "Chiar'oscuro of Nature" in his discourses and in *English Landscape Scenery*, see *John Constable's Discourses*, pp. 5, 9, 11, 40, 46, 62, 63, 71.

141. Constable exhibited this painting at the Royal Academy in 1828 as "Landscape." Not only have the details of the landscape changed from the 1802 version, but Constable has also added a gypsy woman in the foreground.

142. Paulson (*Literary Landscape*, p. 152) likens this process to Freudian "symbolization" and notes that Constable used it in the late works to repress personal content with a more public meaning.

143. *Correspondence*, 4:382.

144. The numerous studies of cottages Constable did roughly between 1832 and 1836 are apropos the subject of ruins in his late works. No longer the neat and snug examples found in the earlier works, these cottages have become picturesque in a way that almost recalls Smith's work.

145. This painting, referred to by Fisher as "Church under a Cloud," was one of Constable's most controversial landscapes. The *Times* called it "a very vigorous and masterly landscape, which somebody has spoiled since it was painted, by putting in such clouds as no human being ever saw, and by spotting the foreground all over with whitewash" (cited in Taylor, *Constable*, p. 212).

146. *John Constable's Discourses*, pp. 9–10.

147. *Correspondence*, 4:258.

148. *John Constable's Discourses*, p. 10.

149. Ibid., p. 21.

150. The series consisted of twenty-two mezzotints that appeared from June 1830 to July 1832 in four issues of four prints each and a fifth issue of six prints. British Museum Publications, Ltd., has recently reproduced these prints, with an introduction and notes by Andrew Wilton, under the title *Constable's "English Landscape Scenery"* (London, 1979).

151. *John Constable's Discourses*, p. 69.

152. E. P. Thompson, *English Working Class*, pp. 441–56. Thompson sees the influence of Methodism in England as the primary force in mediating the "work-discipline" of industrial capitalism. See also his "Time, Work-Discipline, and Industrial Capitalism," *Past and Present* 38 (December 1967): 56–97. Michel Foucault, in *Discipline and Punish: The Birth of the Prison*, trans. Alan Sheridan (London, 1977), studies the development of modern forms of surveillance and discipline through an analysis of their political, social, and ideological apparatuses.

CHAPTER FOUR

1. *Cornhill Magazine* 11 (London, 1865): 291.

2. H. M. Cundall, *A History of British Watercolour Painting* (New York, 1908), p. 93.

3. William Cobbett, *Rural Rides* (Harmondsworth, Middlesex, 1977), p. 91.

4. E. W. Boville, *English Country Life* (London, 1962), p. 118; and F. M. L. Thompson, *English Landed Society in the Nineteenth Century* (London and Toronto, 1963), pp. 238–91.

5. United Kingdom, *Report from His Majesty's Commissioners on the Administration and Practical Operation of the Poor Laws*, Irish University Press Series of British Parliamentary Papers, vols. 9–19 (Shannon, 1970).

6. *Poor Laws*, British Parliamentary Papers, 8:48.

7. David Elliston Allen, *The Naturalist in Britain: A Social History* (Harmondsworth, Middlesex, 1978), pp. 158–75.

8. Raymond Williams, *The Country and the City* (New York, 1973), pp. 165–81.

9. *Poor Laws*, British Parliamentary Papers, 8:4.

10. William Howitt, *Rural Life in England*, 2 vols. (London, 1838), 1:158.

11. Quoted in Howitt, 1:163–64. The passage referred to by Howitt is book 8 ("The Parsonage"), lines 415–31. I am grateful to Robert Folkenflik for this reference.

12. Cobbett, p. 75.

13. Howitt, 1:25.

14. Allen, p. 124.

15. *John Constable's Correspondence*, ed. R. B. Beckett and (for vol. 7) Leslie Parris, Conal Shields, and Ian Fleming-Williams, 7 vols. (Ipswich, Suffolk, 1962–1975), 6:81.

16. Lewis Mumford has noted that throughout history concern for health has been one of the prime motivations for moving from urban centers to the suburbs (*The City in History: Its Origins, Its Transformations, and Its Prospects* [New York, 1961], pp. 488, 494). By the nineteenth century, this reason alone does not account for the enormous growth and popularity of the suburbs. See F. M. L. Thompson, ed., *The Rise of Suburbia* (Leicester, 1982). For a history of Hampstead, see F. M. L. Thompson, *Hampstead: Building a Borough, 1650–1964* (London, 1974).

17. William Hazlitt, *The Plain Speaker* (London and New York, 1905), p. 76.

18. For an account of the speculative builders and developers of Victorian London, see *Exploring the Urban Past: Essays in Urban History by H. J. Dyos*, ed. David Cannadine and David Reeder (Cambridge, Eng., 1982), pp. 154–89.

19. Donald J. Olsen, *The Growth of Victorian London* (New York, 1976), pp. 204–9.

20. For analyses of suburban nostalgia for country and village life, see Walter L. Creese, "Imagination in the Suburb," in *Nature and the Victorian Imagination*, ed. U. C. Knoepflmacher and G. B. Tennyson (Berkeley and Los Angeles, 1977), pp. 49–67; and N. Taylor, *The Village in the City* (London, 1973).

21. Arts Council of Great Britain, *The Idea of the Village* (London, 1976), and F. M. L. Thompson, *The Rise of Suburbia*, p. 15.

22. Arts Council, *Idea of the Village*, pp. 4–8.

23. F. M. L. Thompson, *The Rise of Suburbia*, p. 16.

24. J. M. Richards, in his *Castles on the Ground: The Anatomy of Suburbia* (London, 1973), gives some amusing instances of this phenomenon.

25. John Claudius Loudon, *The Landscape Gardening and Landscape Architecture of the Late Humphry Repton, Esq.* (1840; reprint, London, 1969), pp. viii–ix.

26. Humphry Repton, *An Enquiry into the Changes of Taste in Landscape Gardening* (London, 1806), part 1, pp. 1–42.

27. Loudon, *Humphry Repton*, pp. vii–viii.

28. Ibid., p. viii.

29. Ibid., p. ix.

30. John Claudius Loudon, *The Suburban Gardener and Villa Companion* (London, 1838), p. 8.

31. Arts Council, *Idea of the Village*, pp. 18–23. For an account of Birkenhead, see Creese, in Knoepflmacher and Tennyson, pp. 58–60.

32. For an account of the planning and development of Central Park, see Frederick Law Olmsted, *Public Parks and the Enlargement of Towns* (1870; reprint, New York, 1970), which argues for the positive effect of parkland on the life of city inhabitants. Much of Olmsted's philosophy about the social importance of providing people with pleasurable environments derives from the ideas of Jeremy Bentham.

33. The most significant embodiment of this idea can be found in the writings of the late Victorian city planner Ebenezer Howard, founder of the garden city movement. See his *Tomorrow: A Peaceful Path to Real Reform* (London, 1898). Howard's model of the garden city was a central park ringed by a city that in turn was surrounded by open farmland. Howard's ideas derived from earlier experiments for overseas colonies designed by Granville Sharp (1794) and Edward Gibbon Wakefield (1829), as well as from James Silk Buckingham's proposals for home colonization to resettle poverty-stricken workers in industrial/agricultural villages (1848). These utopian plans were given a more practical turn and application by Howard, whose work set the foundation for the post–World War II new town movement. See Frederic J. Osborn and Arnold Whettick, *The New Towns: The Answer to Megalopolis*, rev. ed. (Cambridge, Mass., 1969), pp. 34–36.

34. The phrase "town pilgrim of nature" is Wilkie Collins's in his novel of 1854 *Hide and Seek* (New York, 1981), p. 16.

35. Kurt Badt believes that Constable's studies of clouds were influenced by Luke Howard's scientific classification of clouds (*John Constable's Clouds* [London, 1950]). Louis Hawes has challenged this belief in "Constable's Sky Sketches," *Journal of the Warburg and Courtauld Institutes* 32 (1969): 351–58. Most recently John Thornes, on the evidence of the published contents of Constable's library, has attempted to set out a complete account of Constable's meteorological understanding. See his "Constable's Clouds," *Burlington Magazine* 121 (November 1979): 697–99.

36. Charles R. Leslie, *Memoirs of the Life of John Constable*, ed. Jonathan Mayne (London, 1951), p. 72.

37. *Ruskin: Rossetti: Pre-Raphaelitism: Papers, 1854 to 1862*, ed. William Michael Rossetti (London, 1899), pp. 38–39.

38. Ford Madox Brown, *The Exhibition of Work and Other Paintings by Ford Madox Brown at the Gallery, 191 Piccadilly*, exhibition catalogue (London, 1865), pp. 7–8.

39. *The Works of John Ruskin*, ed. E. T. Cook and Alexander Wedderburn, 36 vols. (London, 1903), 35:47.

40. John Ruskin, *Modern Painters*, 5 vols. (New York, 1910), "On Ideas of Truth," 1:20–23, and "The Moral Landscape," 3:267–93.

41. Ibid., "Definition of Greatness in Art," 1:11.

42. Ibid., "The Mountain Gloom," 4:309–34, and "The Mountain Glory," 4:335–74.

43. Ibid., "Of Truth of Vegetation," 2:113–36, and "Of Truth of Clouds," 1:205–53.

44. Ibid., "Of Turnerian Topography," 4:17–18.

45. Ibid., "Peace," 5:325–39.

46. Quoted in Raymond Williams, *Culture and Society, 1780–1950* (Harmondsworth, Middlesex, 1968), p. 151.

47. William Michael Rossetti, ed., *Pre-Raphaelite Diaries and Letters* (London, 1900), pp. 188–89.

48. Ibid., p. 131.

49. Ibid., p. 113.

50. Brown, p. 2.

51. Allen Staley, *The Pre-Raphaelite Landscape* (Oxford, 1973), p. 41.

52. Allen, pp. 135–36.

53. See Trevor Levere, "The Rich Economy of Nature: Chemistry in the Nineteenth Century," in Knoepflmacher and Tennyson, pp. 189–200; Philip F. Rehbock, *The Philosophical Naturalists: Themes in Early Nineteenth-Century British Biology* (Madison, Wis., 1983); and Harold I. Sharlin, *The Convergent Century: The Unification of Science in the Nineteenth Century* (London, 1966).

54. William B. Carpenter, "The Argument from Design in the Organic World, Reconsidered in Its Relation to the Doctrines of Evolution and Natural Selection," *Nature and Man: Essays Scientific and Philosophical* (London, 1888), p. 452.

55. Ruskin's own idealistic attitude toward nature is best represented in the five volumes of *Modern Painters*. With impressive insight, Fredrick Kirchoff has argued that Ruskin's approach to the scientific knowledge of his day was highly ambivalent, and hence rather than stress the intellectual dominance of Nature "he must present a way of knowing Nature that implies its opposite: the final elusiveness of all natural phenomena" ("A Science against Sciences: Ruskin's Floral Mythology," in Knoepflmacher and Tennyson, pp. 246–58). Ruskin's desire in the end to preserve Nature's mystery is closely tied to his attitudes toward appearances and his obsessive need to record them. "There is a strong instinct in me," he wrote to his father, "which I cannot analyze—to draw and describe the things I love . . . a sort of instinct like that for eating or drinking" (John Rosenberg, ed., *The Genius of John Ruskin* [New York, 1963], p. 12). The sense of the uncanny that Ruskin located in this *unanalyzable* instinct to "draw and describe the things [he] love[d]" can be interpreted as a desire to preserve the mystery of his own body and its needs. In describing physical appearances, Ruskin continually deferred their meanings and thus confirmed their ultimate unknowability.

56. Charles Dickens, *Dombey and Son* (Harmondsworth, Middlesex, 1970), p. 759.

57. Ibid., and Alfred, Lord Tennyson, *In Memoriam A. H. H.* (London, 1850), part

56, line 15. For a complete study of the effect of Darwinism on Victorian culture, see J. W. Burrow, *Evolution and Society: A Study in Victorian Social Theory* (Cambridge, Eng., 1966).

58. For a substantial modern assessment of Mulready's work, see Kathryn Moore Heleniak, *William Mulready* (New Haven, Conn., 1980).

59. Hughes's *Long Engagement* is in the City Museum and Art Gallery, Birmingham. Hunt's *Hireling Shepherd* is in the City Art Gallery, Manchester. For recent studies of meaning in Victorian paintings, see Susan P. Casteras, "Down the Garden Path: Courtship Culture and Its Imagery in Victorian Painting" (Ph.D. diss., Yale University, 1977), as well as her exhibition catalogue for the Yale Center for British Art, *The Substance or the Shadow: Images of Victorian Womanhood* (New Haven, Conn., 1982); John Dixon Hunt, *The Pre-Raphaelite Imagination, 1848–1900* (Lincoln, Nebr., 1968); George Landow, *William Holman Hunt and Typological Symbolism* (New Haven, Conn., 1979); Jeremy Maas, *Holman Hunt and the Light of the World* (London, 1984); and Leslie Parris, ed., *Pre-Raphaelite Papers* (London, 1984).

60. Staley, pp. 126–27.

61. For a discussion of social realism in Victorian genre paintings, see Casteras, "Down the Garden Path." Studies of the theme of the seamstress include Deborah Cherry, "Surveying Seamstresses," *Feminist Art News* 9 (1983): 37–49, and T. J. Edelstein, "'The Song of the Shirt': The Visual Iconology of the Seamstress," *Victorian Studies* 23 (Winter 1980): 183–210. *The Awakening Conscience* is in the Tate Gallery, London, and Redgrave's *The Seamstress* is in the Forbes Magazine Collection. The plight of the seamstresses was treated in Ralph Barnes Grindrod's thorough and influential exposé *Slaves of the Needle* (1844). Prostitution was often a theme of the Victorian artistic imagination. Dante Gabriel Rossetti's *Found* (1854–1882), based on his earlier poem *Jenny*, deals openly with the subject, as does George Frederic Watt's *Found Drowned* (1848). Sociological studies like Mayhew, *London Labour and London Poor*; William Acton, *Prostitution, Considered in Its Moral, Social, and Sanitary Aspects* (London, 1870); and Joseph Adshead, *Distress in Manchester* (London, 1842), connect prostitution with the social changes brought about by industrialism. Both Adshead's and Grindrod's pamphlets are reprinted in *British Labour Struggles: Contemporary Pamphlets, 1727–1850*, ed. Kenneth E. Carpenter (New York, 1972).

62. Sidney Webb and Beatrice Webb, in *The Story of the King's Highway* (Hamden, Conn., 1963), pp. 165–237, give one of the most complete accounts of stonebreaking and its connection to both the maintenance of the roads and the poor laws. Because stonebreaking was not a profession, it did not appear in the governmental censuses, nor is it mentioned in Henry Mayhew, *London Labour and London Poor*, 4 vols. (London, 1861). Friedrich Engels, in his *Condition of the Working-Class in England*, mentioned the case of a seventy-year-old man attached to a workhouse refusing to break stones (*Karl Marx, Friedrich Engels: Collected Works, 1844–1845*, trans. Florence Kelley-Wischnewetzky [London, New York, and Moscow, 1976], 4:576). The 1859 *Report from the Select*

Committee on the Irremovable Poor mentions stonebreaking as a form of outdoor relief and quotes an interview with George Canning from the office of the Liverpool vestry clerk that reveals the amount of work stonebreakers did and their wages.

Committee:	"You give him an order to break stones at so much per day?"
Canning:	"At so much per tub, which is somewhere about a ton. . . ."
Committee:	"What would he gain by that?"
Canning:	"Married men are allowed to earn a shilling a day at the stone-yard, a single man 10d."

Report from the Select Committee on the Irremovable Poor, United Kingdom, Irish University Press Series of British Parliamentary Papers (Shannon, 1967), 23:619.

63. Reported in Mayhew, *London Labour and London Poor*, 3:319–21. Also see Webb and Webb, pp. 192–213.

64. Webb and Webb, pp. 198–99, 233–34.

65. Ibid., pp. 210–23.

66. A good account of Walker's *Costumes of Yorkshire* is given by F. D. Klingender, *Art and the Industrial Revolution* (New York, 1968), pp. 110–11.

67. T. J. Clark mentions that the subject of stonebreaking in France was treated by many painters; he cites as an example a painting by Adolphe Leleux that appeared in the Salon of 1849, a year before Courbet's great work (*Image of the People: Gustave Courbet and the Second French Republic, 1848–1851* [Greenwich, Conn., 1973], p. 79).

68. No incident or public discussion seems to have inspired the coincidental painting by Brett and Wallis of stonebreakers in 1858. No reports about stonebreaking appear in the parliamentary debates, the *London Times*, or the *London Illustrated News* for the years 1850–1857. It is possible that Brett and Wallis meant their works as counterstatements to Madox Brown's more muscularly optimistic *Work*. Because Brett and Wallis show the men forgotten in Brown's (and society's) celebration of hard work, the sentiments their works express are closer to Ruskin's than to Brown's.

69. The quotation accompanying the painting was: "Hardly entreated, brother! For us was thy back so bent, for us were thy straight limbs and fingers so deformed; thou wert our conscript, on whom the lot fell, and fighting our battles wert so marred. For in thee too lay a god-created form, but it stands with the thick adhesions and defacement of labor; and thy body, like thy soul was not to know freedom" (recorded in Algernon Graves, F.S.A., ed., *The Royal Academy of Arts: A Complete Dictionary of Contributors and Their Work from Its Foundation in 1769 to 1904*, 8 vols. [New York, 1972], 8:115).

70. In the merging of classes and occupations in Brown's *Work* is a similar image of social unity. Brown's account of the painting's meaning is given in his *Exhibition of Work*, p. 7.

SELECT BIBLIOGRAPHY

ART HISTORICAL WORKS

Antal, Frederick. *Classicism and Romanticism, with Other Studies in Art History*. New York, 1966.
Arts Council of Great Britain. *The Idea of the Village*. London, 1976.
————. *The Shock of Recognition: The Landscape of English Romanticism and the Dutch Seventeenth Century*. London, 1971.
Badt, Kurt. *John Constable's Clouds*. London, 1950.
Barrell, John. *The Dark Side of the Landscape: The Rural Poor in English Painting, 1730–1840*. Cambridge, Eng., 1980.
Baskett, John. *Constable Oil Sketches*. London, 1966.
Batey, Mavis. "Oliver Goldsmith: An Indictment of Landscape Gardening." In *Furor Hortensis: Essays on the History of the English Landscape Garden in Memory of P. H. Clark*, edited by Peter Willis. Edinburgh, 1974.
Bell, Quentin. *Victorian Artists*. London, 1967.
Berger, John. *Ways of Seeing*. Harmondsworth, Middlesex, 1972.
Binyon, Laurence. *English Watercolours*. New York, 1969.
Boase, T. R. S. *English Art, 1800–1870*. Oxford, 1959.
Boime, Albert. *The Academy and French Painting in the Nineteenth Century*. London and New York, 1971.
Brown, Ford Madox. *The Exhibition of Work and Other Paintings by Ford Madox Brown at the Gallery, 191 Piccadilly*. Exhibition catalogue. London, 1865.
Bryson, Norman. *Word and Image: French Painting of the Ancien Régime*. Cambridge, Eng., 1981.
Butlin, Martin, and Andrew Wilton. *Turner, 1775–1851*. London, 1974.

Casteras, Susan P. "Down the Garden Path: Courtship Culture and Its Imagery in Victorian Painting." Ph.D. diss., Yale University, 1977.

———. *The Substance or the Shadow: Images of Victorian Womanhood.* Exhibition catalogue for the Yale Center for British Art. New Haven, Conn., 1982.

Cherry, Deborah. "Surveying Seamstresses." *Feminist Art News* 9 (1983): 37–49.

Clark, Kenneth. *Landscape into Art.* 2d ed. New York, 1976.

———. "On the Painting of the English Landscape." *Proceedings of the British Academy* 21 (1935): 27–39.

Clark, T. J. *The Absolute Bourgeois: Art and Politics in France, 1848–1851.* Greenwich, Conn., 1973.

———. *Image of the People: Gustave Courbet and the Second French Republic, 1848–1851.* Greenwich, Conn., 1973.

Clifford, Derek. *A History of Garden Design.* New York, 1963.

Constable, Freda. *John Constable: A Biography, 1776–1837.* Lavenham, Suffolk, 1975.

Constable, John. *John Constable's Correspondence.* Edited by R. B. Beckett and (for vol. 7) Leslie Parris, Conal Shields, and Ian Fleming-Williams. 7 vols. Ipswich, Suffolk, 1962–1975.

———. *John Constable's Discourses.* Edited by R. B. Beckett. Ipswich, Suffolk, 1970.

———. *John Constable's Sketchbooks of 1813 and 1814.* Facsimile edition. Introduction by Graham Reynolds. London, 1973.

———. *Various Subjects of Landscape Characteristic of English Scenery from Pictures Painted by John Constable, R.A.* London, 1830.

Corri, Adrienne. "Gainsborough's Early Career: New Documents and Two Portraits." *Burlington Magazine* 125 (April 1983): 210–16.

Cummings, Frederick, and Allen Staley. *Romantic Art in Britain: Paintings and Drawings, 1760–1860.* Philadelphia, 1968.

Cundall, H. M. *A History of British Watercolour Painting.* New York, 1908.

Cunningham, Allen. *Lives of the Most Eminent British Painters.* London, 1893.

Day, Harold. *John Constable, R.A.: Drawings.* Eastbourne, East Sussex, 1975.

D'Oench, Ellen Gates. "Arthur Devis (1712–1787): Master of the Georgian Conversation Piece." Ph.D. diss., Yale University, 1979.

———. *The Conversation Piece: Arthur Devis and His Contemporaries.* Exhibition catalogue for the Yale Center for British Art. New Haven, Conn., 1980.

Edelstein, T. J. "'The Song of the Shirt': The Visual Iconology of the Seamstress." *Victorian Studies* 23 (Winter 1980): 183–210.

Eitner, Lorenz. "The Open Window and the Storm-Tossed Boat: An Essay in the Iconography of Romanticism." *Art Bulletin* 37 (1955): 281–90.

Fabricant, Carole. "Binding and Dressing Nature's Loose Tresses: The Ideology of Augustan Landscape Design." *Studies in Eighteenth-Century Culture* 8 (1979): 109–35.

Farington, Joseph. *The Farington Diary.* Edited by J. Grieg. 8 vols. London, 1920.

Fleming-Williams, Ian. "Constable Drawings: Some Unfamiliar Examples." *Burlington Magazine* 125 (1983): 219–20.

————. *Constable: Landscape Watercolours and Drawings*. London, 1976.

————. "John Constable at Flatford." *Connoisseur* 204 (1980): 216–19.

————. "A Runover Dungle and a Possible Date for 'Spring.'" *Burlington Magazine* 114 (1972): 386–93.

Fleming-Williams, Ian, and Leslie Parris. *The Discovery of Constable*. London, 1984.

Fried, Michael. *Absorption and Theatricality: Painting and Beholder in the Age of Diderot*. Berkeley and Los Angeles, 1980.

Fulcher, George William. *Life of Thomas Gainsborough, R.A.* London, 1856.

Gadney, Reg. *Constable and His World*. London, 1976.

Gage, John. *Color in Turner: Poetry and Truth*. New York, 1969.

Gainsborough, Thomas. *The Letters of Thomas Gainsborough*. Edited by Mary Woodall. London, 1961.

Galassi, Peter. *Before Photography: Painting and the Invention of Photography*. New York, 1981.

Gaunt, William. *The Great Century of British Painting*. London, 1972.

————. *The Restless Century*. London, 1972.

Gloag, John. *Victorian Comfort: A Social History of Design from 1830–1900*. London, 1961.

Gombrich, Ernst H. *Art and Illusion: A Study in the Psychology of Pictorial Representation*. 2d ed. Princeton, N.J., 1972.

————. *Meditations on a Hobby Horse and Other Essays in the Theory of Art*. London and New York, 1963.

————. *Norm and Form*. London, 1966.

Gowing, Lawrence. *Constable, 1776–1837*. London, 1960.

————. *Turner: Imagination and Reality*. New York, 1966.

Graves, Algernon, F.S.A., ed. *The Royal Academy of Arts: A Complete Dictionary of Contributors and Their Work from Its Foundation in 1769 to 1904*. 8 vols. New York, 1972.

Grigson, Geoffrey. *Britain Observed: The Landscape through Artists' Eyes*. London, 1975.

————. *Samuel Palmer: The Visionary Years*. London, 1947.

Hadfield, Miles. *Gardening in Britain*. London, 1960.

Hardie, Martin. *Watercolour Painting in Britain*. 3 vols. London, 1966–1968.

Harris, John, ed. *The Garden: A Celebration of One Thousand Years of British Gardening*. London, 1979.

Harris, Richard. *Traditional Farm Buildings*. London, n.d.

Hawes, Louis. "Constable's Sky Sketches." *Journal of the Warburg and Courtauld Institutes* 32 (1969): 351–58.

————. *Constable's Stonehenge*. London, 1975.

————. *Presences of Nature: British Landscape, 1780–1830*. New Haven, Conn., 1982.

Hayes, John. "The Drawings of George Frost." *Master Drawings* 4, no. 2 (1966): 163–68.

————. *The Drawings of Thomas Gainsborough*. 2 vols. New Haven, Conn., and London, 1970.

————. *Gainsborough*. New York, 1975.

————. "Gainsborough's Later Landscapes." *Apollo* 95 (August 1964): 20–26.

————. *The Landscape Paintings of Thomas Gainsborough.* 2 vols. London, 1982.

Heleniak, Kathryn Moore. *William Mulready.* New Haven, Conn., 1980.

Herrmann, Luke. *British Landscape Painting of the Eighteenth Century.* London, 1973.

Hilton, Timothy. *The Pre-Raphaelites.* New York, 1970.

Holmes, Charles. *Constable, Gainsborough, and Lucas.* London, 1921.

Honour, Hugh. *Romanticism.* New York, 1979.

Hoozee, Robert. *L'opera completa di Constable.* Milan, 1979.

Hunt, John Dixon. *The Figure in the Landscape: Poetry, Painting, and Gardening during the Eighteenth Century.* Baltimore, 1976.

————. *The Pre-Raphaelite Imagination, 1848–1900.* Lincoln, Nebr., 1968.

Hunt, John Dixon, and Peter Willis, eds. *The Genius of the Place: The English Landscape Garden, 1620–1820.* New York, 1975.

Hunt, William Holman. *Pre-Raphaelitism and the Pre-Raphaelite Brotherhood.* 2 vols. London, 1905.

Hussey, Christopher. *English Gardens and Landscapes, 1700–1750.* London, 1967.

Ironside, Robin, and John Gere. *Pre-Raphaelite Painters.* London, 1948.

Key, Sydney. *Constable.* London, 1948.

Kitson, Michael. "The Inspiration of John Constable." *Royal Society of Arts Journal* 124, no. 5244 (November 1976): 738–53.

————. "John Constable, 1810–1816: A Chronological Study," *Journal of the Warburg and Courtauld Institutes* 20 (1965):338–57.

Klingender, F. D. *Art and the Industrial Revolution.* New York, 1968.

Kroeber, Karl. *Romantic Landscape Vision: Constable and Wordsworth.* Madison, Wis., 1975.

Kubler, George. *The Shape of Time: Remarks on the History of Things.* New Haven, Conn., 1973.

Landow, George. *William Holman Hunt and Typological Symbolism.* New Haven, Conn., 1979.

Lang, Suzi. "The Genesis of the Landscape Garden." In *The Picturesque Garden and Its Influence outside the British Isles,* edited by Nikolaus Pevsner. Washington, D.C., 1974.

Leslie, Charles R. *Memoirs of the Life of John Constable.* Edited by Jonathan Mayne. London, 1951.

Leslie, D. G. *The Inner Life of the Royal Academy.* London, 1914.

Loudon, John Claudius. *The Landscape Gardening and Landscape Architecture of the Late Humphry Repton, Esq.* 1840. Reprint. London, 1969.

Lucas, E. V. *John Constable the Painter.* London, 1924.

Maas, Jeremy. *Holman Hunt and the Light of the World.* London, 1984.

Mansbach, S. A. "An Earthwork of Surprise: The Eighteenth-Century Ha-Ha." *Art Journal* 42 (Fall 1982): 217–21.

Manwaring, Elizabeth Wheeler. *Italian Landscape in Eighteenth-Century England.* New York, 1925.

Nochlin, Linda. *Realism*. Harmondsworth, Middlesex, 1971.

Novotny, Fritz. *Painting and Sculpture in Europe, 1780–1880*. Harmondsworth, Middlesex, 1970.

Oliver, Paul. *English Cottages and Small Farmhouses*. London, 1975.

Parris, Leslie. "Some Recently Discovered Oil Sketches by John Constable." *Burlington Magazine* 125 (1983): 220–23.

———. *The Tate Gallery Constable Collection*. London, 1981.

———, ed. *Pre-Raphaelite Papers*. London, 1984.

Parris, Leslie, and Conal Shields. *Constable: The Art of Nature*. London, 1971.

———. *Landscape in Britain, c. 1750–1850*. Tate Gallery catalogue. London, 1973.

Parris, Leslie, Ian Fleming-Williams, and Conal Shields. *Constable: Paintings, Watercolours, and Drawings*. Tate Gallery catalogue. London, 1976.

Paulson, Ronald. *Emblem and Expression: Meaning in English Art of the Eighteenth Century*. Cambridge, Mass., 1975.

———. *Hogarth: His Life, Art, and Times*. Abridged by Ann Wilde. New Haven, Conn., and London, 1974.

———. *Literary Landscape: Turner and Constable*. New Haven, Conn., 1982.

———. "Toward the Constable Bicentenary: Thoughts on Landscape Theory." *Eighteenth-Century Studies* 10, no. 2 (Winter 1976–77): 256–57.

Pevsner, Nikolaus, ed. *The Picturesque Garden and Its Influence outside the British Isles*. Washington, D.C., 1974.

Phillipson, Barbara, and Phillis Cunnington. *Handbook of English Costume in the Eighteenth Century*. London, 1936.

Plymouth, Robert G. (Lord Windsor). *John Constable, R.A.* London, 1905.

Pointon, Marcia. "Gainsborough and the Landscape of Retirement." *Art History* (December 1979): 441–55.

Praz, Mario. *The Conversation Piece*. London, 1974.

Pyne, W. H. *Etchings of Rustic Figures for the Embellishment of Landscape*. London, 1814–1815.

Redgrave, Richard, and Samuel Redgrave. *A Century of Painters of the English School*. 2 vols. London, 1866.

Reynolds, Graham. *Catalogue of the Constable Collection in the Victoria and Albert Museum*. London, 1973.

———. *Constable: The Natural Painter*. London, 1965.

———. *The Later Paintings and Drawings of John Constable*. 2 vols. New Haven, Conn., 1984.

———. *Victorian Painting*. London, 1966.

Reynolds, Joshua. *Discourses on Art*. Edited by Robert Wark. London, 1969.

Rhyne, Charles. "Constable Drawings and Watercolours in the Collections of Mr. and Mrs. Paul Mellon and the Yale Center for British Art": part 1, "Authentic Works"; part 2, "Reattributed Works." *Master Drawings* 19 (Summer and Winter 1981): 123–45, 391–425.

———. "Fresh Light on John Constable." *Apollo* 87 (1968): 227–30.

Riely, John. "Shenstone's Walks: The Genesis of the Leasowes." *Apollo* 110 (September 1979): 202–9.

Rorschach, Kimerly. *The Early Georgian Landscape Garden.* Exhibition catalogue for the Yale Center for British Art. New Haven, Conn., 1983.

Rosenberg, John, ed. *The Genius of John Ruskin.* New York, 1963.

Rosenblum, Robert. *Modern Painting and the Northern Romantic Tradition: Friedrich to Rothko.* New York, 1975.

———. *Transformations in Late Eighteenth-Century Art.* Princeton, N.J., 1967.

Rosenthal, Michael. *British Landscape Painting.* Ithaca, N.Y., 1982.

———. *Constable: The Painter and His Landscape.* New Haven, Conn., 1983.

———. "Copies after Constable." *Burlington Magazine* 124 (1982): 629–33.

———. "Golding Constable's Gardens." *The Connoisseur* 187 (October 1974): 89–91.

Rossetti, William Michael, ed. *Pre-Raphaelite Diaries and Letters.* London, 1900.

———, ed. *Ruskin: Rossetti: Pre-Raphaelitism: Papers, 1854 to 1862.* London, 1899.

Rothenstein, John, and Martin Butlin. *Turner.* New York, 1964.

Ruskin, John. *Modern Painters.* 5 vols. New York, 1910.

———. *The Works of John Ruskin.* Edited by E. T. Cook and Alexander Wedderburn. 36 vols. London, 1903.

Sartin, Stephen V. *Polite Society: Portraits of the English Country Gentleman and His Family by Arthur Devis, 1712–1787.* Exhibition catalogue for the Harris Museum and Art Gallery. Preston, Lancashire, 1983.

Sellars, James. *Samuel Palmer.* London, 1974.

Shesgreen, Sean. *Engravings by Hogarth.* New York, 1973.

Shields, Conal, and Leslie Parris. *John Constable 1776–1837.* London, 1969.

Sitwell, Sacheverell. *Conversation Pieces: A Survey of English Domestic Portraits and Their Painters.* London, 1936.

———. *Narrative Pictures: A Survey of English Genre and Its Painters.* London and New York, 1969.

Smart, Alastair, and Attfield Brooks. *Constable and His Country.* London, 1976.

Solkin, David H. *Richard Wilson: The Landscape of Reaction.* Tate Gallery catalogue. London, 1982.

Staley, Allen. *The Pre-Raphaelite Landscape.* Oxford, 1973.

Streatfield, David C. "Art and Nature in the English Landscape Garden: Design, Theory, and Practice, 1700–1818." In *Landscape in the Gardens and the Literature of Eighteenth-Century England.* Los Angeles, 1981.

Stroud, Dorothy. *Capability Brown.* London, 1965.

———. *Humphry Repton.* London, 1962.

Surtess, Virginia, ed. *The Diary of Ford Madox Brown.* London, 1981.

Taylor, Basil. *Constable: Paintings, Drawings, and Watercolours.* London, 1973.

———. *Painting in England, 1700–1850: From the Collection of Mr. and Mrs. Paul Mellon.* Richmond, Va., 1963.

Thicknesse, Philip. *A Sketch of the Life and Paintings of Thomas Gainsborough, Esq.* London, 1788.

Thornes, John. "Constable's Clouds." *Burlington Magazine* 121 (November 1979): 697–704.

Walker, John. *John Constable*. New York, 1978.

Walton, Paul H. *The Drawings of John Ruskin*. Oxford, 1972.

Wark, Robert. *Ten British Pictures, 1740–1840*. San Marino, Calif., 1971.

Waterhouse, Ellis. *Gainsborough*. London, 1958.

———. *Painting in Britain, 1530–1790*. Harmondsworth, Middlesex, 1969.

White, Christopher. *English Landscape, 1630–1850*. Exhibition catalogue for the Yale Center for British Art. New Haven, Conn., 1977.

Whitley, William T. *Art in England, 1800–1820*. 2 vols. New York, 1968.

Wiebenson, Dora. *The Picturesque Garden in France*. Princeton, N.J., 1978.

Williamson, G. C. *English Conversation Pictures of the Eighteenth and Early Nineteenth Centuries*. New York, 1975.

Willis, Peter. *Charles Bridgeman and the English Landscape Garden*. London, 1977.

———, ed. *Furor Hortensis: Essays on the History of the English Landscape Garden in Memory of P. H. Clark*. Edinburgh, 1974.

Wilton, Andrew, ed. *Constable's "English Landscape Scenery."* London, 1979.

Woodall, Mary. "A Note on Gainsborough and Ruisdael." *Burlington Magazine* 66 (January 1935): 40–45.

———, ed. *The Letters of Thomas Gainsborough*. London, 1961.

Zerner, Henri, and Charles Rosen. *Romanticism and Realism: The Mythology of Nineteenth-Century Art*. New York, 1984.

HISTORICAL WORKS

Allen, David Elliston. *The Naturalist in Britain: A Social History*. Harmondsworth, Middlesex, 1978.

Ariès, Philippe. *Centuries of Childhood: A Social History of Family Life*. Translated by Robert Baldick. New York, 1962.

Boville, E. W. *English Country Life*. London and Toronto, 1962.

Briggs, Asa. *Victorian People: A Reassessment of Persons and Themes, 1851–67*. Harmondsworth, Middlesex, 1977.

Carpenter, Kenneth E., ed. *British Labour Struggles: Contemporary Pamphlets, 1727–1850*. New York, 1972.

Chambers, J. D., and G. E. Mingay. *The Agricultural Revolution, 1750–1880*. London, 1966.

Curtler, W. H. R. *The Enclosure and Redistribution of Our Land*. Oxford, 1920.

Davies, David. *The Case of Labourers in Husbandry*. London, 1795.

Eden, Fredrick Morton. *The State of the Poor*. London, 1797.

Elias, Norbert. *The Civilizing Process: The History of Manners*. New York, 1978.

Engels, Friedrich. *The Condition of the Working-Class in England*. Vol. 4 of *Karl Marx, Friedrich Engels: Collected Works, 1844–1845*. Translated by Florence Kelley-Wischnewetzky. London, New York, and Moscow, 1976.

Foucault, Michel. *Discipline and Punish: The Birth of the Prison*. Translated by Alan Sheridan. London, 1977.

Hammond, J. L., and Barbara Hammond. *The Village Labourer, 1760–1832*. London, 1920.

Himmelfarb, Gertrude. *The Idea of Poverty: England in the Early Industrial Age*. New York, 1984.

Hobsbawm, Eric J., and George Rudé. *Captain Swing*. New York, 1968.

Hoskins, G. W. *The Making of the English Landscape*. London, 1955.

Marcus, Steven. *Engels, Manchester, and the Working Class*. New York, 1975.

Marx, Karl. *Capital*. Vol. 1. Translated by Ben Fowkes. New York, 1977.

———. *Grundrisse: Introduction to the Critique of Political Economy*. Translated by Martin Nicolaus. New York, 1973.

———. *Surveys from Exile*. Edited by David Fernbach. Translated by Ben Fowkes and Paul Jackson. New York, 1974.

Mason, John E. *Gentlefolk in the Making: Studies in the History of English Courtesy Literature and Related Topics, 1531–1774*. Philadelphia, 1935.

Mayhew, Henry. *London Labour and London Poor*. 4 vols. London, 1861.

Mingay, G. E. *English Landed Society in the Eighteenth Century*. London, 1963.

Olsen, Donald J. *The Growth of Victorian London*. New York, 1976.

Peacock, Alfred James. *Bread or Blood: A Study of the Agrarian Riots in East Anglia in 1816*. London, 1965.

Plumb, J. H. *England in the Eighteenth Century*. Harmondsworth, Middlesex, 1974.

Ruggles, Thomas. *The History of the Poor*. 2 vols. London, 1795.

Sharp, Thomas. *The English Panorama*. London, 1955.

Slater, Gilbert. *The English Peasantry and the Enclosure of the Common Fields*. London, 1907.

Smart, W. "Antecedents of the Corn Law of 1815." *English Historical Review* 24 (1909): 470–87.

Stone, Lawrence. *The Family, Sex, and Marriage in England, 1500–1800*. New York, 1977.

Tate, W. E. *The English Village Community and the Enclosure Movements*. London, 1967.

Thompson, E. P. *The Making of the English Working Class*. Harmondsworth, Middlesex, 1977.

———. "Time, Work-Discipline, and Industrial Capitalism." *Past and Present* 38 (December 1967): 56–97.

Thompson, F. M. L. *English Landed Society in the Nineteenth Century*. London and Toronto, 1963.

Thomson, David. *England in the Nineteenth Century*. Harmondsworth, Middlesex, 1950.

Thrisk, Joan, ed. *Suffolk Farming in the Nineteenth Century*. Ipswich, Suffolk, 1958.

Trevelyan, G. M. *English Social History*. Harmondsworth, Middlesex, 1967.

United Kingdom. *Report from His Majesty's Commissioners on the Administration and Practical Operation of the Poor Laws.* Irish University Press Series of British Parliamentary Papers. Vols. 9–19. Shannon, 1970.

———. *Report from the Select Committee on the Irremovable Poor.* Irish University Press Series of British Parliamentary Papers. Vol. 23. Shannon, 1967.

Webb, Sidney, and Beatrice Webb. *The Story of the King's Highway.* Hamden, Conn., 1963.

Young, Arthur. *Agriculture in Suffolk.* London, 1798.

———. *Farmer's Tour through the East of England.* London, 1771.

———. *General View of the Agriculture of the County of Lincoln.* London, 1799.

———, ed. *The Annals of Agriculture.* 46 vols. London, 1770–1813.

GENERAL WORKS

Abrams, Meyer H. *The Mirror and the Lamp: Romantic Theory and the Critical Tradition.* New York, 1953.

Acton, William. *Prostitution, Considered in Its Moral, Social, and Sanitary Aspects.* London, 1870.

Addison, Joseph. *Selections from Addison's Papers Contributed to the Spectator.* Edited by Thomas Arnold. Oxford, 1886.

Alison, Archibald. *Essay on the Nature and Principles of Taste.* Edinburgh, 1825.

Althusser, Louis. *For Marx.* Translated by Ben Brewster. New York, 1969.

———. *Lenin and Philosophy and Other Essays.* Translated by Ben Brewster. New York and London, 1971.

Althusser, Louis, and Etienne Balibar. *Reading Capital.* Translated by Ben Brewster. London, 1977.

Appleton, Jay. *The Experience of Landscape.* London and New York, 1975.

Austen, Jane. *Northanger Abbey.* Edited by R. W. Chapman. London, 1971.

Barrell, John. *The Idea of Landscape and a Sense of Place, 1730–1840: An Approach to the Poetry of John Clare.* Cambridge, Eng., 1972.

Barthes, Roland. *Camera Lucida: Reflections on Photography.* Translated by Richard Howard. New York, 1981.

———. *Elements of Semiology.* Translated by Annette Lavers and Colin Smith. New York, 1980.

———. *Image, Music, Text.* Translated by Stephen Heath. New York, 1977.

———. *Mythologies.* Translated by Annette Lavers. New York, 1972.

———. *S/Z: An Essay.* Translated by Richard Miller. New York, 1974.

———. *Writing Degree Zero.* Translated by Annette Lavers and Colin Smith. New York, 1977.

Baudrillard, Jean. *Le Système des objets*. Paris, 1968.

Baxandall, Lee, and Stefan Morawski, eds. *Marx and Engels on Literature and Art: A Selection of Writings*. St. Louis, Mo., 1973.

Bewick, Thomas. *Memoir of Thomas Bewick* (1862). London, 1961.

Bloom, Harold. *The Anxiety of Influence: A Theory of Poetry*. Oxford and New York, 1973.

Burke, Edmund. *A Philosophical Enquiry into the Origin of Our Ideas of the Sublime and Beautiful*. Edited by J. T. Boulton. Notre Dame, Ind., 1968.

Burrow, J. W. *Evolution and Society: A Study in Victorian Social Theory*. Cambridge, Eng., 1966.

Cobbett, William. *Rural Rides* (1830). Harmondsworth, Middlesex, 1977.

Dickens, Charles. *Dombey and Son*. Harmondsworth, Middlesex, 1970.

Donzelot, Jacques. *The Policing of Families*. Translated by Robert Hurley. New York, 1979.

Du Bos, Jean-Baptiste. *Réflexions critiques sur la poésie et sur la peinture*. 3 vols. Paris, 1755.

Dyos, Harold J. *Exploring the Urban Past: Essays in Urban History by H. J. Dyos*. Edited by David Cannadine and David Reeder. Cambridge, Eng., 1982.

Dyos, Harold J., and Michael Wolff, eds. *The Victorian City: Images and Realities*. London, 1973.

Eagleton, Terry. *Criticism and Ideology*. London, 1976.

Fabricant, Carole. *Swift's Landscape*. Baltimore, 1982.

Foucault, Michel. *The Order of Things: An Archaeology of the Human Sciences*. Translated anonymously. London, 1970.

Freud, Sigmund. *Civilization and Its Discontents*. Translated and edited by James Strachey. New York, 1962.

———. *On Creativity and the Unconscious: Papers on the Psychology of Art, Literature, Love, Religion*. Edited by Benjamin Nelson. New York, 1958.

———. *Sexuality and the Psychology of Love*. Edited by Philip Rieff. New York, 1972.

———. *Three Essays on the Theory of Sexuality*. Translated and edited by James Strachey. New York, 1962.

Fromm, Erich. "The Theory of Mother Right and Its Relevance for Social Psychology." In *Crisis of Psychoanalysis*. New York, 1934.

Gadamer, Hans-Georg. "The Problem of Historical Consciousness." Translated by Jeff L. Close. *Graduate Faculty Philosophy Journal* 5, no. 1 (Fall 1975): 8–56.

Genette, Gerard. *Figures II*. Paris, 1969.

Gilpin, William. *Three Essays: On Picturesque Beauty; On Picturesque Travel; and On Sketching Landscape*. London, 1803.

Girouard, Mark. *Life in the English Country House*. New Haven, Conn., and London, 1978.

Goldsmith, Oliver. *Poems and Plays of Oliver Goldsmith*. Edited by Austin Dobson. 27 vols. London, 1891.

Hartman, Geoffrey H. *Wordsworth's Poetry, 1787–1814*. New Haven, Conn., and London, 1977.

Hazlitt, William. *The Plain Speaker*. London and New York, 1905.

Hipple, Walter John, Jr. *The Beautiful, the Sublime, and the Picturesque in Eighteenth-Century British Aesthetic Theory*. Carbondale, Ill., 1957.

Home, Henry (Lord Kames). *Elements of Criticism*. New York, 1866.

Horkheimer, Max. "Authority and the Family." In *Critical Theory: Selected Essays*. Translated by Matthew J. O'Connell and others. New York, 1972.

Horkheimer, Max, and Theodor W. Adorno. *Dialectic of Enlightenment*. Translated by John Cumming. New York, 1972.

Howard, Ebenezer. *Tomorrow: A Peaceful Path to Real Reform*. London, 1898.

Howitt, William. *Rural Life in England*. 2 vols. London, 1838.

Hussey, Christopher. *The Picturesque: Studies in a Point of View*. London, 1927.

Kant, Immanuel. *Observations on the Feeling of the Beautiful and Sublime*. Translated by John T. Goldthwait. Berkeley and Los Angeles, 1965.

Knight, Richard Payne. *An Analytical Inquiry into the Principles of Taste*. London, 1805.

Knoepflmacher, U. C., and G. B. Tennyson, eds. *Nature and the Victorian Imagination*. Berkeley and Los Angeles, 1977.

Lasch, Christopher. *Haven in a Heartless World: The Family Besieged*. New York, 1979.

Lipking, Lawrence. *The Ordering of the Arts in Eighteenth-Century England*. Princeton, N.J., 1970.

Loudon, John Claudius. *The Suburban Gardener and Villa Companion*. London, 1838.

Macherey, Pierre. *A Theory of Literary Production*. Translated by Geoffrey Wall. London, 1978.

Mack, Maynard. *The Garden and the City: Retirement and Politics in the Later Poetry of Pope, 1731–1743*. Toronto, 1969.

Marcuse, Herbert. *Eros and Civilization*. New York, 1962.

Miller, D. A. "Discipline in Different Voices: Bureaucracy, Police, Family, and *Bleak House*." *Representations* 1 (February 1983): 59–89.

Monk, Samuel H. *The Sublime*. Ann Arbor, Mich., 1962.

Mumford, Lewis. *The City in History: Its Origins, Its Transformations, and Its Prospects*. New York, 1961.

Nicolson, Marjorie Hope. *Mountain Gloom and Mountain Glory: The Development of the Aesthetics of the Infinite*. New York, 1963.

Nivelon, Francis. *Rudiments of Genteel Behavior*. London, 1737.

Olmsted, Frederick Law. *Public Parks and the Enlargement of Towns*. 1870. Reprint. New York, 1970.

Osborn, Frederic J., and Arnold Whettick. *The New Towns: The Answer to Megalopolis*. Rev. ed. Cambridge, Mass., 1969.

Pinkerton, John, ed. *A General Collection of Voyages and Travels*. London, 1808.

Poggioli, Renato. *The Theory of the Avant-Garde*. New York, 1971.

Price, Martin. "The Picturesque Moment." In *From Sensibility to Romanticism: Essays Presented to Frederick A. Pottle*, edited by Fredrick W. Hilles and Harold Bloom. Oxford, 1965.

Price, Uvedale. *An Essay on the Picturesque As Compared with the Sublime and the Beautiful.* London, 1842.

Rehbock, Philip F. *The Philosophical Naturalists: Themes in Early Nineteenth-Century British Biology.* Madison, Wis., 1983.

Repton, Humphry. *An Enquiry into the Changes of Taste in Landscape Gardening.* London, 1806.

Richards, J. M. *Castles on the Ground: The Anatomy of Suburbia.* London, 1973.

Røstvig, Maren-Sofie. *The Happy Man: Studies in the Metamorphoses of a Classical Ideal.* 2 vols. New York, 1954.

Sharlin, Harold I. *The Convergent Century: The Unification of Science in the Nineteenth Century.* London, 1966.

Shenstone, William. *The Letters of William Shenstone.* Edited by Marjorie Williams. Oxford, 1939.

————. *The Works in Verse and Prose of William Shenstone, Esq.* Edited by Robert Dodsley. 3 vols. London, 1765.

Sheridan, Thomas. *Courses of Lectures on Elocution.* Providence, R.I., 1796.

Smith, John Thomas. *Remarks on Rural Scenery.* London, 1797.

Stanhope, Philip Dormer. *Letters Written by Lord Chesterfield to His Son.* Edited by Ernest Rhys. London, 1889.

Starobinski, Jean. *L'Invention de la liberté, 1700–1789.* Geneva, 1964.

Swift, Jonathan. *Works.* 9 vols. Dublin, 1747.

Taylor, N. *The Village in the City.* London, 1973.

Thompson, F. M. L., ed. *The Rise of Suburbia.* Leicester, 1982.

Towle, Mathew. *The Young Gentleman and Lady's Private Tutor.* London, 1770.

Turner, James. *The Politics of Landscape: Rural Scenery and Society in English Poetry, 1630–1660.* Oxford, 1979.

Whately, Thomas. *Observations on Modern Gardening.* London, 1770.

Williams, Raymond. *The Country and the City.* New York, 1973.

————. *Culture and Society, 1780–1950.* Harmondsworth, Middlesex, 1968.

————. *Keywords: A Vocabulary of Culture and Society.* New York, 1976.

————. *Problems in Materialism and Culture.* London, 1980.

INDEX

Designer: Mark Ong
Compositor: Wilsted & Taylor
Text: 11/13 Garamond
Printer: Malloy Lithographing
Binder: John H. Dekker & Sons